Web
Designer's

D1517429

Guide to

Typography

Hayden
Books

**Michael Leary,
Dan Hale, and
Andrew DeVigal**

Associate Publisher
John Pierce

Publishing Manager
Laurie Petrycki

Managing Editor
Lisa Wilson

Marketing Manager
Stacey Oldham

Acquisitions Editor
Michelle Reed

Development Editor
Robyn Holtzman

Copy Editor
Meshell Dinn

Production Editor
Kevin Laseau

Technical Editor
Tim Webster

Publishing Coordinator
Karen Flowers

Cover Designer
Aren Howell

Book Designer
Sandra Schroeder

Illustrations
Steve Zafarana

**Manufacturing
Coordinator**
Brook Farling

**Production Team
Supervisors**
Laurie Casey
Joe Millay

Production Team
Lori Cliburn
Janelle Herber
Linda Knose
Elizabeth SanMiguel
Scott Tullis
Megan Wade

Indexer
Rebecca Hornyak

Web Designer's Guide to Typography

©1997 Hayden Books

Library of Congress Catalog Number: 96-78593
ISBN: 1-56830-337-8

Copyright © 1997 Hayden Books

Printed in the United States of America 1 2 3 4 5 6 7 8 9 0

Warning and Disclaimer

Dedication

This book is dedicated to my parents, Leo and Martha Leary. Their selfless love and guidance have taught me to trust in my abilities and to never stop dreaming. They are with me always. —Michael

For Ganeith Albriktson —Dan

Thank you God for giving me the energy. To my family and friends for putting up with me, especially to my brother and my moonlighting partner, Angelo, for giving me constant inspiration. A round of applause definitely goes out to the people that keep the software at the bleeding edge, Adobe and Macromedia, and for the true designers and artists that keep pushing me to learn and grow.—Drew

About the Authors

Michael Leary is co-owner and Principal Designer at Galápagos Design Group, a digital font foundry in Littleton, Massachusetts. He serves on their Board of Directors. He has been in the type industry since 1984, having made significant contributions to the development of font libraries both at Agfa Corporation and Bitstream, Inc., before founding Galápagos. He is also a member of Association Typographique International (ATypI) and the Type Director's Club.

Daniel Hale (dhale@pobox.com) is a type freak and inveterate road-tripper. After receiving a degree from the Evergreen State College, he went to work at his father's publishing company, where he taught himself typesetting and fell in love with letters. Though he enjoys the Web (especially now that CSS exists), he dreams of owning a Philadelphia hand press and several hundred pounds of Dante and Joanna. He lives in Seattle with Emmy, the Spaz Cat from Hell, whom he found abandoned in a campground in Butte, Montana.

Andrew DeVigal is co-principal at DeVigal Design (http://www.devigal.com), a visual communications firm specializing in graphic design and information architecture both in print and digital format including the World Wide Web. DeVigal is also a Web producer/site and interface designer for Knight-Ridder New Media in San Jose. Prior to San Jose, he was an informational graphic journalist for the *Chicago Tribune* for three years before becoming a producer/art director for the Internet version of the *Tribune*.

Acknowledgments

To Michelle Reed, who gave me this opportunity at Hayden Books. Your energy and support were invaluable.

To Robyn Holtzman, Kevin Laseau, and the entire staff of editors who worked on this book—thank you for your patience and diligence. I have learned so much having worked with you.

To Steve Zafarana, an artist and friend whose abundant talent and generosity have allowed me to share with you his extraordinary world. His illustrations, which grace this book, come from a place we should all be lucky enough to visit. They bring laughter and joy. Thank you, Steve-O.

To Dennis Pasternak, whose knowledge and design skills for the letterform are beyond approach. Thank you friend, for allowing me to walk the corridors of your mind, gathering valuable information for this book. Your passion and drive are to be admired.

To Larry Oppenberg, whose words and advice have guided me through this journey. Working with you has been a great experience. You have been both a teacher and a friend and I will continue to learn from you. (Even though you are a Yankee fan!)

To George Ryan, the John Wayne of Fonts. You are a true craftsman. I have been lucky enough to get to know the caring soul that you are. Thank you for letting me share in your knowledge and experience. Your wonderful storytelling ability can turn the most stressful day into a laughter and smile. There is a writer in you, Jorgé.

To Sue Zafarana, my dear friend, whose loving support and belief in me has made all the difference. There are few words to say. You grace my life and I thank you.

To all of my friends—your positive words and thoughts have inspired me and kept me from straying off course. I cannot spend enough time with all of you. This work is an outgrowth of your kindness and friendship. Thank you all.

And last, to my family—who are my strength and focus. You have always opened your lives to me and my soul has been enriched because of that. To my brother Leo, sisters Orianne, Jane, Cathy, to their respective families, to my Aunt Mary, and to Dean—I thank you all. I am so very lucky to have so many shoulders to lean on. This book is yours to share. —Michael Leary

Thanks go to Robyn Holtzman, my development editor at Hayden Books, for her patience and encouragement; Todd Fahrner, for recommending this project to me, and giving me a swift kick when I needed it—I am in your debt; and Alison, for putting up with my preoccupation and amazingly dull conversation over the past month.

Trademark Acknowledgments

All terms mentioned in this book that are known to be trademarks or services marks have been appropriately capitalized. Hayden Books cannot attest to the accuracy of this information. Use of a term in this book should not be regarded as affecting the validity of any trademark or service mark.

Hayden Books

The staff of Hayden Books is committed to bringing you the best computer books. What our readers think of Hayden is important to our ability to serve our customers. If you have any comments, no matter how great or how small, we'd appreciate your taking the time to send us a note.

You can reach Hayden Books at the following:

Hayden Books
201 West 103rd Street
Indianapolis, IN 46290
317-581-3833

Email addresses:

America Online: Hayden Bks
Internet: hayden@hayden.com

Visit the Hayden Books Web site at http://www.hayden.com

Contents at a Glance

Table of Contents

PART 1

Getting Started with Typography

Typography Basics

Introduction to the Font

It is everywhere. The written word, printed on a page or on a screen, addresses the human race. It touches all ages, all cultures. Why is the written word so engrained in our daily lives? Because these words are so effective at delivering a message or telling a story. Words succeed in their mission because of their voice—a voice that speaks to us, informs, persuades, questions, and makes us laugh. Beyond the connection of nouns, verbs, and other grammatical structures that make up our sentences, much of this voice is born of the typestyle chosen by the designer. An author uses the words to tell the story, but a designer uses his typestyle to reflect the feelings within those words.

Importance of Type as Message

Type performs a valuable service—it acts as a connection between the word and message. It enhances the content. Type enables the author to compose words with regard to their expressive intent.

The typographic styles we use are a reflection of our society, of how we work and play. As generations change, so do our ways and means of expressing ourselves. Yet even in this age of multimedia, sound-bytes, and quick-flash imagery, the printed word is still an important vehicle for transporting our thoughts. And although the words are the vehicle, the type is the make and model—the color and personality of the vehicle. It reflects its owner and the community surrounding it.

How Type Enhances Content

The typestyle you choose to represent your words is affected by a number of attributes: style, size, weight, and posture. When these attributes are set correctly (and there is a correct way, depending on the function), the typestyle complements the words; it doesn't distract the reader from them. It is the author (the writer, typesetter, Web designer, or the person making the typographic decisions) who must choose the type with great sensitivity and intelligence.

Type's voice can be strong and persuasive, or light and humorous. It can evoke a serious tone, or put the reader at ease. Again, this can all be achieved through the skillful hand of the type's author. When the author infuses emotion through his choice of typestyle, a relationship is born that breathes life onto the page or screen.

How Type Is Taken for Granted

Most people see the written word on a page, screen, or billboard and think little or nothing of the effect the typography has within each context. Yet a person is baffled as to why he purchased several items he didn't need after seeing a large storefront sign that read:

"CLOSE OUT SALE! 60% OFF ALL STOCK! EVERYTHING MUST GO!"

The viewer may think it was the sale that drew him into the store for all the bargains. Yet if it wasn't for the correct typographic decisions (choosing style, size, weight, and posture), the sign wouldn't impart that fevered urgency needed to capture its audience. It is perfectly acceptable for the reader to see the message in the words and be oblivious to the typestyles used.

When incorrect typographic decisions are made, the results can be quite horrifying. If the reader becomes distracted enough from the words' message because of poorly executed typography, she loses interest. When you lose the reader, the words are invisible.

Difference between a Font and a Typeface

The terms font and typeface are generally used to mean the same thing. This leads to some confusion. Whereas a font is meant to describe one style (see Figure 1.1), a typeface can mean one font or an entire family of fonts of the same style but with varying attributes. Typeface is best used to describe a family of fonts; variations of one typestyle.

abcdefghijklmnopqrstuvwxyz
ABCDEFGHIJKLMNOPQRSTUVWXYZ
123457890(".;:.*"?!£)ÆŒæœ&[]
The evolution and permanence of type

Figure 1.1

Characters within a font—set in Maiandra Demi Bold.

Type design houses continue to be called "foundries." The word font derives from the word foundry. A font is a set of characters set in one style, one variation of weight, width, and posture.

The word typeface (also known as typeface family) is defined as a collection of fonts having the same typestyle but varying weights, widths, and postures.

Anatomy of Type

Whether it be a font or a typeface, the main ingredient in both is the character (see Figure 1.2).

Figure 1.2

The uppercase G, set in Kennedy Book.

A character is the basic element upon which all fonts and typeface families are based. When a type designer creates a collection of characters (many of them beyond what you find visible on your computer keyboard), it is called a character set. The major type foundries deliver their typefaces in industry standard character sets, predetermined collections that most customers have become familiar with. They may also provide, at the customer's request, fonts in custom character sets, with the requirements determined by the customer. Appendix A provides some examples of standard character sets.

To understand how a body of type works, we must examine its anatomy. To understand the underlying structure is to understand the total mechanism.

Anatomy

The following is a list of pieces that make up the structure of a character, illustrated in Figure 1.3.

➡ Arm—The horizontal stroke that is free on one end, as on the uppercase E.

➡ Ascender—Part of the lowercase letter that extends above the x-height, as in the lowercase b, h, and l. The distance from the top of the x-height to the top of the ascender height characters, such as the b, h, and l.

➡ Baseline—The imaginary line upon which all characters in a font rest or align.

➡ Bowl—The round and/or elliptical forms that make up the basic shape of letters such as the uppercase C and O and the lowercase b, o, and p.

➡ Cap height—The height of the uppercase letters. The cap height is usually a bit shorter than the height of the ascenders.

➡ Counter—The partially or fully enclosed parts of a letter, such as the defined space within the uppercase H and lowercase n and u.

➡ Crossbar—The straight horizontal stroke extending across two vertical or diagonal stems. This is seen in the uppercase H.

➡ Descender—Part of the lowercase letter that extends below the baseline, as with the lowercase g, j, p, and q. The distance from the baseline to the bottom of descender characters such as the lowercase g, j, p, and q.

➡ Ear—The small extension that projects from the top-right of the lowercase g.

➡ Figure—The distance from the baseline to the top of the figures (numerals). This height is usually the equivalent of the cap height.

➡ Hairline—The thin horizontal stroke located at the top and bottom of round characters such as the uppercase and lowercase o, c, and s.

➡ Kerns—The negative letterspacing between specific character combinations that is applied to reduce the space between them.

➡ Link—A stroke joining the upper and lower body of the lowercase g.

➡ Point size—Type is measured in units with the same name as the traditional printer's unit of measurement, the point. In desktop publishing, the point is equivalent to .3528 millimeters or .01389 of an inch (1/72 inch). This is an imperial measurement used in typewriter technology. The traditional point, still used by most British and North American printers, is .351 millimeters, or .01383 of an inch (1/72.27 inch). The point is usually combined with a larger scale unit, the pica. The pica is equivalent to 12 points.

➡ Serif—The beginning and/or finishing strokes on a stem drawn at a right (or oblique if the style is italic) angle to the stem. The serif guides the eye from one letter to the next. The use of serifs in a text typeface makes it much easier to read.

➡ Set width—The total width of the character, including the white space on either side. This does not include kerns.

➡ Shoulder—The curved stroke between two vertical stems, such as on the lowercase h, m, and n. Its weight may taper as it leaves one stem and connects to the other.

➡ Spine—The main diagonal stroke on a upper- and lowercase s.

➡ Stem—The straight vertical strokes of a letter, such as the uppercase I and T and lowercase l and r.

➡ Stress—The orientation, measured in degrees, upon which the thin and thick strokes of a character are aligned. This is most noticeable in closed characters such as the lowercase b, o, and p, but it is reflected in all of the characters within a typeface.

➡ Tail—The descending stroke on an uppercase Q or the diagonal stroke of the uppercase R. The tail usually extends below the baseline.

➡ Terminal—The end of a stroke that is not finished with a serif, as on the lowercase t and e.

➡ X-height—The height of the lowercase letters from the baseline. This does not include the ascender or descender heights.

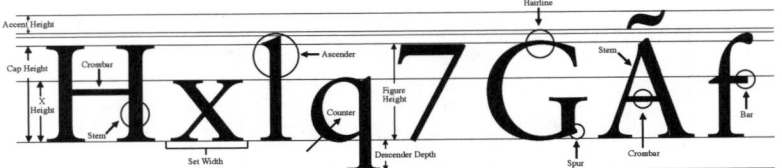

Figure 1.3

The anatomy of type. Each character part is a typographic structure that, with its corresponding features, defines a letter. The point size waterfall is a proofing tool designers use to see that the font's weight, color (overall tone), and alignment are correct.

Font Styles

Variation of weight, width, and posture create font styles. Let's take a look at these variations and how they are used.

Weight

The term weight refers to the lightness or darkness of a typestyle, which is determined by the design and the thickness (or thinness) of the line. Weight is a stylistic element that can range from light to dark with a series of gradations between the two. The standard levels of weight are extralight, light, semilight, regular, medium, semibold, bold, extrabold, and ultrabold (also referred to as black).

Roman

The "normal" weight, also referred to as the roman weight or style, is the most common. It is an attribute with little stylistic variation, as does an italic or bold weight. Roman weight dates back to the mid-1400s. Today, Roman is used as a term to define plain text.

abcdefghijklmnopqrstuvwxyz
ABCDEFGHIJKLMNOPQRSTUVWXYZ
123457890(".;:.*"?!£)ÆŒæœ&[]
The evolution and permanence of type

Figure 1.4

An example of a Roman weight font, set in Swiss 721 Roman (also known as Helvetica Roman).

Bold

The bold style is a 20th century creation. It has a secondary role—such as that of the italics—to be used for emphasis. Bold serves as a signal to its reader. Frequent use of bold type was not a common occurrence until the middle of this century, as magazines started featuring display advertising.

Bold type is most effective when it has been derived from its roman counterpart. It is best used in headings, captions, and logos and should only be used when the entire word or phrase can be set in this weight. The bolder the weight, the louder the voice. If it is used incorrectly, it can ruin the continuity of the text. Within a paragraph of text, it is best to use italics, instead of the bold weight, to emphasize.

abcdefghijklmnopqrstuvwxyz
ABCDEFGHIJKLMNOPQRSTUVWXYZ
123457890(".;:.*"?!£)ÆŒæœ&[]
The evolution and permanence of type

Figure 1.5

Swiss 721 Bold, also known as Helvetica Bold.

Light

Light is a more delicate weight than Roman or Bold. It has a gentle, airy feeling, and is used almost exclusively for display purposes. Light weight type is used less frequently than Roman or Bold. If the text is set at a small size, it can be difficult to read. If, however, a gentle, quiet tone is what you wish to impart to your reader, a light weighted font is appropriate.

abcdefghijklmnopqrstuvwxyz
ABCDEFGHIJKLMNOPQRSTUVWXYZ
123457890(".;:.*"?!£)ÆŒæœ&[]
The evolution and permanence of type

Figure 1.6

An example of a light weighted font, Swiss 721 Light (also known as Helvetica Light).

Widths

Width differs from weight in that width deals with the amount of horizontal space the typestyle utilizes. Characters that are narrower or tighter than those in a Roman font are called condensed or compressed. Characters that are wider than the Roman style are called expanded or extended.

Posture

The posture of a typestyle is determined by the angle of its characters; the tilt, left or right, of the character strokes. If a font is not "Roman" in posture (having no angle to the straight vertical stems), it is either considered "italic" or "oblique."

Italic

The italic style is based on a cursive handwriting style. It refers to the right-slant of characters in a particular typestyle (see Figure 1.7). The posture or angle of the strokes within a font should be the same, but it can vary between different typestyles. The earliest use of italics took place in the late 15th and early 16th centuries. Today, the italic style has taken a secondary role. Designed to stylistically complement the Roman weight, the italic style functions to emphasize a word or phrase, to introduce or indicate.

abcdefghijklmnopqrstuvwxyz
ABCDEFGHIJKLMNOPQRSTUVWXYZ
123457890(".;:."?!£)ÆŒææ&[]*
The evolution and permanence of type

Figure 1.7

An italic font, ITC Galliard Italic.

Oblique

Oblique or "matching" italics are characters generated from their Roman counterparts. They are not considered "pure" italics, which are designed. Because obliqued characters are electronically drawn, the proportions have a tendency to be distorted.

Backslanting (tilting characters to the left) serves little or no purpose because it goes against the normal flow of reading. Unless it is being used for a very specific reason (referring to someone's atrocious handwriting!), backslanting should not be designed or used.

abcdefghijklmnopqrstuvwxyz
ABCDEFGHIJKLMNOPQRSTUVWXYZ
123457890(".;:.*"?!£)ÆŒœœ&[]
The evolution and permanence of type

Figure 1.8

A sloped roman font set in ITC Berkeley Oldstyle.

Font Classification

Classifying type has presented problems for many years. There have been few classification systems that have successfully and thoroughly categorized each style from type's earliest beginnings through today's usage. The Vox Classification System, developed in 1954, was fairly successful at categorizing each style and is followed by many present–day designers. Type foundries have also attempted to construct their own classification plans, some with favorable results. Each system has its own names for categorizing and the number of categories is not always consistent.

In this book, you will be introduced to the core classifications, and review other categories of specialized design. This should give you a strong base of knowledge to work from when choosing a font for your Web page.

Serifs

Serif type has been around for about 500 years. These styles are classified historically, rather than functionally. They were developed much earlier than sans serif designs.

Oldstyles

Oldstyles are based on type designs from both the 15th and 16th centuries. Their tone is often friendly and warm, imparting a romantic, classical feel. Structurally, their features include the fairly pronounced difference between the thick and thin strokes. Oldstyles are ideal for almost any text meant for extensive reading. Books, newsletters, manuals, and articles are acceptable environments for oldstyle usage. They also work well at much larger sizes, suitable for display uses such as headlines and signage.

abcdefghijklmnopqrstuvwxyz
ABCDEFGHIJKLMNOPQRSTUVWXYZ
123457890(".;:.*"?!£)ÆŒæœ&[]
The evolution and permanence of type

Figure 1.9

ITC Galliard, an oldstyle font.

Transitionals

Transitionals are based on the designs from the late 17th and 18th centuries. They are classified historically, taking their place between the oldstyle and modern periods, hence the name Transitional. This period of design was referred to as neo-classical.

Transitional style is quite popular and often seen in magazine design. It remains a favorite in the advertising industry as well. Common applications for a transitional style are headlines, posters, and signage. Transitionals combine well with geometric sans serifs.

The appearance of transitionals is not as romantic as oldstyles, possessing an almost business-like quality. Structurally, transitionals are based more on mathematics than on hand-drawn lettering. The lines look more mechanical and geometric, and the serifs tend to be symmetrical. The difference between the height of the uppercase and lowercase characters is much less pronounced than that of an oldstyle design.

At lower resolutions (as with onscreen images), traditional designs appear and reproduce much better than other styles. They are less complex and do not possess the contrasting thick and thin strokes of an oldstyle.

abcdefghijklmnopqrstuvwxyz
ABCDEFGHIJKLMNOPQRSTUVWXYZ
123457890(".;:.*"?!£)ÆŒæœ&[]
The evolution and permanence of type

Figure 1.10

Baskerville, a transitional font.

Moderns

The modern style is based upon designs from the late 18th and 19th centuries. They have a very stylized, refined appearance. There is a sophistication and elegance about moderns. Structurally, they have exaggerated features. The relationship between thick and thin strokes is quite pronounced. This style can also be known as "hairline serif," with very thin hairlines.

abcdefghijklmnopqrstuvwxyz
ABCDEFGHIJKLMNOPQRSTUVWXYZ
123457890(".;:.*"?!£)ÆŒæœ&[]
The evolution and permanence of type

Figure 1.11

Bodoni, a modern font.

Slab Serifs

Slab serifs are a subclass of the modern style. They were developed in the 19th century for use as display faces. Slab serifs share most of the same proportions of the modern style. Slab serifs can be used effectively for logotypes and corporate identity projects. They are a preferred design choice when using short amounts of text and when a high level of legibility is critical. Slab serifs combine well with both grotesque and geometric sans serifs.

abcdefghijklmnopqrstuvwxyz
ABCDEFGHIJKLMNOPQRSTUVWXYZ
123457890(".;:.*"?!£)ÆŒæœ&[]
The evolution and permanence of type

Figure 1.12

Serifa Bold, a slab serif font.

Sans Serifs

Sans serif styles have been around for the past 100 years and have been classified functionally rather than historically. This classification, based solely on form, has three basic categories: geometric, grotesque, and humanist.

Geometric

Geometric sans serifs are based on simple geometric principles. There is little or no variation in stroke width. The x-height is similar to that of the modern style, being much smaller in relationship to its own cap height. The horizontal and vertical strokes of the geometric character are straight. The curved portions of the characters are quite intriguing. They follow a line that is almost circular. This design attribute is unique to geometrics.

abcdefghijklmnopqrstuvwxyz
ABCDEFGHIJKLMNOPQRSTUVWXYZ
123457890(".;:.*"?!£)ÆŒœœ&[]
The evolution and permanence of type

Figure 1.13

A geometric font, set in ITC Avant Garde.

abcdefghijklmnopqrstuvwxyz
ABCDEFGHIJKLMNOPQRSTUVWXYZ
123457890(".;:.*"?!£)ÆŒæœ&[]
The evolution and permanence of type

Figure 1.14

A geometric font, set in Futura Book.

Grotesque

Grotesques have proportions quite similar to serif typefaces. In comparison to the geometric style, they have more variation in the weight of their strokes and the lowercase x-height is larger.

abcdefghijklmnopqrstuvwxyz
ABCDEFGHIJKLMNOPQRSTUVWXYZ
123457890(".;:.*"?!£)ÆŒæœ&[]
The evolution and permanence of type

Figure 1.15

A grotesque font set in Univers.

abcdefghijklmnopqrstuvwxyz
ABCDEFGHIJKLMNOPQRSTUVWXYZ
123457890(".;:.*"?!£)ÆŒæœ&[]
The evolution and permanence of type

Figure 1.16

A grotesque font set in ITC Franklin Gothic.

Humanist

The humanist style is probably the most versatile of the three sans serif styles mentioned here. It is an effective text face, as well as a successful choice for use as a headline, subhead, or caption. An interesting comparison has been made between the humanist style and the oldstyles. Humanists are much like oldstyle serifs, but without the serifs.

Mixing Serifs and Sans Serifs

When the basic text is set in a serif typeface, a related sans serif is frequently useful for other elements such as tables, captions, or notes. Try keeping your serif-sans serif combinations down to two fonts, one of each. By introducing two similar serifs or sans serifs, they will not only share many of the same attributes, but they tend to make the page look untidy. If you have chosen a family that includes a matched sans serif font, your problems may be solved.

Some font styles provide both a serif and sans serif version of the same type style. Stone Sans and Stone Serif, created by Sumner Stone, are an example of this.

Jazz music over the years

Jazz music has changed dramatically over the years. From big band to be-bop, straight-ahead jazz to fusion, jazz has transformed itself over time. What hasn't changed is the intensity in which jazz musicians approach their music. When you hear the timeless sound of Miles Davis' ***Kind of Blue*** or John Coltrane's ***Giant Steps*** you hear the passion in the voice and it carries through from vision to instrument to art.

Serif and sans serif versions of the same type style.

Do not mix body type styles. Stick with the same body text. To start with a Baskerville and switch over to a Helvetica is a travesty. Body text is meant to flow smoothly. By changing body text styles, the flow is interrupted. Attention is broken and the successful use of the body text is lost. The only place where such a change is allowed is if the two styles are completely separated (an example of this would be when a box of text is introduced on a page to highlight a point).

Oldstyle serif designs combine well with humanist sans serif designs because they share similarly shaped characters and proportions (see Figure 1.17).

Jazz music over the years

Jazz music has changed dramatically over the years. From big band to be-bop, straight-ahead jazz to fusion, jazz has transformed itself over time. What hasn't changed is the intensity in which jazz musicians approach their music. When you hear the timeless sound of Miles Davis' Kind of Blue or John Coltrane's Giant Steps you hear the passion in the voice and it carries through from vision to instrument to art.

Oldstyle serif type style combined with humanist sans serif typeface.

Transitional serif designs combine well with grotesque sans serif designs. Transitionals combine the best of both oldstyle and modern serif styles whereas a grotesque sans serif has proportions similar to serif styles. There is a greater variation of strokes in the grotesque style.

Jazz music over the years

Jazz music has changed dramatically over the years. From big band to be-bop, straight-ahead jazz to fusion, jazz has transformed itself over time. What hasn't changed is the intensity in which jazz musicians approach their music. When you hear the timeless sound of Miles Davis' Kind of Blue or John Coltrane's Giant Steps you hear the passion in the voice and it carries through from vision to instrument to art.

Figure 1.19

Transitional serif types combined with grotesque sans serif typeface.

Modern serif designs combine well with geometric sans serif designs. In fact, it is the the heavier weights of the geometric styles that complement the modern style best because of the exaggerated strokes, wide in variation of weight, from thick to thin.

Jazz music over the years

Jazz music has changed dramatically over the years. From big band to be-bop, straight-ahead jazz to fusion, jazz has transformed itself over time. What hasn't changed is the intensity in which jazz musicians approach their music. When you hear the timeless sound of Miles Davis' Kind of Blue or John Coltrane's Giant Steps you hear the passion in the voice and it carries through from vision to instrument to art.

Figure 1.20

Modern serif typeface used with geometric sans serif design.

If you are familiar with a type designer's work, choosing a serif and sans serif design from the portfolio may provide the cohesive look needed. A designer's work will have a certain look and feel to it. This look and feel will run through several if not many of their designs. This consistent quality between styles is what you are looking for.

Scripts

Scripts are quite possibly the most beautiful of all typefaces. Some of them are exquisite in their ornate design. Scripts work well in formal presentations, such as invitations, and as a decorative style for use in signage, menus, and titling. They look best with tight letter spacing, which in turn helps the reading flow. Scripts should not be used for setting long lines of text. Extended reading of a script style can be hard on the reader's eye. Also, setting scripts in all uppercase characters is a no-no! Script uppercase characters are meant to connect to lowercase characters. By setting in just uppercase, there will be no connection between characters and the effect of the script style is lost.

abcdefghijklmnopqrstuvwxyz
ABCDEFGHIJKLMNOPQRSTUVWXYZ
*123457890(".;:. *"?!£)ÆŒææ&//*
The evolution and permanence of type

An elegant script font set in Snell Roundhand.

Uncials

European scribes originally designed uncials, dating back to the 4th century. These alphabets commonly carry only a single case (instead of an uppercase and lowercase), as did most European typefaces designed during the Middle Ages. Uncial's unique designs show a reliance on hand-lettering style. Although they are decorative in nature, uncials tend to be quite readable. They are effective as both a display (titling) style and for use as initial drop caps. Some authors use an uncial style for their text when they are attempting to evoke a medieval tone. Uncials combine well with oldstyle text.

abcdefghijklmnopqrstuvwxyz
abcdefghijklmnopqrstuvwxyz
123457890[".;:.*"?!£]æœæœ&[]
the evolution and permanence of type

An uncial font set in Libra.

Blackletter

Blackletter style originated as a written form from northern Europe in the 12th century. Also known as Gothic, or Fraktur, Blackletter became more popular as a text face and eventually replaced other handwritten styles, such as uncials, for common text usage. We now find blackletters difficult to read, and they are no longer a solution for text. Blackletter characters are generally tall and narrow (see Figure 1.22), working well as titles, headlines, and initial drop caps. Avoid using blackletter with words in all caps. Also, do not add space between the letters. Blackletters look best when the characters are tightly spaced.

abcdefghijklmnopqrstuvwxyz
ABCDEFGHIJKLMNOPQRSTUVWXYZ
123457890(".,;.*"?!£)ÆŒæœ&[]
The evolution and permanence of type

Cloister Black, a blackletter font.

Symbol Typefaces/Pi Fonts

Symbol or pi fonts do not contain letters of the Roman alphabet. Rather, they are collections of graphic symbols including arrows, squares, circles, bullets, stars, and other symbolic elements. Some pi fonts have symbols that relate to a theme or profession, such as mathematic, cartographic, and navigational symbols. These types of fonts exists for just about any usage. Designers who manufacture pi fonts can customize the character set to your needs.

Where did the term pi font originate? Back when hot metal type was the standard, "pi" referred to the type of a single style that had been mistakenly put into the drawer of another style. The pi word referred to any type that may have spilled to the floor.

Figure 1.24

A symbol/pi font set in ITC Zapf Dingbats.

Decorative Type

This classification has the widest variety of designs. There are no rules of classification for this grouping, except to be decorative. These fonts are useful in signage, posters, logos, menus, titling, and video applications. Decorative types shouldn't be used for text. As with script styles, the user must be thoughtful about selection, as decorative type is often overused.

abcdefghijklmnopqrstuvwxyz
ABCDEFGHIJKLMNOPQRSTUVWXYZ
123457890(".;:.*''?!£)ÆŒæœ&[]
The evolution and permanence of type

Figure 1.25

A decorative font set in Cloister Openface.

Other Differentiations

Although the terms *text* and *display*—mentioned several times in this chapter—are not considered classifications, they are very important categories to consider. They are defined by their usage.

Text Style

Text fonts are used in body copy, the main portion of a book, newsletter, or newspaper. These fonts must be legible and readable at small sizes, as most body copy is set in 9 or 10 point. Their function is to be pleasing to the eye and easy to read. A more decorative type style may be more attractive to the eye, but there is distraction in its attractiveness. Text must have a flow and rhythm to it, keeping the eye moving along the line, undisturbed. Though the variations of text styles are far more subtle than display type, they have a character all their own.

Traditionally, text types are serif in design, rather than san serifs (though sans serif type is used frequently in European design). There are quite a few sans serif designs that work well, but the serif style is safer for extended passages of text. It is much less taxing to the eye.

abcdefghijklmnopqrstuvwxyz
ABCDEFGHIJKLMNOPQRSTUVWXYZ
123457890(".;:.★"?!£)ÆŒæœ&[ ]
The evolution and permanence of type

A text font set in Aldine 401 (also known as Bembo).

Display Style

The idea behind the display style is to catch the reader's attention. Display fonts are extremely effective for titling, advertising, posters, and many other eye-catching uses. Whereas most of the text styles are serif fonts, display fonts tend to be sans serif. Display fonts are used at larger sizes for emphasis. Bolder weights are often used, too, holding up better than light weights at the larger point sizes. These stronger features make the eye drag over the type, ensuring that the reader takes notice.

There are type styles that cross over effectively from the text to display category. These are usually serif styles with a bit more exaggerated features. Many of the more distinctive display fonts could be categorized in the decorative classification. It is rare to see a display style cross over into text.

ABCDEFGHIJKLMNOPQRSTUVWXYZ
ABCDEFGHIJKLMNOPQRSTUVWXYZ
123457890(".;:.*"?!£)ÆŒ&[]
THE EVOLUTION AND PERMANENCE OF TYPE

A display font set in ITC Rennie Mackintosh.

Proportional Spacing

Most typefaces have proportional spacing. In these fonts, different characters take up different amounts of horizontal space; their set widths are different. The set width consists of the character's width and the white space to the left and right. Thin characters have thinner spacing whereas wider ones have wider set widths. The letter m in a proportional font, for example, has a greater horizontal spacing than the letter t. Proportionally spaced fonts are more readable than monospaced fonts. The change in character widths gives a line of text a light to dark rhythm that is pleasant to the eye. The numerals in a proportional font are usually monospace because of their usage. If numbers are to be used in a column, they need to line up. Same set widths enable this.

abcdefghijklmnopqrstuvwxyz
ABCDEFGHIJKLMNOPQRSTUVWXYZ
123457890(".;:.*"?!£)ÆŒæœ&[]
The evolution and permanence of type

Figure 1.28

A proportional font set in Swiss 721 Medium (also known as Helvetica Medium).

Monospacing

Monospacing refers to fonts where thin and wide characters share the same set widths, unlike proportional fonts. The width of the lowercase i is the same as the lowercase w. To compensate for this, thin letters are widened with large serifs and wider letters are condensed. Monospacing doesn't make for a pretty typeface, but there are functional uses for it. Monospace fonts are mechanical looking, as if a machine or a typewriter stamped them out, and are enjoying a spirited revival of sorts. More and more Web designers are using monospaced fonts as "grunge" fonts, giving their hard-edged Web pages an industrial look.

abcdefghijklmnopqrstuvwxyz
ABCDEFGHIJKLMNOPQRSTUVWXYZ
123457890(".;:.*"?!£)ÆŒæœ&[]
The evolution and permanence of type

Figure 1.29

A monospaced font set in Letter Gothic 12 Pitch.

Form and Function

Design and technology—the two become one in this world of digital communication. They are inseparable entities. To design effectively within this context, you must understand the principles for delivering quality images and the technology with which to deliver them. You cannot succeed with digital media unless you understand the constraints as well as the opportunities. This understanding comes from learning the technology for which you are designing and the tools that are available to you.

Principles of Effective Design

Some design knowledge transcends the media in which the designer works. These core understandings provide an origin from which design can grow and evolve. Although some of these principles touch on aesthetics, many of them deal with human nature and design functionality.

There are some very important typographic and page layout principles that you should follow when creating a great Web page:

➡ Your goal is to attract an audience's attention toward the ideas you wish to convey. This is crucial to successful Web page design.

➡ Never assume that the reader of your Web site is going to stick around for a long time, browsing each and every morsel of each and every page. Much of the time, the reader will be moving between pages and between sites.

➡ It is easier for the reader to digest smaller portions and will enable him to move more efficiently through the information provided.

➡ Choose typefaces that consist of varying styles and weights. They should not only work together, but also succeed at attracting the reader's attention. Try matching the type to your content.

➡ Hypertext links should be used. These links provide an interesting way to hold the reader's attention and provide additional information at the same time.

The Internet is no longer an environment for just words on a screen, but it has become a world where verbal and visual elements are integrated and intertwined. Yet even with the rise in the use of graphics, sound, and animation as effective digital communication devices, text continues to be the most popular way to communicate and still rules the digital frontier.

There are some very good reasons for this:

➡ Text is familiar to people. We are comfortable with giving and receiving information using written language. It is a primary method of communication.

➡ Images are always left to subjective interpretation, whereas text is more straightforward. You can speak candidly and succinctly when using text.

➡ In the world of computers, text is universal. Every platform supports it. Also, it requires substantially less bandwidth to transmit type than images.

Always keep in mind that the space that surrounds every letter on the page and that peeks through each and every character you use must be considered as carefully as selecting a type style. Your decisions on how that space will be addressed with text will help determine your success at building a quality Web document.

Proportion

You must be cognizant of the fact that there is a difference between the proportions of letters. For example, although it may appear that the relationship of the lowercase height to the type size is satisfactory at one size, it may not be so at other sizes. Some font styles have quite large lowercase counters. At the same point size, other font styles will have smaller lowercase counters. You should recognize this and make adjustments accordingly.

Measurement System

In most desktop publishing applications, type is measured in units with the same name as the traditional printers' unit of measurement—the point. A point is .3528 mm, or $1/72$ of an inch (.01389 inch). The traditional point used by most printers in North America and England is .351 mm, or $1/72.27$ of an inch. Although these differences are small, they can have a cumulative effect, providing discrepancies in the position of elements in documents produced with differing technologies. Type specimens produced using traditional printing methods will not be appropriate for comparison with desktop publishing samples. Because of these small cumulative differences, the two samples may not match.

The point system of measuring type has produced many benefits. One of them is the fact that both type and spaces from different type foundries could be mixed together with a common language for description. Another was the fact that different typestyles could be placed together on a basis of simple arithmetic.

The human eye finds it simple to read certain point sizes. Twelve or 10 point seems most comfortable, while 8 point needs more effort and text as small as 6 point is rather difficult to read. Type designers have learned to help readers by adjusting the proportions of letters according to size. Remember this when you are choosing your type for a Web page. Always take into consideration what is best and easiest for the reader.

Although type is measured in points and picas, the page or field upon which the type will appear is likely to be specified in either millimeters or inches. Usually, the position of the type is specified as margins or page number positions in millimeters or inches.

Nominal versus Optical Size Differences

The nominal size of a font is not related to any measurable part of the character. In most typefaces, there is a small allowance of space above the ascender extent and below the descender extent of the letterform of characters. If you were to measure the distance between these two extents, you will not always come up with the same point measurement as is the nominal point size.

Optical size refers to how the reader's eye views the characters. Though the point size of a font may be 12 point, if it has a larger x-height it may look a point or two larger.

Just as the uppercase and lowercase limits of letterforms cannot be predicted from the nominal point size, so too the other vertical dimensions, such as cap height, x-height, and distance between ascender and lowercase, vary in their relative proportions, according to the design of the typeface.

An example of this is the difference in the x-height of a geometric sans serif and that of a grotesque sans serif. The geometric style has a smaller x-height in relation to its cap height. The grotesque style contains an x-height quite large in comparison to its cap height.

Point size refers to an imaginary bounding box extending from the descender line to the ascender line. The actual character sizes may vary greatly within the bounding box, which is why two fonts of the same size can be different in optimal size.

Horizontal Spacing

This section defines the spacing of typographic characters on the horizontal axis, from left to right.

Letterspacing

Letterspacing, which is also referred to as tracking, is the addition or subtraction of an equal amount of space horizontally between all letters in a line of text. It is the presetting of universal negative or positive letterspacing values into degrees of space to enable a designer to determine the overall look or tone of the text. You can adjust tracking to squeeze a line of type into a narrow column or to expand a word to fill a given space in a design. Most desktop publishing applications allow for adjustments to letterspacing, although the default letterspacing provided is usually more than acceptable.

Kerning

Most page layout programs allow for spacing adjustments to character pairs. This is called kerning. Choosing this formatting option will automatically close up the space between character combinations that commonly appear too widely spaced. Examples of this can be seen in the character pairs "To" and "Va" (see Figure 1.28). Certain character combinations will always appear widely spaced even when they are kerned so that they touch each other. Examples of these are the "vy" and "ry."

AT AV LV RA
Va WA Wo YO
fo ge ry ye

Figure 1.30

Frequently used kerning pairs.

Kerning character pairs within a page layout program should be done cautiously. It may help give a smoother appearance to titles and headings. Always pay attention to the overall balance of spacing in the text when making interventions at the level of individual characters (see Figure 1.29).

YOU'RE ELATED WHEN YOU
SEE GOOD KERNING...
AND BOTHERED WHEN YOU
SEE BAD KERNING!

Figure 1.31

Example of good and bad kerning within text.

Kerning changes are contained in "kerning tables," which are already programmed into a typeface. A designer will subtract a certain number of units from the width of a character (like the uppercase W) and the software (a type design application) moves fewer units than would normally be required for that character. The subsequent letter will then overlap to visually decrease the intercharacter space. Kerning tables (or data) refers to pairs of charactares that sit next to each other.

Most word processing and desktop publishing systems can kern hundreds of pairs automatically. Some designers, having great experience with kerning, will kern well over 1,000 pairs so as to better balance most pairs encountered in text. They feel that the more kerning pairs you have, the better-looking your text. However, if one cannot kern indefinitely, it is best to kern only the most egregious of pairs. As a designer kerns more and more pairs, the possiblity of a greater imbalance between those pairs kerned and those left unkerned will increase.

Kerning information is contained within the font itself. Therefore, kerning cannot be specified or declared within HTML or when using style sheets.

Effects on Readability

If you choose to manipulate the letterspacing (see Figures 1.30 and 1.37), here are some considerations:

➡ If you are using tracking to create a closer fit to a font, beware! You may find that global changes improve the cohesion of some character combinations but make others worse. Rounded characters like the e-a or o-e combinations will look worse if tightened too much because they sit tight naturally. On the other hand, tightening a w-n or r-t combination will aid its interspacing.

➡ Avoid increasing letterspacing in lowercase body text; looser spacing always decreases legibility of small type.

➡ Though most programs have features that increase the tracking, only use these options for text set in all caps, small caps, or display text, where looser spacing may increase legibility.

➡ Capitalized text or small caps that appear with normal text can look too tight and crowded compared to surrounding text. You may want to adjust the letterspacing of the caps in this situation.

➡ You may be able to substitute ligatures for particular character clusters that appear unevenly spaced, as an alternative to letterspacing. Ligatures are character combinations made into one character. This can help the reader's eye flow along a line of text. Some fonts contain ff or fl combinations.

This is example of good letterspacing.

Figure 1.32

Example of good letterspacing.

This is an example of bad letterspacing.

Figure 1.33

Example of bad letterspacing.

Vertical Spacing

Vertical spacing is also referred to as leading. The term leading comes from the days of hot metal type. A printer used thin strips of lead to add space between lines of type.

Measuring Vertical Space

Vertical space is defined as the total distance from the baseline of one row of type to the baseline of the next row of type (see Figures 1.32 and 1.33). It is not only important for readability, but also for appearance. Even when characters include a small amount of vertical space above and below the ascender and descender lines, rows of type will appear to be very close together. That is, unless they are set within a vertical distance considerably larger than that of the nominal point size. This problem varies greatly among fonts. As a general rule, the amount of space between lines, as expressed as a percentage of point size, should be no less than 120%. For example, if your text is 10–point, you should consider a leading of at least 12 points.

Leading, like kerning, cannot be specified with HTML.

Text reads well with a suitable font that enhances your subject matter. Bold and italic versions of your chosen font design add subtle *emphasis* to the text when used in a sensible way.

Text with very tight vertical spacing.

Text reads well with a suitable font that enhances your subject matter. Bold and italic versions of your chosen font design add subtle *emphasis* to the text when used in a sensible way.

Text with proper amnount of vertical spacing.

Effects on Readability

As each type style is different, the leading you choose will change based on the style you consider. A common problem is too little leading on very long lines of type. Leading should increase proportionally as line length increases.

Here are some important tips regarding your leading choices and how they will affect the type styles you choose:

➡ Body text can handle greater leading better than less leading.

➡ Display faces, such as headlines, look appropriate when little leading, or sometimes negative leading, is used. In this instance, the characters are so much larger than the body text that the tightness of the lines is not as apparent.

➡ Typefaces with small x–heights do not require leading beyond the 120% as was mentioned earlier because the small height provides enough vertical space above it.

➡ Typefaces with standard or above average x-height require a bit more leading.

➡ Typefaces with large x–heights require even more leading because the tall x–height requires it.

➡ If sans serifs are used for body text, leading needs to be increased, sometimes as much as 135–140% of the nominal point size. Because of the lack of a serif, the stem of a sans serif will be more striking to the reader's eye and may appear larger.

➡ Typefaces with larger x-heights have larger appearance sizes, and therefore, require more vertical space. This is what happens when a Modern style is used.

➡ Vertical space may need to be increased for texts with tall ascenders, descenders, or caps.

➡ There should be adequate vertical space for diacritical marks (accents).

➡ If you combine different fonts within a row of text you need to be sure that the combination does not interfere with the regular vertical spacing of the row in relation to the other rows. Fonts from different typeface families may be aligned to different vertical positions within the overall vertical space set in the leading option.

Wordspacing and Body Text Alignment

Wordspacing is the amount of space between words in a paragraph. Wordspacing should always be consistent and even, aiding in the rhythm of reading. The belief most commonly held and adhered to is that when words are set to be read in sequence, they should always be closely spaced. Lines and pages are easier to read when wordspacing is close than when spacing between words is too wide. Close wordspacing greatly improves the color (the degree of blackness) of a line.

Usage

A carefully composed text page appears as an orderly series of black strips separated by horizontal channels of white space. Open wordspacing keeps short letters and serifs from performing their important function—that of keeping the eye moving along the line.

First rule of wordspacing—if you notice the spacing, there are problems. Any feeling of vertical emphasis is absent in a well-composed page. The close wordspacing ensures that the white space is available for use between the lines where it serves its purpose of aiding readability. On the other hand, if words are spaced too closely, they can appear as one giant indistinguishable word.

Screen resolution, being much less than that of printed output, can make words appear closer than they are. When printed, however, the wordspacing may be fine. Take this into consideration when designing a font or using it in the layout of your Web page. The goal is to keep the eye moving as it does normally, scanning left to right. An interruption of that rhythm stops the flow of information and the viewer may move on to other sites.

Justification

Body text can be aligned in the following ways—justified left (which is flush left, ragged right), justifed right (which is flush right, ragged left), justified (which is flush left and right), and centered (which is ragged left and right). Body text is usually aligned in one of two ways—justified or justified left.

Justified text is flush on both sides, with even margins. Justified text often appears more professional. It imparts a more formal, business-like tone. However, wordspacing issues are much more evident in justified text. The effects can be quite drastic. Justifying text causes words to be pushed and pulled together. If text is justified, wordspace will expand or contract as necessary in order to align characters at the left side and the right side of the text column.

Unfortunately, most page layout programs do not allow for much control over wordspacing within justified text. The resulting disruption between character relationships and word and line spacing can reduce the legibility of the text (see Figures 1.34 and 1.35). This is very noticeable in narrow columns. The narrower the column, the greater the opportunity for word spacing problems.

It has been said that justified text is easier to read than justified left text. I would submit that this may be the case if and only if the wordspacing is excellent.

He who first shortened the labor of copyists by device of movable types was disbanding hired armies, and cashiering most kings and senates, and creating a whole new democratic world: he had invented the art of printing.

Figure 1.36

Justified text with poor wordspacing.

He who first shortened the labor of copyists by device of movable types was disbanding hired armies, and cashiering most kings and senates, and creating a whole new democratic world: he had invented the art of printing.

Figure 1.37

Justified text with proper wordspacing.

Margins and Other Options

One of your options to make justified text look better is to take control of your margins.

Take care to work the margins, decreasing or increasing them by $\frac{1}{8}$ of an inch at a time until the wordspacing is acceptable. A good column width for single column pages is about 4.25–4.5 inches, roughly 26 to 28 picas.

Decreasing or increasing your body text point size by 1 point could correct bad wordspacing. If you do this, be careful not to size your type too much—very small or very large body text reads poorly.

Another option for better-looking justified text is hyphenation, which is discussed more thoroughly later in this chapter.

Ragged Text

Justifed left text, also referred to as ragged text, can solve much of the difficulty of wordspacing because of the ragged right side (see Figure 1.36). Odd line breaks are always preferable to bad wordspacing. Ragged text is more casual and more personal than justified text. It is commonly used.

He who first shortened the labor of copyists by device of movable types was disbanding hired armies, and cashiering most kings and senates, and creating a whole new democratic world: he had invented the art of printing.

Justified left text.

Centered text (see Figure 1.37), which is ragged on both left and right sides, is used less often. The eye is used to beginning each line at the same left position and centered alignment disrupts this. You will see it used in special cases, such as when setting text for poetry, business cards, or invitations.

He who first shortened the labor of copyists by device of movable types was disbanding hired armies, and cashiering most kings and senates, and creating a whole new democratic world: he had invented the art of printing.

Figure 1.39

Centered text.

Justified right text (see Figure 1.38) is rarely used. It too goes against the eyes' desire to start each line at a certain launching point, reading left to right. Justified right text could be used at the top of a letter. A person's name and address usually aligns left at the top of the page. Additional information like the date can be right aligned.

He who first shortened the labor of copyists by device of movable types was disbanding hired armies, and cashiering most kings and senates, and creating a whole new democratic world: he had invented the art of printing.

Figure 1.40

Justified right text.

Paragraph Blocking

The style in which you lay out your paragraphs is less critical than wordspacing, but still should be treated seriously and with great care.

Block Style

Block style paragraphs do not begin with an indent, they simply have a blank space between paragraphs. These are generally easier to read because the eye always starts along the left edge rather than having to jump in at the starting line of each paragraph. They also look cleaner and add white space to the page.

Some important things to remember when using block paragraphs:

➡ Always make sure there is a blank space between block style paragraphs. Ignoring this rule leads to very long text blocks that are too tiring to read.

➡ Although it is natural to put an extra return between paragraphs by pressing Enter, it is a better idea to allow your software to do the inter-paragraph spacing. If you press Enter, you are locked into normal line spacing. If your software does it, you can specify exactly how much space you leave between paragraphs.

He [the writer] must teach himself that the basest of all things is to be afraid; and, teaching himself that, forget it forever, leaving no room in his workshop for anything but the old verities and truths of the heart, the old universal truths lacking which any story is ephemeral and doomed — love and honor and pity and pride and compassion and sacrifice.

Figure 1.41

An example of block style paragraph.

Indented Style

The accepted size of a paragraph indent is one em (see Figure 1.40). That means that if your body text is 12 point, you indent the first line 12 points, or about .17 inches (or the width of two tabs). If your software does not enable you to enter a measurement in points (and most of them do), approximate.

Here are some additional tips for using indented style paragraphs:

➡ The depth of the indent is relative to the width of the column. You can use a larger indent for effect, but a smaller one will look like a mistake.

➡ Do not use deep indents on narrow columns. Columns that are too narrow interrupt the eye too frequently to be successful.

➡ If you are setting short paragraphs, do not use an indent because it is too distracting.

➡ Do not indent using spaces. It is much easier to make errors by indenting too much or too little.

➡ When indentation is called for, the first line of the commencing paragraph should be set full out (no indent). This treatment gives the page a strong and clean beginning. Similarly, the first line of a paragraph immediately below a subheading should be full set out.

➡ When body text wraps around an image or another element, pay close attention to the indentation of the affected paragraphs. Wrapping can eliminate indentation in certain cases, so you'll want to adjust the indents manually, perhaps differently in each paragraph.

He [the writer] must teach himself that the basest of all things is to be afraid; and, teaching himself that, forget it forever, leaving no room in his workshop for anything but the old verities and truths of the heart, the old universal truths lacking which any story is ephemeral and doomed — love and honor and pity and pride and compassion and sacrifice.

Figure 1.42

Indented text.

Boxed Text

If an important note or statement must be made and you want to set it apart from the rest of your text, you may want to use boxed text.

Boxed text is an effect used to separate and emphasize words within the enclosure (see Figure 1.41). However, merely setting the text apart from the rest by encircling it with a box is not enough. It must be done correctly.

➡ Make sure to leave a border of white space inside and outside the box. It provides the eye with a barrier around the text and makes it look more professional.

➡ Do not let the text touch the borders of the box. This leads the reader to believe that some of the text may be hidden underneath the box. It will also look rather unsightly. A clean, even space surrounding the text focuses the reader's eyes within the box toward the words.

This is an example of boxed text. This is an example of boxed text. This is an example of boxed text. This is an example of boxed text.

Figure 1.43

Boxed text.

Copyfitting

Copyfitting is the process of estimating (or "fitting") the selected type size and leading in which the copy can be set to fill a predetermined area (see Figure 1.42).

Copyfitting is not as critical to a Web page designer as it is to a printer because the number of pages that need to be set is not the main concern of a Web page designer. Space is seldom an issue. However, if a Web page designer does limit herself to a specific amount of space, then the concern is a valid one.

Novice typesetters will often compress or expand a typeface to achieve copyfitting. Although this may work for certain decorative typestyles, this technique is frowned upon for the proper setting of regular body text. It is always better to use effective tracking and spacing techniques or adjust your column width than to play around with the proper proportions of a font. Any extreme modifications to the height or width creates a distortion of the font, which is displeasing viewing material to any reader.

If the text is too long, adjust the point size in small increments. This is a fast and easy way to adjust the length of your text. Remember, all of your body text should be the same size, so if you adjust it at all, the new point size must be reflected in all of the body text.

Adjusting margins by a small amount may allow for better-fitting text. The same rule applies for margins; any adjustment in size must be reflected throughout your document.

If the text is too short, you can also adjust the point size. It works just as well for lengthening your text as it does for shortening. You may also consider adding subheads. This will make the text longer and break it up, ridding it of an overall grey look. Adjusting margins is yet another option.

Typography can be used to express your own voice. At the same time, it should represent the message you are delivering. It takes some time and skill to familiarize yourself with different typestyles. You must do this to convey your messages.

Typography can be used to express your own voice. At the same time, it should represent the message you are delivering. It takes some time and skill to familiarize yourself with different typestyles. You must do this to convey your messages.

Figure 1.44

Copyfitting to make text "fit" into a pre-determined area.

Hyphenation

Hyphenation is an essential part of justified text. It also improves the appearance of justified left text. Without hyphenation, justification routines tend to open spacing excessively, giving you very obvious areas of space between words or characters.

Most page layout programs have the capability to hyphenate text automatically. However, the automatic mechanism follows what is contextually legal to do. Most do not take into consideration the reader's keen eye for what is too much hyphenation and what looks best (see Figure 1.43).

Some rules for using hyphenation include the following:

➡ Beware of too much hyphenation; too many consecutively hyphenated lines can be rather unsightly.

➡ Rely on your own eye to make sure that your decisions to hyphenate are valid ones. These decisions should be based upon aestethics.

➡ Do not hyphenate a word if the latter part of the word is less than three characters and the former part is less than two characters.

➡ Hyphens should never be used as dashes. Hyphens are used for breaking words on syllable at the end of lines. The en dash is used as a substitute to define the word "to" or "through" such as in "pages 10–20" or "Dec. 12–15." It can also be used to replace the colon. The em dash is used parenthetically to show a break in thought or to emphasize, such as "Bye—she thought to herself." Like the en dash, it too can take the place of a colon.

> Typography can be used to ex-press your own voice. At the same time, it should always re-present the message you are de-livering. It takes some experi-ence to familiarize yourself with different typestyles.

> Typography can be used to express your own voice. At the same time, it should always represent the message you are delivering. It takes some experi-ence to familiarize yourself with different typestyles.

Figure 1.45

Examples of hyphenation.

Conclusion

In this chapter, you learned the basics of letterform anatomy, type history, and font classification. You also learned the importance of letter spacing, word spacing, and other conventions as they relate to readability. Now that you're armed with this knowledge, in the next chapter you'll learn the finer points of identifying and choosing font characteristics to achieve effective composition.

Effective Composition

Many aspects of document content influence how well typefaces perform. By drawing attention to these different influences, we are reminded that it usually takes several fonts to provide you with the choices you need in developing a page.

The standard rule has been to limit your font usage in a layout to two fonts, thus providing consistency across the page. Web pages, however, can contain great amounts of information and need to grab the reader's attention, much like that of a billboard. If your Web documents are intended to contain mostly text, one or two fonts is enough. If your pages are to be used as a marketing or showcasing tool, you may want to add more font choices.

The typographic and page layout choices we discuss in this chapter help in defining your message, your voice. They are about giving your page personality. And although attracting an audience is vital to a successful Web page, the organization of that page and how best to present information is equally important.

You want to inspire your audience. The content and the message must be clear. This chapter will attempt to employ those features that can lend a hand in building effective Web pages.

Character Options

There are several unique types of characters that, when integrated into a printed or Web design, can act as a focus or an entry point for a larger composition. Some can act as supporting players in combination with other typographic elements or images. But it is important to choose these characters carefully, noting their strengths and weaknesses in different arrangements.

Drop Caps

The use of initial letters goes back to their artistic and elaborate application in the earliest of books. The Gutenberg Bible, for example, contains colorful initials drawn by hand.

Drop caps are the oldest style of initial. They are used primarily to break up the grey monotony of long text blocks. Drop caps provide an excellent way to start an article or chapter because they attract attention and add graphic interest to the page (see Figure 2.1). A drop cap is the first letter of a word that drops into the body of the text. It is set down within the copy.

The most important aspect in the use of initial letters is 'fit'—the space surrounding the initial should be optically the same on the side as it is on the bottom. Because drop caps are usually large (24 to 72 point), you should use a typestyle that is graphically interesting, not just big. The bottom of the drop cap should not float between the lines of the paragraph but should sit on the same baseline as one of the lines of text. If quotes are to be set around a drop cap, they should be set in a size between the text size and the initial letter size.

T here is a sumptuous variety about the New England weather that compels the stranger's admiration —and regret. There weather is always doing something there; always attending strictly to business; always getting up new designs and trying them on people to see how they will go. But if gets through more business in spring than in any other season. In the spring I have counted one hundred and thirty-six different kinds of weather inside of twenty four hours.

Figure 2.1

An example of a drop cap.

To make a drop cap, follow these steps:

1. Select the first letter in the paragraph, choosing a large point size and the bold style from the appropriate menu or sub-menu.

2. From the Style menu, make the character a subscript.

3. Return to the main document window and place a tab stop in the document ruler so that you can place a few lines of the opening paragraph's text to the right of the drop cap.

4. You may have to adjust the drop cap size or adjust the amount of subscripting to raise or lower the letter to the proper height.

The other type of initial is the "raised cap." A raised cap is a first character that is raised above the body of a paragraph (see Figure 2.2). Raised letters also can be indented.

In many cases, image files are used to create the effect of drop caps, particularly on Web pages. Later chapters discuss how to create such image files.

During the whole of a dull, dark and soundless day in the autumn of the year, when the clouds hung oppressively low in the heavens, I had been passing alone, on hordeback, through a singularly dreary tract of country, and at length found myself, as the shades of evening drew on, within view of the melancholy House of Usher.

Figure 2.2

An example of a raised cap.

Small Caps

A small cap is an uppercase character that is about 70–80 percent of the height of the existing uppercase characters. Small caps work effectively for titling. They work with normal text, but only when you want to convey a more formal, elegant tone. Small caps work well for abbreviations of awards, decorations, honors, and titles that follow a person's name.

Note | Titling is similar to a heading, presenting the title of a film or the name of the book. It showcases the title or phrase that is represented.

Some typographers prefer to use small caps for postal abbreviations and geographical acronyms longer than two letters.

True-drawn small caps are the same height as the x-height and usually equal to the normal cap width. They also resemble regular caps in stroke weight, designed for easy integration as a natural complement to the regular cap character. True-drawn small caps are not available in most fonts with standard character sets. Some applications (such as QuarkXPress and Adobe PageMaker) enable you to create small caps. Depending on the type style you use, you may need the small caps to be larger than 70–80 percent of the true caps. If 70 percent begins bringing the small caps close to the lowercase in height and you want them to remain distinctive, a small cap that is 80–90 percent of the cap height may be more suitable. Experiment with what looks best to you. Adjust the point size down for a set of caps as an alternative way to simulate true-drawn small caps.

Some fonts are sold with both small caps and oldstyle figures, taking the place of the lowercase and standard lining figures, respectively. Adobe Systems refers to these fonts as SCOsF fonts, or Small Caps and Oldstyle Figure fonts.

Small caps are preferable in typefaces with fine features and a small x-height whereas full-size caps are more suitable in typefaces with larger x-heights and a more robust form. Words in text generally look better as a combination of small and regular caps, rather than all caps. Using full-size caps in combination with small caps enhances the strengths of both letterforms to produce more readable text.

Adobe's Janson Text Roman SCOsF and Adobe Caslon SCOsF are two examples of fonts whose lowercase and lining figures are replaced with small caps and oldstyle figures. The oldstyle figure works well with the classical look of the small cap.

> Do not slope small caps! Their size and shape do not lend themselves to such manipulation.

AaBbCcDdEeFfGgHhIiJjKkLlMm NnOoPpQqRrSsTtUuVvWwXxYyZz

Figure 2.3

An example of small caps used as lowercase letterforms.

Lining and Oldstyle Figures

First, a little history. The set of figures we use, Arabic numerals (numbers or numerals as they are known to many people), have been commonly used throughout the world since ancient Arabic scholars first used them.

Because figures are used extensively for lists and tables, they need to have the same set widths to align properly. Because of this, the figure 1, which is narrow, looks lost in the white space to the left and the right of the character. Most fonts have a fitted figure 1, which means it is allowed to have a tighter set width—the white space to the left and right of the character fit to space it better (see Figure 2.5).

Lining figures are just that—figures that align together to the same baseline. They are also the same height. Lining figures have become a permanent feature of typeface design since the 18th century. They are more a matter of function and necessity, rather than aesthetics.

411.25
2,435.00
1,007.25
$3,853.50

32MB/2.5GB/150MHz

Figure 2.4

Notice the spacing around the figure 1.

Oldstyle figures have similarities to lowercase characters, having ascenders, descenders, and x-heights. They are appropriate for a more elegant look. These figures are better substitutes than lining figures in many text situations, such as passages of text where numbers, dates, and dollar amounts are intermixed.

Oldstyle figures are always legible, for the same reason lowercase letters are legible—the variation in size plays an integral part in the role of recognition. Lowercase characters are distinctive in shape and size through their variation in round and square features and their ascender and descender features. Oldstyle figures benefit from a similar variation in size of shape by having ascending and descending features. Oldstyle figures should be used whenever the surrounding text is set in lowercase or small caps. They are aesthetically pleasing when they are set with lowercase characters.

Oldstyle figures are inappropriate for use when you are dealing with many rows of numbers (for example, forms or price lists). The effect of the descending or ascending parts of the oldstyle figures repeated over and over again in a list or form is irritating to the eye (see Figure 2.6). They are seldom seen in sans serif types as well. Sans serif styles are much more uniform in their style and appearance than serif styles. The oldstyle figure does not lend itself to a uniform look.

$$0123456789$$

$$0123456789$$

Figure 2.5

An example of variations among oldstyle numerals.

360 degrees   1-508-555-1212

February 9, 1996   1895-1962

Figure 2.6

The alignment of these characters does not recommend the typeface for use in a list.

Swash Characters

The swash is an element of the character. It means "flourished." Swash characters are generally more of an aesthetic choice rather than a functional one. They have disappeared to some extent in modern times. Today's reader has a much shorter attention span, and some of the need to accentuate our text (that is, adding flourishes to characters to decorate) has been lost in today's mad-dash world of providing great amounts of information fast. You will, however, see swash characters used. They are beautifully drawn weapons that graphic designers like to have in their design arsenal. In typographic terms, a flourish is a very wide bold stroke, meant to accentuate.

Swash characters are usually cursive. Hence, swash typefaces are usually italic. These characters have long fluid shapes, leading the eye around the curves, highlighting its beauty. They can be used for display and titling, but only sparingly because the simple beauty of the stroke is lost when repeated over and over again. It becomes more of a distraction than an attraction.

There are several types of swash letters:

➡ Logotypes—swash initial followed by an italic lowercase letter.

➡ Two attached lowercase letters.

➡ A variation of single swash characters, some of which are required to be used in the middle or end of a word.

Me

ck

a e t z

v w

We-lcome

Style Effects

Every page layout program has a number of style effects that you can add to (or detract from) your text by highlighting the text and choosing a style option from the menu or submenu. These options can provide weight, posture, and special effect attributes from which to choose. The style effects we will discuss are:

➡ Underlining

➡ Outline

➡ Shadow

➡ Strikethru

➡ Plain

➡ Bold

➡ Italic

➡ Reverse

Underlining

Underlining is a feature available in most applications, but it should only be used in certain situations. Financial or academic publications are environments where underlining may be applicable. When it comes to normal body text, underlining is very distracting.

Underlining can disrupt the flow of words if the underline is positioned too closely to the character's baseline. The underline cuts throught the descenders and can disrupt vertical spacing as well. Therefore, other means of emphasis should be used (such as emboldening or italisizing a font) if possible. Because the typewriter has a very limited palette for emphasizing, the underline is used to a great extent.

Word underlining is a similar attribute that does not extend the underline between words, leaving the interspacing free of any line. Usage of word underlining should follow that of the underline explained in the previous paragraphs.

<u>underline</u>

Outline

This effect drops out the black from the inside of the highlighted characters. Outline fonts commonly are used in display work. Some fonts, such as Caslon Open, are specifically designed as outline fonts. Outlining works well for both serif and sans serif typefaces.

Shadow

This seldom-used effect puts a drop shadow on highlighted characters. Unless you are designing a newsletter for home or for other non-professional uses (such as a birthday party invitation, an informal document, or community announcements) where it is acceptable, do not use it; it is a garish looking effect that compromises readability.

shadow

Strikethru

This effect is most commonly used by editors to cross out words. The strikeout line extends across both the words and the space in between. Strikethru can also be used effectively as a marketing tool. Allowing the customer to see a sales announcement that says "20% OFF" with a strikethru effect and then a final line that says "60% OFF" shows the reader that prices are being slashed.

~~strikethrough~~

Plain

This is the default choice, keeping your font as it is with no alteration to style. Plain is chosen when another style effect has been applied to your font and you want to return to the original style.

plain

Bold

This attribute emboldens your font. If there is a bold version of your font installed on the computer system, the application will intelligently grab the true bold weight, instead of emboldening the Roman weight. Depending on how your bold font has been made, it will either appear in the font style window as "Pine Bold," or as "Pine," which is the font name. If it appears as "Pine," the weight will have to be chosen within the style effect menu.

It is always preferable to use a real bold font (one that was originally designed at the actual bold weight) rather than emboldening a Roman weight font. Emboldening is an algorithm that adds weight to a font by a certain percentage. It does not take into consideration all the idiosyncracies of a design as a type designer does when he creates the bold font.

bold

Italic

Italics are used to emphasize, to attract attention when pointing out a key word or phrase. The italic option works like the bold choice. It will slope the roman or bold font you have chosen. If, however, there is a true italic version of your font on the computer system, it will intelligently grab the true italic, rather than slope the roman postured font. Here again, you want to use a real italic font if it exists on your computer system, rather than slope a Roman font. Sloping just slants the Roman features. There are many adjustments a designer makes when creating an italic font that the sloping algorithm does not, such as the stresses on a round curve or the positioning of already diagonal strokes.

Reverse

This effect reverses the highlighted text from black to white. Reverse is used when the background color is a color other than white and you want the text to be white. Readability can be adversely affected if the contrast between the background and the white text is not great enough (as with a bright yellow or pink background). If the background is dark enough, white text can sometimes be easier on the eye than black text on a very bright white background.

I would suggest using sans serif styles over serif styles when using this affect. If your characters have small or delicate serifs, they can get lost in the reverse process.

Content Organization

Page structure can have as much impact on readability as character appearance. It determines, to a large extent, whether the viewer makes the proper associations, performs the designated tasks, or reaches the intended conclusion. There are a variety of typographic features that can be used to construct a hierarchy of information on your Web page.

Headings

Headings are the front door to your Web page. They are the entryways through which a reader begins to read the text that follows. The point size of the heading should be larger than the body text, enabling it to stand out.

Headings should be consistently aligned throughout the publication or document. They need to relate to the rest of the page. Otherwise, they look unorganized, as if they've been haphazardly scattered. If you stand back and look at the page, the headings should line up with the text. Being off by even a small amount will be noticeable.

Here are some important points regarding headings:

➡ Headings can take many forms, but one of the first decisions is whether they will be symmetrical to the page, or asymmetrical. Symmetrical headings, centered on the page, are called cross-heads. Centering headlines works with justified text.

➡ Asymmetrical headings usually take the form of left-side headings, which are set flush left. Right alignment of a heading is rare for readability; left alignment is most common.

➡ Make sure to break any long headings at a sensible spot. What counts is that the message is conveyed to the reader as effectively as possible.

➡ Headings should not have periods.

> # Symmetrical Heading

> # Asymmetrical Heading

> # ❖❧Ornate Crossheading❧❖

Bullets

The bullet character is used to list or mark text that is important and needs to be highlighted. Bullets are used to give emphasis to a text segment or word and are either flush left or indented slightly from the left margin. The text following the bullet should be indented further past the bullet.

Bullets should align as close to the x-height as possible if they are full size and center on the x-height if not full size. Make sure that the bullet is not too big relative to the type it is addressing or it will stand out too much.

Bullets can be filled (black) or open (an outline).

○ number one	• number one
○ number two	• number two
○ number three	• number three
○ number four	• number four
○ number five	• number five
○ number six	• number six

Boxes

Boxes, like bullets, are used to give emphasis to a text segment or word. They should be as close to the type's x-height as possible if full size and center on the x-height if not full size. Boxes are used to indicate the end of a story in a magazine or book and can be filled (black) or open (an outline).

▫ number one	▪ number one
▫ number two	▪ number two
▫ number three	▪ number three
▫ number four	▪ number four
▫ number five	▪ number five
▫ number six	▪ number six

Borders

Borders are frames placed around type, graphics, or other material in Web pages for decoration as well as to separate text.

Your border should reflect the typography it is framing or separating. If your type is ornate, a delicate, ornate border will be successful. A delicate, ornate border would not work on a Web page about pro football, for example.

The most important consideration is that the corners of a border meet properly. Also, they should never visually overpower the text that is contained with them.

When using a border, place it with your text and take a step back to look at your page. The weight of the border has a great affect on its success at working with your type. If the border is too heavy, it overpowers the text. If it is too light, it loses its usefullness as a place separator.

You can create your own border by selecting a single ornament and repeating it horizontally and vertically. An ornament is a graphic shape that takes its place within a font as would any other character. When the key it has been mapped to is selected, the ornament appears.

Superscripts/Subscripts

Superscripts and subscripts (also referred to as superiors and inferiors) are usually set in a smaller point size than the typeface in use and positioned above or below the baseline. Superscripts and subscripts are typographical asides—small in relative importance to the regular text and raised to keep them out of the flow of the main text. Common uses for superscript include:

➡ When a numeral is used to indicate a number raised to a certain power.

➡ When a name or phrase is registered or trademarked.

➡ To indicate elements on the periodic chart.

Many fonts include sets of superscript figures, but these are not always of satisfactory size.

Text figures set at a reduced size and elevated baseline are sometimes the better choice. They can be manufactured by changing them to a smaller point size and increasing or reducing line spacing for positioning. Adjusting your text figure in size, weight, and spacing to make superscripts will take some care.

Superscripts and subscripts are often numerals, but alphabetic characters are sometimes used. Numeric superscripts are used for chemical equations and mathematics. They are also used for footnote reference and product pricing.

0123456789 0123456789 0123456789
0123456789 0123456789 0123456789

Grid Systems

A grid is a basic method of measurement that helps a document maintain consistency. Page organization is what grids are all about. They are a great starting point when designing a page and are often used in publication design and other situations where graphic elements must be combined with text. Grids are most important in creating a cohesive page.

If you choose a six column grid, it doesn't mean that you must have six columns of text. It means that the width of those columns is your main unit of measurement. Therefore, you can combine two or more columns for your text and use a single narrow column for the white space. The width of the column could also be used for vertical measurement. This leaves the document or page looking very uniform.

If you want to have a large number of columns, you need a grid with many columns. Remember, if your page is limited (8×11 inches as compared with a newspaper-size page), too many columns of text lead to a lack of readability, so prepare your grid system with this in mind. If your page is as wide as a newspaper, you can afford a grid with more columns. To provide narrow white space between colors, you need a grid with many columns because each column is your main unit of measurement.

Visualize how you want your page to be laid out. If you have the text ready, visualize it in columns on the page. This gives you a better idea as to how the page should be laid out.

Type for Communication

Fonts help express our written message in the same way that a palette of colors helps to express a painting. Knowing what fonts to use, similar to choosing color, depends on the nature of the work. Whether you're designing for the Web or printing a birthday card, fonts should convey the mood, importance, and context of the message.

Finding a Common Thread

Consistency is one form of typographic beauty. Contrast is another. A given page can be set from beginning to end in one type style and in one size. It can also be filled with variety. Onscreen, pages are comprised of many different elements such as text, headings, lists, captions, and so on. Some of these elements need to be differentiated typographically, but at the same time, these different elements should form a visual unity.

Typeface families are designed to do just that. Most pages can be set perfectly well with only one family of type. Different text elements set in roman, bold, italic, condensed, or other variants of a typeface should be instantly distinguishable, though clearly related in style (see Figure 2.8). A single font cannot represent all the elements of a document effectively, so you may need to combine two or three fonts.

Jazz music over the years

Jazz music has changed dramatically over the years. From big band to be-bop, straight-ahead jazz to fusion, jazz has transformed itself over time. What hasn't changed is the intensity in which jazz musicians approach their music. When you hear the timeless sound of Miles Davis' *Kind of Blue* or John Coltrane's *Giant Steps* you hear the passion in the voice and it carries through from vision to instrument to art.

Figure 2.8

Varying weights and sizes help to accentuate content.

It takes time to get a feel for how well fonts will perform together, and guidelines exist that can help you when considering mixing fonts.

It can be quite difficult to get more than three typefaces to work together in a single layout. Start with two typefaces, one being a serif style and the other a sans serif.

Starting with two serif fonts or two sans serif fonts gives you two fonts that inherently maintain a number of style and usage similarities. These similarities may outweigh any distinctiveness each font possesses. These fonts may not provide enough contrast. The idea is to take contrasting styles (serif and sans serif) and make them work harmoniously.

The effectiveness with which different typefaces work together depends, in part, on the features of their letterforms. Combinations of fonts are expected to show either a sharp contrast or a great similarity of character. If you mix typefaces with similar appearance to show distinctions, there is a risk that the change in typeface may go unnoticed. If you alternate typefaces to emphasize headings within a text, you should ensure that the vertical spacing of the headings clearly signals their relationship to the text that follows them.

If your page requires elements such as titles, headings, subheads, or math equations, an extended family of fonts, supporting many weights and widths, would be a preferred choice. Avoid using pairs of styles that are too close in weight. Your typeface will provide you with many shapes and sizes but will perform as a single typographic entity.

You may find that choosing one typeface family limits you. In this case, you will need to choose several cohesive families. The importance here is that your mixing and matching of fonts be done carefully (see Figure 2.9).

Packers, 21 Dallas 10

Green Bay, Wisconsin - It took all but two minutes at the end of the fourth quarter for Green Bay Packers to finally put the Dallas Cowboys away. With one minute fifty-eight seconds left, Brett Favre threw a sixteen yard pass to Andre Rison for the winning touchdown. The win put the Packers in the playoffs.

Figure 2.9

Careful use of different font families.

Getting the Desired Results

The typography of each element within the text should fit the element's purpose, whether it is used for sustained reading, skimming, or just to assist a reader's navigation through the text. Different text elements within a document may be distinguished by typefaces that have or do not have serifs, or by fonts with varying degrees of contrast in the width of vertical and horizontal strokes, such as Bodoni Poster.

Contrast is created by mixing typestyles and sizes that are significantly different from each other; this helps to ensure that the eye does not get bored. When dealing with display faces, it is not necessary for the fonts you use on the same page to be inherently similar. There should, however, be some compatibility. A geometrically shaped face such as Bauer Bodoni has little promise as a titling face when the accompanying text face is set in a low-contrast design, where horizontal and vertical strokes are similar in weight.

Packers, 21 Dallas 10

Green Bay, Wisconsin - It took all but two minutes at the end of the fourth quarter for Green Bay Packers to finally put the Dallas Cowboys away. With one minute fifty-eight seconds left, Brett Favre threw a sixteen yard pass to Andre Rison for the winning touchdown. The win put the Packers in the playoffs.

Figure 2.10

Creating contrast between serif and sans serif typefaces.

Appropriateness is important. If you are using an elegant-looking typestyle for your body text, you do not want to use a contrasting font that detracts from the more elegant face. The use of a very heavy font as a heading does not work well with very light text— there will be too much distraction.

You can only be sure that certain fonts work within a text by seeing how they perform. If you are designing for the screen, make sure you study the way your fonts work onscreen. I would suggest that you print your page as well. Proofing can help you determine whether your heavier weights are holding up adequately and that lighter weights are not disappearing.

Point size and screen resolution are integral considerations when choosing type for your page. If you decide to use a subtle design whose features are quiet and refined, those features may get lost on-screen at crude resolutions. However, if the same font is being used at a larger point size as a heading or display font, this may correct the problem.

Mixing and Matching

Typefaces with blunt and substantial serifs, open counters, and little in the way of pretensions, stand the best chance of surviving the inadequacies of low-resolution onscreen use. Always consider a font that can perform well within the crude environment of the screen. Optima, a sans serif style, has very subtle design features. The stems taper and the curves slowly change in weight. These slight changes in design can only be seen at much higher resolutions. Fonts such as this are not recommended for Web use because their personality is lost onscreen. Though the tapers are lost at low resolution, rendering the font with much less personality, it will print well.

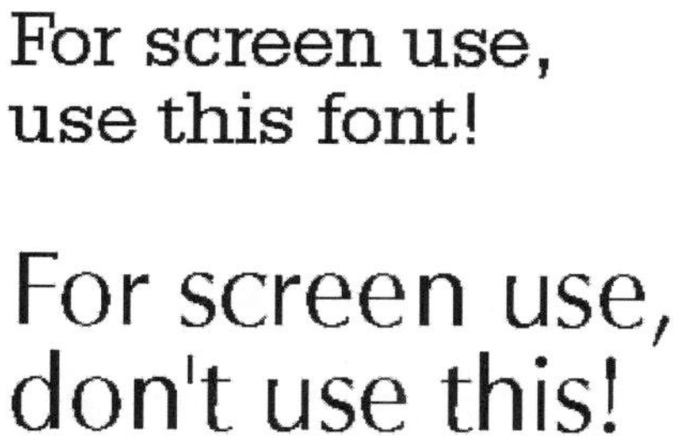

For screen use,
use this font!

For screen use,
don't use this!

Figure 2.11

An example of low-resolution versus high-resolution use.

Monospace typewriter fonts, lacking little in the way of voice and style, have begun to achieve cult status in this age of screen communication. Their bland, uniform look is being hailed as a "grunge" style, working well with other fonts to support and aid in the deliverance of the message.

Grunge
rock.

Approach the mixing of type sensibly, as you would in choosing your own daily attire. (Wait a minute, this may not be sound advice without knowing how you dress!) Look to your message for hints at what might work well with the content you are presenting. Most of all, enjoy the process.

Different Messages

The typefaces you choose should reflect the subject of your text. If your message is about movies, your typographic choices should be sympathetic to that idea. The type should be dramatic and engaging, evoking emotion. The message you contain in your text will be better served by typographic choices that support your theme. There are a few ways to educate yourself in the making of proper typographic choices. One way is to peruse a font catalog that can be obtained from any of the major font foundries. Choose a few fonts you think impart a certain feeling to your text. The other is to consult your neighborhood Web site. Companies such as Adobe Systems, Inc. provide Web pages developed to assist in choosing type effectively (`www.adobe.com/type/browser/info/info0.html`).

Love! Drama! Action! Terror!
This movie has it all and more!

What makes a font dramatic? Dramatic features. Longer ascenders and descenders, graceful lines. A font that is *engaging* grabs your attention; its features stand out. They aren't as long and dramatic but are sharp and distinctive. If your Web page is of an athletic nature, the type you choose should have strong features, maybe even a slick look. Italic sans serifs tend to have a sleeker, slick look. There should be little baggage or ornament to the fonts you use for this theme. As an athlete wears his muscularity, your text should wear its typographic look. A bold, heavy, or ultra weight font is a strong-looking font. I cannot state with enough emphasis how important these choices are. In fact, your readers may not even be aware of the choices you make—but they will inevitably be attracted to the combination of type and message.

Another important choice is the figures in the font. If your Web page supports the use of many numbers, use a selection of fonts that have strong sets of figures.

Ask yourself, when you are trying to decide which fonts to use for your content, whether your content is of a formal or informal nature. Answering this dramatically reduces the number of appropriate typefaces. Formal looking fonts are more traditional and conventional. Serif fonts are more formal than sans serif fonts. Casual looking fonts are informal and friendly. Sans serif fonts are more informal. Fonts with rounder features such as Park Avenue have a softer, more intimate feel to them. Fonts with sharper edges as in a blackletter font have a stronger, cold feel to them. Fonts whose vertical strokes do not sit uniformly on the baseline (such as Dom Casual) tend to be funnier, friendlier. A monospace font (such as Courier) takes on an informative look. Fonts with large round features evoke a lighter mood.

Take care to know a bit about the fonts you are using. Everyone who browses the Web knows intimately what a Times Roman font looks like. Yet there are many typefaces that the lay person would find similar to Times Roman but have many features that define them differently. Your intent and knowing how best to support that intent will decide whether your page is effective.

Warning

> The typestyle should support your composition and assist the reader in enjoying the content. It should not become part of the message or get in the way. Rather, it should act as a well-tuned vehicle for transporting your content across the page.

Cultural Considerations

It is a small world indeed. Languages criss-cross the continents via the Internet and fight for familiarity. Using and mixing different languages will continue to become an issue in the 21st century.

Mixing Foreign Languages

Your audience, particularly on the Web, may be one of differing languages. Mixing Latin letters, however, with Hebrew, Arabic, or Cyrillic is, in principle, scarcely different from mixing a Latin serif font with a sans serif one. Although they may look different and may even read in different directions, these different alphabets spring from the same source and are written with the same tools.

Though the differences in a Latin and non-Latin fonts are usually obvious, there are many structural similarities. Because of this, the same questions and decisions made for developing a page of Latin text must be made for a multilingual one. A TrueType font with a standard character set contains a number of European characters.

One of the most important decisions is whether to emphasize or minimize the differences in the languages. It is a general rule that if a typographer wants to mix the different alphabets closely, they must be close in color and size. The Latin, Greek, and Cyrillic alphabets are closely related in structure. Most Cyrillic fonts have much of the same color and shape as Latin small caps.

Asian fonts are different from the fonts we previously mentioned. Japanese and Chinese fonts have character sets that contain anywhere from 3,000 to 6,000 characters. These fonts are built differently from Latin, European, Middle Eastern, or Indic fonts because of the sheer scope of the character set. Because of the enormous amount of characters, the way the characters are encoded is completely different as well.

Fonts beyond Latin and European languages have special keyboard layouts and special considerations when using them in a Web page. Localized versions of computer system software deal with their own type of fonts much more efficiently. Many of these language issues are still being addressed. There is no global solution yet.

ABCDEFG
ЉЊЋЂЏБГДЖЗ
бвгджзикфљ

Ligatures

Ligatures can be found in both Latin and non-Latin typefaces. Ligatures are characters made up of two or more characters. Some typestyles, especially oldstyle designs, look considerably better when ligatures are used. They conserve space and help keep the eye moving. They are made for fine typography and are truly a mark of a sophisticated user.

Although they are not seen as often today as they were in olden days, ligatures can add a touch of refinement to your page.

Certain character pairs lend themselves to ligature use. The "fi" and "fl" are commonly joined to present a more pleasing look. Here are some examples of ligatures you will find in most typefaces with standard character sets:

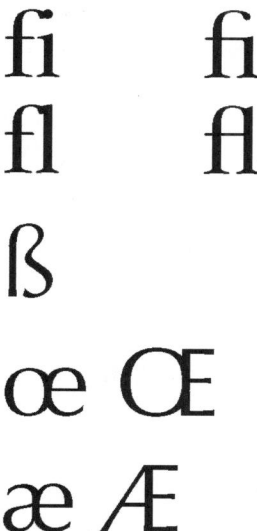

A few words of caution when using ligatures:

➡ Avoid using ligatures with fixed width fonts.

➡ Ligatures are generally only effective at text sizes from 8–14 point.

➡ Avoid using ligatures in all letterspaced type (such as expanded or condensed typefaces).

➡ Most word processors do not have spell checkers sophisticated enough to check for ligatures.

Accents

Typography was once a fluently multilingual and multicultural calling. Within the last 50 years, the digital revolution in typography and the technological breakthroughs in transferring and receiving data in a moment's notice mean we must consider other cultures and languages in our fonts. With the Web as Main Street to the world, we are faced with other cultures and languages at a click of the mouse button.

One of the most striking differences among texts of varying languages is the presence of diacritical marks (accents). Most fonts today have diacritics that are applied in foreign language use. They are formed primarily for pronunciation and stored as separate characters in most fonts. Accents have no width value, but they float above or below the character position. Accents used in this manner are designed for the weight, style, and height of a typeface.

Accented characters can be keyed in two different ways: as the complete character (the alphabetic character and its corresponding accents positioned above or below); or as two keys—one for the accent and one for the alphabetic character. The latter case selects the accent, positions it with no width, and then positions it over or under the alphabetic character. For use with Web pages, the complete character needs to be used.

Character Sets

A character set is a collection of characters brought together for use as a single font. Many of the characters in a character set are not visible on the keyboard, but they can be produced by using the Option, Alt, Control, or a combination of those keys with the Shift key. (Appendix A shows which characters can be accessed from both the Mac and PC keyboard and what keys access them.)

Standard Character Sets

Depending on your needs, a standard character set may or may not supply you with all of the characters you need. If it does not, you may consider producing them yourself in a dedicated font design program. It takes a great deal of skill and training to produce a high-quality font. However, if it is one or two special characters you need added to your set and you are proficient with other design applications (that is, Adobe Illustrator and Photoshop, Macromedia FreeHand), you will find the retail font packages (like Macromedia Fontographer or Pyrus Software's FontLab) both comprehensive and understandable. You can use existing characters to build other characters, like taking a lowercase n and j to compose an n-hook character.

Most type foundries have a standard character set for all of their typefaces. (Appendix A provides a standard PostScript, TrueType, and WGL character set. These are system-wide standards, accepted by the vast audience of font users on both the PC and Mac platforms.)

Expanded Character Sets

Typefaces containing additional characters such as ligatures, fractions, superscripts, subscripts, and other international symbols not normally available in a standard set are considered "expanded" sets. Expert sets do not contain the normal keyboard or alphabetic characters. They are traditionally used in fine typography or for very specific needs.

Getting Noticed

Display typefaces feature bold, eye-catching letters designed to capture the reader's attention. Display fonts are used for headings, titling, posters, advertisements, and other instances where attention grabbing is necessary.

Display type is often sans serif and bolder than the surrounding text. Stylistic extremes are often employed in display styles, making long passages of this type virtually unreadable. Exaggerated serifs, round or elongated characters, or calligraphic flourishes adorn the display style, showing off its sometimes beautiful, sometimes garish appearance.

As showy as it tends to be, display type should be neutral and flexible enough to work well with text faces.

Text typefaces can make the cross over into display type. Rarely does the opposite take place—a true display font crossing into body text. When a text font is set in an ultra-bold weight or expanded or compressed width, it can take on the appearance of a display font. The exaggerated weight and width make the font less readable, but this is not a concern for display fonts, which are used in samples no longer than a line at a time. Whereas body text requires you to look at the typeface set in a paragraph, display text requires you to look at the typeface letter by letter.

ABCDEFGHIJKLMNOPQRSTUVWXYZ
abcdefghijklmnopqrstuvwxyz
0123456789

ABCDEFGHIJKLMNOPQRSTUVWXYZ
abcdefghijklmnopqrstuvwxyz
0123456789

Decorative typestyles overlap into the display arena. Although some designers use decorative faces as display type, these faces generally have so much personality that they monopolize the page design and distract the reader from the message. A decorative font used in a formal setting like that of a business letter or serious presentation sticks out like a sore thumb.

ABCDEFGHIJKLMNOPQRSTUVWXYZ
0123456789
°ₒ°⸰?!()[]#$%&*-

ABCDEFGHIJKLMNOPQRSTUVWXYZ
abcdefghijklmnopqrstuvwxyz
0123456789

ABCDEFGHIJKLMNOPQRSTUVWXYZ
abcdefghijklmnopqrstuvwxyz
0123456789

ABCDEFGHIJKLMNOPQRSTUVWXYZ
°ₒ°?@#$%&()[]+—=13579

Here is a good exercise. Write the words that will be set in the display type. You may also want to write words that describe the style of your document. At the same time, look over many different display fonts. Do any of the fonts you are viewing conjure up an image that reflects your message? Are the letters you are looking at speaking to you in a voice that matches that message? Try several typestyles and get a feel for what you are looking for. It may take some time. There are vast amounts of display (and decorative) fonts available but few that will answer your needs specifically. Your decision should be a font style that enhances your words.

The Web has a number of font foundry sites where you can view font styles online. Some of them offer guidelines on selecting the fontstyle for your needs. The following are Web sites providing high-quality fonts online:

www.letraset.com/itc

www.adobe.com/type

www.microsoft.com/truetype

www.bitstream.com

www.fontbureau.com

Conclusion

This chapter discussed several unique types of characters (drop caps, oldstyle figures, swash characters) that, when combined with more standard typographic elements, provide effective composition. This chapter also covered:

- ➡ Style effects to enhance your text
- ➡ Typographic elements to organize your content (bullets and boxes)
- ➡ Making decisions to mix and match font styles to your content
- ➡ Foreign language considerations

These topics work together to enable the designer to provide his/her content in the most effective way by making informed decisions. The next section deals with the presentation of your content on-screen, how that content is affected by onscreen readability, hinting considerations, and anti-aliasing.

CHAPTER 3

Form and Function

Type is meant to communicate. It also can become noise. When type does not deliver its information simply and clearly, it has failed. As our ways of communicating have evolved from typesetting to laser printing to the computer screen, a type designer's solutions to highly effective type have changed. With the computer screen as one of today's premier communication tools, concerns range from screen clarity and legibility to methods of hinting and antialiasing to provide high-quality screen fonts for use at low resolutions.

The last thing we need is to clutter our screens with bad type. When type becomes noise, it has failed. Over the years, typography has been subject to the same cultural changes that we all face—fashion, music, style—all trends that alter our outlook and define our times. Type changes with time. Although the classics remain, new styles flourish. During the sixties and seventies, the 'mod' and 'hip' trends of fashion and music made their way into the printed word. The late eighties and early nineties experienced a 'grunge' trend, and we see it in the type that has been made available from font foundries. Minimalist designs, where portions of characters represent whole letters and the concept is as important as the typeface itself, have opened the door for more graphic designers to jump into the typographic culture. Figure 3.1 is a good example. Because of this, we not only see some very good type designs, but some very bad ones as well. Without strong backgrounds in typography, these artists are creating many low-quality fonts that are surfacing on the Internet. Figure 3.2 shows a freeware font that was found on the Internet. The quality of the design is fairly low. The weights vary from character to character. Height alignments are off as well. There are several factors that go into quality onscreen type. We will be discussing them and other ways to make the shapes of characters clean and legible on the computer screen.

Figure 3.1

Big Clyde, a well-designed decorative typestyle.

Figure 3.2

Medieval Plain, a freeware font found on the Internet.

The best way to determine a good quality freeware font from a bad one is to look at a paragraph or more of text.

➡ The color (level of blackness as the text is read across the page) of the paragraph should not waver in its darkness. It shouldn't look spotty.

➡ The font should look smooth and consistent. Features such as serifs should be consistent in shape and heights should align. You should also use as many characters as possible from the keyboard.

The Mac comes with a utility called KeyCaps that enables you to see how to access characters beyond the ones designated on the keyboard (using combinations of the Option, Control, or Alt keys). Windows carries a utility called Character Map that provides a similar function. Try them and see if your freeware fonts have any of the characters beyond those designated on the keyboard.

We are a culture of fads and trends. The cyclical motion of these fads seems to accelerate in unison with the speed at which technology changes. The environment in which we are introduced to the latest styles and trends has changed. Today's book, magazine, library, cafe, mall—those places we go to learn, watch, chat, laugh, and shop, are moving in great leaps and bounds to the computer screen. And because of this, the Web is the emerging studio where the artist, designer, writer, and musician will go to create. Our ideas, words, styles, and trends will be developed and communicated on the Web and shared by its large audience.

The screen has become our canvas. We paint images, words, messages onto the screen to evoke emotion, understanding, even excitement. Although print will never go away, the computer and television screens have become the way that most of us gather information. We see our world onscreen, and it is up to us to define it.

In defining this new medium called the Web, issues involving type such as page layout, font availability, and font security need to be addressed. The standardization of a scripting language such as cascading style sheets has provided the designer a strong foundation to start with. High-quality screen fonts that have been hinted and/or antialiased to reduce graphic noise and provide clean, legible text are being developed by several reputable font foundries, such as Galapagos Design Group and Microsoft Corporation. Font security issues continue to be discussed and may be addressed with the advent of OpenType. OpenType will be discussed in full in Chapter 14. As more and more fonts are being downloaded and used on the Web, the type designer needs to know that his/her fonts are safe and will not be stolen or used without license.

What this all comes down to is trying to make the computer screen as effective a communications tool as the printed word. In fact, the attempt should be to provide screen output that can deliver a close representation to what the same content would look like on paper. This is called WYSIWYG (What You See Is What You Get).

Most desktop publishing systems have WYSIWYG screen displays that deliver screen representations of fonts, approximating their appearance on paper. Even these WYSIWYG displays give only an impression of the appearance of type on paper—most are unlikely to accurately represent either the letterforms of characters or their spacing.

Fonts such as Geneva, Monaco, and Courier on the Mac or Arial and Times New Roman on the PC are system fonts that come installed with the computer system. These bitmaps are there to give the designer a core set of quality screen fonts to start with. Bitmaps, however, are low-resolution fonts that are point size and resolution specific. We will discuss bitmaps in more detail later in this chapter.

As technology began providing for better outline fonts, bitmaps fell by the wayside. Outlines are scalable representations of fonts, which allow a designer to use the font at any size. A bitmap is created for use at one specific size. Outlines are very economical for storing character and shape information. They are only transformed or scaled when the typesetter instructs them to do so. Scalable outlines made their introduction into the font industry in the mid-1980s. As users saw the benefits of an outline font as size- and resolution-independent, it became apparent that outlines would be the font format of choice.

The way an outline font works is simple. In fact, anyone who has been a computer user for the last 10 years has been using outline fonts for some time. When you enter an application and type some text, you simply highlight the text and select your font and point size from the appropriate menu. All of the complex transformations that go on to bring a size-independent font file to your prescribed size and resolution takes place behind the scenes. We will discuss outlines in more detail later in the chapter.

High-quality screen fonts are the most important tool in designing typography for the Web. Although the majority of type has always been produced by printers and typesetters, usually at resolutions above 300 dpi (dots per inch), type is now being viewed on low-resolution screens. The computer screens that accompany PCs normally have a screen resolution of 96×96 dots per inch. The Macintosh monitor has a screen resolution of 72×72 dots per inch. Because of the low resolution of these monitors, it is critical how screen size letter appears.

Legibility

Legibility refers to how well a typeface suppports the process of fluent reading. A reader's eyes make a series of fixations across a row of text, taking in a cluster of words at each fixation. Words within a cluster are recognized by their overall contour, not by the design of each letter. Reading words by their overall shape is much faster than reading letter by letter. Sequential letter-by-letter reading is very difficult.

For reading to progress smoothly, the characters of a typeface should harmonize with one another, both in their letterforms and their spatial characteristics. Words of harmonious text should always appear to be whole units, and eye movements should not be disrupted by characters that "jump out" of the text.

A typeface with a larger x-height is likely to be more legible. Most of the characters' details are at a relatively larger size. The larger x-height of the lowercase characers provide more room for the stems, hairlines, and other structural features to be recognizable. Vertically, a lowercase "a" will have more room for its three hairline features if the x-height is larger. Horizontally, a lowercase "m" will benefit from a taller x-height because the width of a character will open up somewhat if the height is larger. Because of this, there will be more room (left to right) for its three stems to render. At too small a point size, the lowercase "m" stems collide and the character becomes unrecognizable.

Type designers make design and spacing decisions based on viewing dark characters on a light background, as in Figure 3.3. If you reverse out the type so that it appears against a black background you may find that the horizontal spacing is not generous enough. Consequently, characters appear to run together. This is partly due to the brightness and glare of the white letterform against a black background. White characters do not appear as sharp and recognizable at small sizes like black or dark characters do. Some adjustments may need to be made to increase character spacing.

Reversed out type

Figure 3.3

Reversed out type.

Text set in all uppercase characters needs more generous horizontal spacing to ensure that individual character shapes are clear.

When your Web content is mostly text, typography is the tool you use to "paint" patterns of organization on the page. The first thing your readers see is not the titling, headings, or other details of the page; they see the overall pattern and contrast of the page. The reader's eye scans the page first as a graphical pattern. Then it begins to track and decode the type and its elements. The regular repeating patterns established through carefully organized pages of text and graphics help the reader to quickly establish the location of your information. It also increases the overall legibility of the page.

A few notes on checking for legibility:

➡ Legibility checks are more difficult to carry out onscreen than they are on paper. You should check on characters as they appear in context. When you decide on the text you are going to use in your Web document, type some of it onscreen to see how the letterforms appear on your page. This gives you a better feel for how a typeface will work when it is read.

➡ Legibility checks should include specimens of text as they will look in your finished document. A specimen of text can contain a row of uppercase characters, lowercase characters figures, punctuation, and other international and symbol characters within the font. It also should contain a paragraph or two of words that utilize most of the uppercase and lowercase letters of the alphabet. I would also add a paragraph or two of text.

Readability

Readability refers to ease of reading in continuous blocks of text and is often more a function of the arrangement of type than of the typeface itself. Normally, we read by recognizing shapes. Making it easy for the eye to scan a line and go to the next line is the key to readability. Lines that are too short, too long, too close together, or otherwise adversely altered make scanning difficult and tiring. This slows down the flow of the information to the brain.

Americans find serif text more readable than san serifs. Europeans find sans serifs more readable. Why the difference? It all comes down to what you are used to, what you grew up reading. This is where readability defines itself beyond legibility. A typeface and the way it is displayed on a page or onscreen may be quite legible. However, if it is a style and layout that is not familiar to someone, he may find it unreadable.

Sans serifs can be difficult to read over long stretches because they are too monotonous. Serifs give letters a more distinctive appearance and shape, and the serif feature itself leads the eye from one letter-form to the other.

Clarity

Typographic design for the computer screen is difficult because of the relatively low resolution of the monitors. Compromises in the resolution and visual contrast of screen typography result in reduced reading speed and comprehension. Proper typographic design can do a great deal to relieve the difficulties of text in onscreen documents.

Good typography depends on both the visual contrast between one font and another, and the contrast between text blocks and the surrounding empty space. Nothing attracts the eye and brain of a reader like strong contrast and distinctive patterns. This is true of Web documents as well. Give consideration to the patterns your text will make in your Web page and to the surrounding space. You only get these attributes by carefully designing them into your page.

Resolution must be considered before deciding on something as important as the main text of your page. Some typefaces look good at almost any size or resolution. Display and script typefaces are less affected by resolution constraints because they are typically set at larger sizes (above 14 point). At small sizes, display faces will suffer regardless of the resolution.

If your Web page is teeming with bold type, everything onscreen will appear similar. It will look like you are just screaming at your audience. If every page is crammed with text, readers will view the page as a wall of gray and will reject the lack of visual contrast. By carefully considering the surrounding space as well as the text, you will avoid filling your pages with text, which does not give the eye anywhere to rest. Make sure to use bold type only where you really need emphasis.

Quality Screen Type

When you are printing a typeface or working with a typestyle on-screen at a very large point size, you are working with large numbers of pixels, which are those dots (or squares as they are seen onscreen) that make up the black character.

When using type at high resolutions, as you would with printers, the pixels are barely recognizable because these units are so small. Yet when you view characters at low resolutions as you would onscreen, you can actually see the patterns that form the character. Although pixel patterns are not such an issue at printer resolutions, they are of great concern as seen onscreen.

When you can see the building blocks of every letter you use, it becomes apparent that their location and configuration are extremely important. We want clean looking characters to grace our Web pages so that the shapes are instantly recognizable. Figures 3.4 and 3.5 contrast a highly unreadable line of text with a much more readable one. Even if we only have a limited number of pixels to work with in painting each letter, we need those pixels to be positioned as best as possible to deliver a recognizable set of letters through which our words will emerge. This means that all of the features of a letterform should be recognizable. A lowercase "e" counter should be open. A lowercase "m" should have space between each of its three stems.

Poor looking screen type

Figure 3.4

Low-quality screen type.

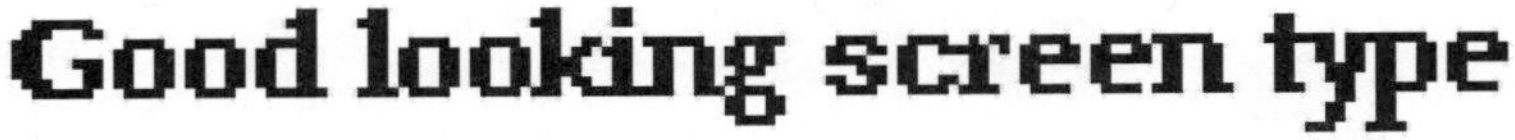

Good looking screen type

Figure 3.5

High-quality screen type.

How do we affect the way the pixel patterns fall on the screen to shape our letters? A good starting point is to make sure you are using a high-quality font, such as those purchased from larger font foundries. You will want to browse the libraries of several type foundries before deciding on where to purchase your typefaces.

But ensuring the quality of a font is not enough. A high-quality font may deliver beautiful letters onto the printed page, but it may fall apart onscreen when limited by the resolution. The way to affect typographic characters onscreen is through the use of hinting, which is covered later in this chapter.

Bitmaps and Outlines

Bitmaps are size-dependent and resolution-dependent representations of our letterforms. A bitmap records the entire description of every cell of the character. This information is stored in the computer system and then rendered directly by the output device. Bitmaps are a precise way to specify a letterform's appearance. They can also be extremely demanding on storage capacity. This is quite true at larger sizes and resolutions. A separate description must be available for each size and resolution that you want your characters to appear. Computer monitors vary in resolution and you must provide a bitmap for each resolution if you want to work in that environment.

Outlines are independent of size and resolution restrictions. They record only a description of the lines and curves that make up the character. It is the output device that fills in the outline of each character as it is being rendered. Outline fonts reside within the computer system in outline form and are only scaled and transformed when the size instructions are given to the application. They are economical in terms of storage because you have access to almost any choice of sizes (only being restricted there by your application's limitiations). The advantage to the outline is its flexibility. If you want to transform an outline character at 12.5 point, as long as your application supports such control, it is possible. Depending on your choice of application, you may be able to manipulate your outlines even further.

Hinting

Hinting is the name for the set of techniques designed to restore, as much as possible, an outline's character legibility. Because bitmaps are size- and resolution-dependent, they can be edited by the type designer to make sure each letterform is readable. The type designer cannot edit an outline for any particular point size or resolution. To help the outline with screen recognition, there is hinting. Hinting is a typographic technology applied to a font when it is being developed into a character set. The technique consists of careful and usually small adjustments in the outline filling process (the rasterization). Before hinting, an outline will be filled based on where the curves and contour is rendered. This can lead to shapes that are often unaesthetic or illegible (see Figure 3.8). At low resolutions, undesirable rounding effects mean that part of some characters can disappear and other parts may appear too thin or too thick. Diagonals, for example, suffer greatly when an outline is rasterized as a black character.

Ever since software designers and typographers were given the task of rendering scalable type on low resolution devices, hinting has been an acknowledged way of dealing with resolution limitations. Hints attempt to correct onscreen anomalies by equalizing the weight of stems and hairlines, preventing parts of characters from disappearing and generally maintaining aesthetic appearance and legibility down to as low a resolution as possible (see Figure 3.6).

Well hinted screen type

Figure 3.6

Hinted screen type.

Fonts That Include Hinting

The goal of hinting is to improve quality. A hinted font will provide text where the stroke weights are consistent, diagonals and curves are controlled, and the overall effect is more appealing.

There are two standard font formats that include different types of hinting—PostScript Type 1 and TrueType.

PostScript Type 1

There are two kinds of PostScript fonts: Type 1 and Type 3. Type 1 is Adobe Systems hinted PostScript font. Type 3 is a PostScript font that is unhinted. With regard to this discussion, anytime PostScript is used it is meant to describe Type 1 hinting. There are no Type 2 fonts.

PostScript Type 1 fonts truly fueled the desktop publishing explosion. The PostScript technology came from Adobe Systems, Inc. Adobe had once owned PostScript, which is a device independent language that enables text and graphics to be printed at any resolution on any PostScript-based output device. PostScript fonts have been around for over a decade. There are thousands of them. In PostScript Type 1s, each character is stored as a scalable outline made up of curves and control points.

The hinting of a font can be done automatically by designing a font with a retail type development tool such as Fontographer or FontLab or by proprietary tools that font foundries use when they create their designs. Hints can also be added manually within the aforementioned tools.

Type 1 hints make for high-quality typographic images when those images are output to a printer or if those images are used at a higher point size on the screen. It has been my experience, however, that Type 1 hints do not do enough to assist a font's appearance onscreen at small sizes (see Figure 3.7). At screen sizes, you still get pixel dropout (missing pixels) along the baseline, as well as heavy diagonals. This is because the Type 1 hints do not provide enough control over character features at small sizes.

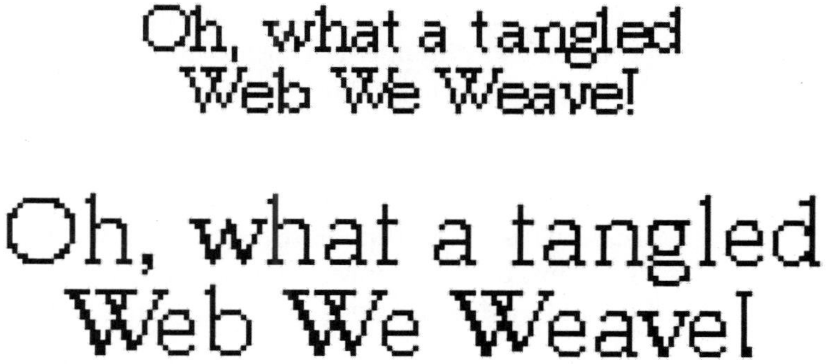

Figure 3.7

PostScript font at screen sizes.

TrueType

TrueType hints address many of the issues surrounding onscreen display of text. The TrueType format was developed by Apple Computer, Inc. in 1990. Apple made TrueType an open environment. This meant that anyone could develop TrueType. The computer code that made up the TrueType font format was made available to all font developers. This was in direct contrast to PostScript, which was a proprietary format that Adobe wished to keep as their own.

No one outside of Adobe developers could produce PostScript fonts. Much of TrueType's success has to do with its backing and development from Microsoft Corporation. Because of this, Adobe was forced to open their hint architecture to the masses.

The TrueType format is now well established and supported by many Web applications. It has a publicly available font specification. The documentation on how to create and manipulate a TrueType font is contained within the TrueType specification. TrueType instructions try to preserve a character's shape as closely as possible when the character is rendered at any size or resolution (see Figure 3.8). It has a more comprehensive way of dealing with stem and hairline weights, alignments, and diagonal shapes. In effect, the shapes and features of a TrueType font at screen sizes are more recognizable than those within a PostScript font.

TrueType is actually a programming language as well as a hinting format. For most designers, native TrueType hinting is a daunting task. This is because the manual application of TrueType hints onto a font is a much more complex process than applying PostScript hints. There are also a number of tables that must be edited within the font to provide values for height alignment, minimum weight for horizontal and vertical features, and so on. TrueType hinting can be carried out using off-the-shelf font design and manipulation tools. Some font foundries have developed their own proprietary software that provides a suite of tools to use in their creation of TrueType fonts. Most of these conversion tools can take a PostScript Type 1 fonts and use it as a starting point to making a TrueType.

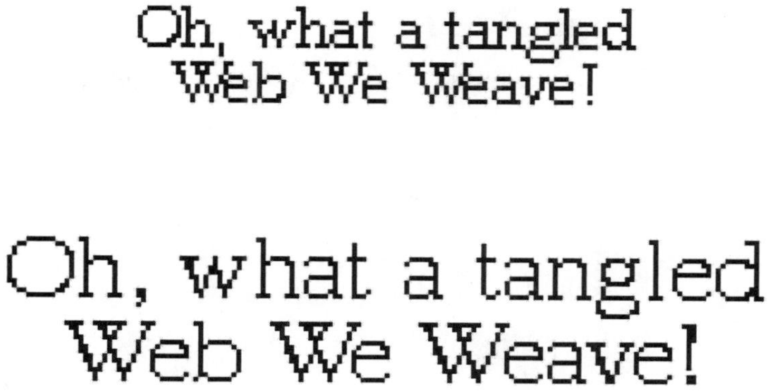

Oh, what a tangled
Web We Weave!

Oh, what a tangled
Web We Weave!

Figure 3.8

TrueType font at screen sizes.

Which format is best? Both formats can be used in the same document successfully. It is not desirable to use both PostScript and True-
Type formats within the same typestyle. As far as quality issues go,
both formats provide good quality output from a printer of 300 dpi
or higher. At screen sizes, TrueType's more robust hinting instructions provide better looking low-resolution images. For this reason
alone I would choose a TrueType font for use in a Web document. It
provides higher quality screen output. As for size, a PostScript font is
usually smaller in file size than a TrueType font, which allows it to be
printed faster. However, most of the Web pages that are viewed are
never output to a printer. If you are running a non–Pentium or non–
PowerPC computer, this may be of some importance to you. However, if you are running one of these faster systems, the speed and
size issues are negligible. Again, both formats maintain excellent output when the device is a printer. A TrueType font will output to a
printer slower than a PostScript but it is due to the TrueType font
containing additional information with it to provide for better
screen output.

Although PostScript was developed to provide higher quality fonts,
and TrueType took that quality to the screen, there exists no font
format exclusively for use on the Web.

OpenType

OpenType could be the answer. OpenType is being developed by the two companies directly responsible for the success of both True-Type and PostScript—Microsoft Corporation and Adobe System, Inc. Microsoft's Windows products support TrueType almost exclusively. OpenType is a new font format that attempts to include both TrueType and PostScript font formats within it, as well as providing additional technology specifically designed to handle the concerns of fonts on the Web. OpenType will be covered thoroughly in Chapter 14.

Aliasing

Aliasing is that jagged boundary along the edge of a character. It is the well-known effect on computer screens where diagonals and curved lines are displayed as a series of zigzagging horizontal and vertical lines (see Figures 3.9 and 3.10). Aliasing is not an effect that is applied to the font. Rather, it is the actual description of the low-resolution contour as it appears onscreen. When the pixels are too large, as they are on low-resolution computer screens, the jaggedness distracts the reader. Figure 3.9 illustrates how aliased text appears sharp and jagged to the eye. Especially at very small sizes, when you are dealing with few pixels to represent the shapes of your characters, the round curve of an O or a C will not look smooth at all. This can be distracting to the eye.

Figure 3.9

Aliased font at screen size, showing the jaggies.

Aliasing is sharper in appearance
because all characters reveal their
true bitmap forms for screen usage.

Aliased text.

Antialiasing

Antialiasing is the name for the technique designed to reduce or eliminate that jagged effect by shading the pixels along the borders of graphical elements (see Figure 3.11). This is usually done by inserting pixels that blend at the boundaries between the image and background colors.

Antialiasing is smoother in appearance
because grayscale pixels optically alter
the characters' true bitmapped forms.

Antialiased text.

Antialiasing smoothes a character's edge by adding partially transparent pixels to fill in the stairstepping pattern normally found on screen size characters. Figure 3.12 shows a closeup of antialiased text. Notice how the pixel pattern is supported by varying shades of gray. It increases the apparent resolution of a device. Antialiasing can be a function of an application or system software. Microsoft Corporation calls the antialiasing of fonts, font-smoothing. They deliver a font-smoothing utility with Windows 95 and Windows NT system software. The smoothing areas are only applied to curves, serifs, and common diagonal problem areas. To use this utility, you need to be running a screen mode of more than 256 colors.

An antialiased image (which has soft edges) will pick up parts of the colors it was created against to develop that soft look. If the background in Photoshop was white and your text was blue, the blue letterforms will pick up some white when they are antialiased.

When the antialiasing is turned on, these partially clear pixels pick up some color from the ones they cover, so they end up looking like a blend of the colors on both sides of the new pixels.

With black type, your antialiasing pixels will be varying shades of gray. The gray is a blend of the black character and the white background. But sometimes your text may be a color other than black. Quality antialiasing depends on screens that can display many colors. Screens managing only 256 colors (which is also know as "8-bit" color) generally cannot display good antialiasing. A screen that has 16-bit (65,000+ colors) or 24-bit (32 million+ colors) color will be much more successful at displaying antialiasing.

If you are in an application like Photoshop and are working with text, antialiasing can be selected for application to your text.

Within Photoshop:

1. Enter your text using the Type tool in the tool box.
2. Select the antialiased Style option in the Type tool dialog box.

This will smooth the edges.

Antialiasing can become a problem when it comes to the Web. This occurs when your Photoshop image (whether it be of a typographic nature or not) is converted to a transparent GIF file. A transparent GIF is defined as a compressed image that when rendered, will appear against any background and have no border highlighting the image. It's as if the image was dropped on top of the background. If the letterforms in the image have picked up some of the white from the Photoshop background and your Web page's background is another color, those letterforms will appear as if they have a halo around them.

The solution to this is to build your images against the same color background that will appear in your Web document. It may appear unattractive when you are building it in Photoshop but it will look great when overlaid onto your final background.

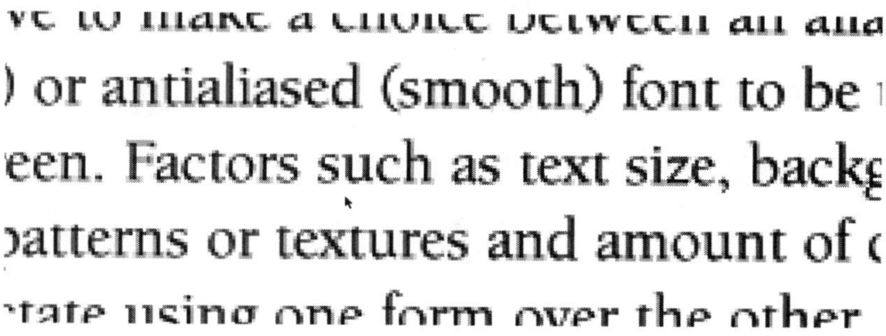

ve to make a choice between all ana

) or antialiased (smooth) font to be

een. Factors such as text size, backg

)atterns or textures and amount of (

state using one form over the other

Figure 3.12

Closeup of antialiased text.

Conclusion

This chapter covered how type can be developed and manipulated to make for quality screen presentation. We spoke of the changing styles and trends in how we display our typestyles. We touched on what we should look for in a quality font and covered two very important aspects of effective screen representation—legibilty (how well a typeface supports the process of fluent reading) and readability (the ease of reading continuous blocks of text). You were introduced to the bitmap and outline font format and we discussed the positives and negatives of two hinting technologies: PostScript type 1 and TrueType. We finished the chapter with a discussion on aliasing (the actual rough contour of a screen size image) and antialiasing (the technique to smooth the rough contours of an image).

CHAPTER 4

Web Fonts and Gallery

Fonts for the Web

If you search the Web, you will find a myriad of typefaces available as shareware and freeware. You will also find that digital type foundries sell their fonts on the Web. Purchasing a font from a reputable font foundry is the best way to ensure that your typeface has been created by skillful designers. This is important for a number of reasons.

First of all, you want to make sure that the font is technically accurate. This means the font should be able to work in a number of varying applications, from desktop publishing, to illustration programs, to paint and image manipulation software. Your font should install smoothly. It should also work on different versions of system software (such as Windows 3.1 and Window 95 if it is in a PC format).

You also want to make sure that the character set is correct. Typefaces formatted for the Mac contain many of the same characters in a PC formatted font. They are not exactly the same, however. It is true that most people will not be using characters beyond the ones accessible on the keyboard. But you should get what you pay for. Because most commercial fonts conform to a standard set of formats and character sets (see Figure 4.1), you should take the time to see that your font purchases contain the proper characters and styles. Otherwise you might wind up with an incomplete character set, as seen in Figure 4.2.

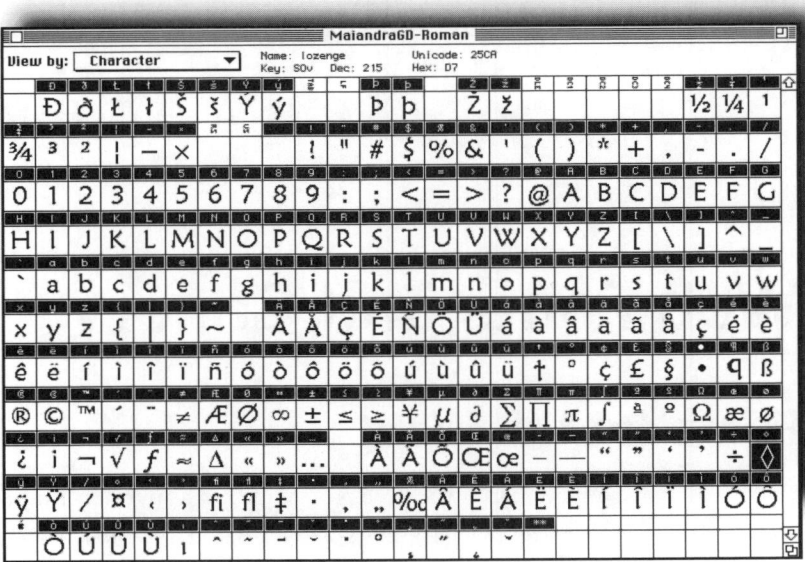

Figure 4.1

A complete character set.

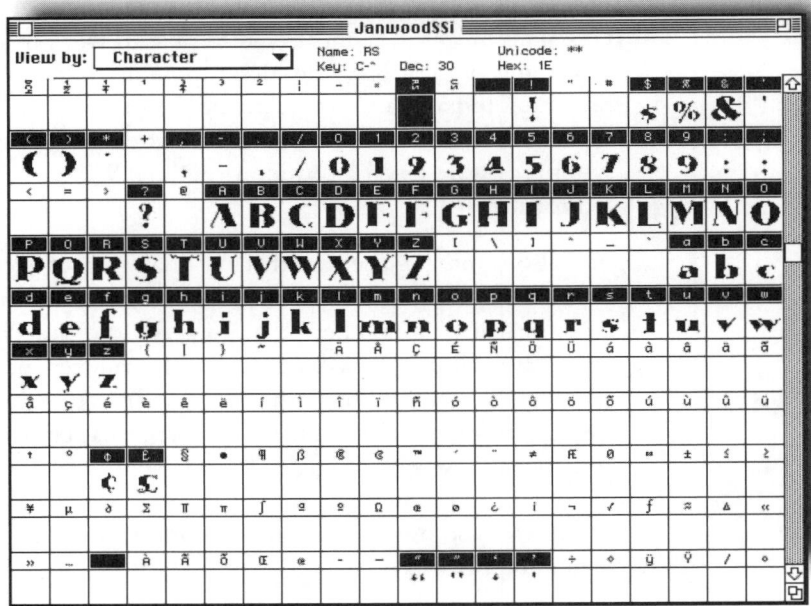

Figure 4.2

An incomplete character set.

Keys such as ß, Æ, Œ, œ, and æ are just a few of the keys not accessible without a multiple key input such as (Option-E-A)[Alt-E-A] for the á (lowercase a acute) on the Mac or Numlock-Alt-0-1-4-9 for the • (bullet), on the PC. There are a few utilities that show other characters and how to access them. On the PC, Character Map enables you to call on any installed font and click enables the character you wish to see. It displays its multiple key command for accessing it. On the Mac, KeyCaps, which comes with the system software, gives you visual access to characters beyond the standard keyboard.

A number of type and design magazines run yearly listings of font foundries that are reputable and have libraries of fonts to choose from. Publish, Desktop Publishing, HOW, and U&lc are just a few magazines that do this.

Font Quality

It has been my experience that many of the shareware and freeware fonts found on the Web do not meet the criteria of proper design, alignment, weight, and standard character sets (see Figure 4.2). Many of these fonts have not been tested on printers or screens of varying resolutions. Because there is no way of knowing what environment a font is going to be used in when it is purchased, it is important to test the font in a number of applications and output devices. Without the ability to do extensive testing, many designers must rely on their own personal computer systems for quality assurance. This may not be a robust enough testing process. As a purchaser of fonts, you must make sure to test your typefaces as thoroughly as possible.

First, I would open up a word processing or desktop publishing application and begin typing out all of the uppercase, lowercase, figure, punctuation, and other symbol characters available from the standard keyboard. The uppercase characters should be on the first line, the lowercase on the second, the figures on third, and so on. Highlight all of the characters and change the point size to 10 point. I would then copy each line of characters directly below itself. Change the point size of the newly pasted line to 12 point. Continue this copy pasting until you have character groups that are at 14, 18, and 24 points. These point sizes get used quite often for text and display purposes. Do this for each of your character groups. This will give you a good range of sizes to review. Highlight all of your text and select your font style from the appropriate menu.

What you will be looking at (see Figure 4.2) is a waterfall effect, each successive size getting bigger. Make sure none of the characters disappear from the line (a sure sign that something is wrong). Then print the page out and look at the higher-resolution output. This will give you some level of comfort that the body of characters you are dealing with are working correctly.

ABCDEFGHIJKLMNOPQRSTUVWXYZ

ABCDEFGHIJKLMNOPQRSTUVWXYZ

ABCDEFGHIJKLMNOPQRSTUVWXYZ

ABCDEFGHIJKLMNOPQRSTU
VWXYZ

ABCDEFGHIJKLMNOPQR
STUVWXYZ

abcdefghijklmnopqrstuvwxyz

abcdefghijklmnopqrstuvwxyz

abcdefghijklmnopqrstuvwxyz

abcdefghijklmnopqrstuvwxyz

abcdefghijklmnopqrstuvwxyz

0123456789

0123456789

0123456789

0123456789

0123456789

.,;:'''?!★()[]{}\/|_–

.,;:'''?!★()[]{}\/|_–

.,;:'''?!★()[]{}\/|_–

.,;:'''?!★()[]{}\/|_–

.,;:'''?!★()[]{}\/|_–

@#$%^&+<>~

@#$%^&+<>~

@#$%^&+<>~

@#$%^&+<>~

@#$%^&+<>~

Figure 4.3

Waterfalls of characters.

To access the rest of the font, use one of the utilities we mentioned earlier or consult your application documentation.

Stolen Designs

Unfortuately, there are a few bad apples out there, trying to make it a little more difficult for the rest of us by selling stolen designs. When you purchase fonts, beware of those that do not contain their own copyright. You can check for a copyright in a Mac font by selecting the font file and choosing Get Info from the File menu (see Figure 4.4). If you are a PC/Windows 95 user, you can obtain copyright information in a font by double clicking a TrueType font file. If it is a PC PostScript font, double clicking the .afm (Adobe Font Metrics) file will give you additional information about the font. This is not a guarantee that the font design has not been stolen. It should, however, alleviate some concern about the origins of the font.

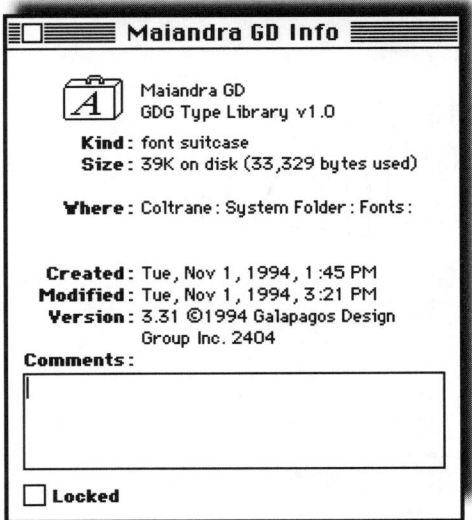

Figure 4.4

The Mac Get Info dialog box for a font file.

Finding High-Quality Web Fonts

Now let's say you have found fonts you like and they contain quality designs and the proper character sets. How can you tell that they would make good fonts for Web use? Remember that a great-looking printed font does not necessarily make a great-looking Web font. A Web font's concerns are geared toward screen use, rather than printed output. So how do we find Web fonts?

Web page design continues to evolve. Along with this evolution comes a greater desire to have access to more Web fonts. There are also concerns regarding how these Web fonts will be transported to the Web and how anti-aliasing will affect their look. There are a number of digital type foundries that have worked together to address these issues. They have built TrueType libraries containing fonts that were developed for extensive screen use. Galápagos Design Group, the Font Bureau, Emigre, Agfa, Bitstream, Monotype, and Microsoft (just to name a few) have developed fonts to deal with the low resolution of the computer screen. These fonts have been hinted extensively so that the important features of each letter shine through at very small sizes. To get a better idea of some of the new type designs that are making for great Web fonts, let's look at Microsoft's latest offering.

Web Core Fonts

In a grand effort to create a common Web font repertoire, Microsoft Corporation has taken it upon themselves to provide a set of PC and Mac TrueType fonts. The maker of Windows refers to these new type designs as "Web core fonts," similar to the system core fonts that accompany both the Mac and PC system software. These fonts are being distributed on the Internet, via Mirosoft's Web site (`www.microsoft.com`), and can be downloaded at no cost to the user (except for the time spent online). Microsoft's intent is to make these fonts widely available so they will make it into everyone's computer systems. This would enable a Web designer to call upon a greater number of fonts when developing a page and his audience would have those same fonts on their systems.

Several other font foundries, including Galápagos Design Group, from Littleton, Massachusetts, have also started creating high-quality fonts for use on the Web.

The next few pages will show you some of Microsoft's and Galápagos' Web fonts. These fonts have been developed for use on the Web, having been extensively hinted for quality screen output. They are all being shown close-up, at 14 point.

Comic Sans

Comic Sans is a font based on a cartoonist's style. The design is informal yet quite expressive. Its simple strokes have been carefully tailored to work well onscreen at small sizes.

ABCDEFGHIJKLMNOPQRSTUVWXYZ
abcdefghijklmnopqrstuvwxyz
0123456789$¢.,:;?!&

Figure 4.5

Comic Sans.

Here is a close-up of Comic Sans at 14 point.

Figure 4.6

Comic Sans close-up.

Comic Sans Bold

Comic Sans Bold is a bit more expressive, its heavier weight making it a good choice for a display font.

Figure 4.7

Comic Sans Bold.

Here is a close-up of Comic Sans Bold at 14 point.

Figure 4.8

Comic Sans Bold close-up.

Georgia

Georgia is one of two serif font families released for Web use by Microsoft Corporation. It has some similarities to Century Schoolbook. It could be classified as a Transitional style.

ABCDEFGHIJKLMNOPQRSTUVWXYZ
abcdefghijklmnopqrstuvwxyz
0123456789$¢.,:;?!&

Figure 4.9

Microsoft's Georgia.

Here is a close-up of Georgia at 14 point.

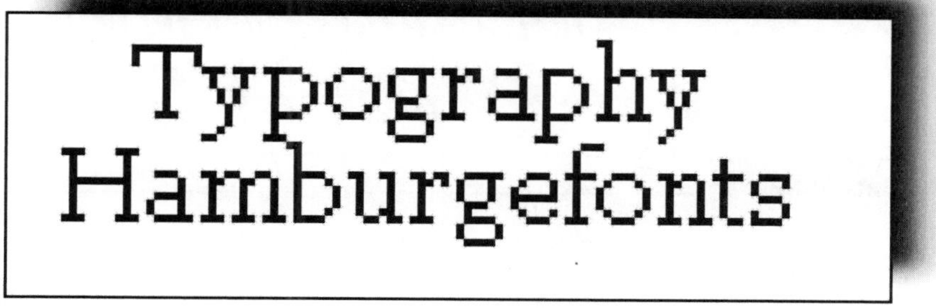

Typography
Hamburgefonts

Figure 4.10

Georgia close-up.

Georgia Bold

**ABCDEFGHIJKLMNOPQRSTUVWXYZ
abcdefghijklmnopqrstuvwxyz
0123456789$¢.,:;?!&**

Figure 4.11

Georgia Bold.

Here is a close-up of Georgia Bold at 14 point.

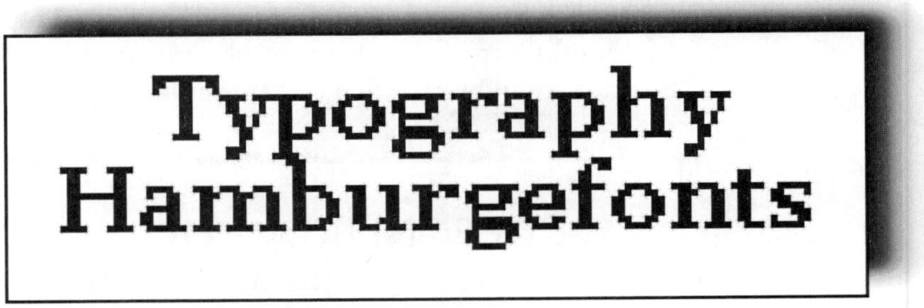

Figure 4.12

Georgia Bold close-up.

Georgia Italic

Figure 4.13

Georgia Italic.

Here is a close-up of Georgia Italic at 14 point.

Figure 4.14

Georgia Italic close-up.

Georgia Bold Italic

ABCDEFGHIJKLMNOPQRSTUVWXYZ
abcdefghijklmnopqrstuvwxyz
0123456789$¢.,:;?!&

Figure 4.15

Georgia Bold Italic.

Here is a close-up of Georgia Bold Italic at 14 point.

Typography
Hamburgefonts

Figure 4.16

Georgia Bold Italic close-up.

Impact

Impact is a sans serif displace typestyle. It imparts a very strong image with letters that are dark and condensed.

ABCDEFGHIJKLMNOPQRSTUVWXYZ
abcdefghijklmnopqrstuvwxyz
0123456789$¢.,:;?!&

Figure 4.17

Impact.

Here is a close-up of Impact at 14 point.

Figure 4.18

Impact close-up.

Verdana

Verdana is a sans serif design along the lines of Gill Sans. It is Humanist by classification and is quite readable at small sizes.

Figure 4.19

Verdana.

Here is a close-up of Verdana at 14 point.

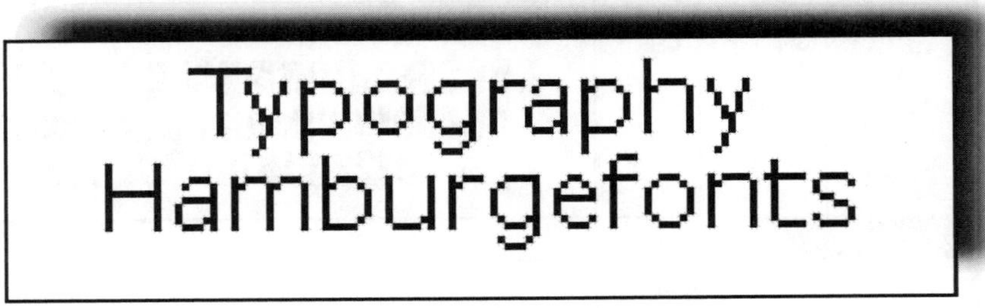

Figure 4.20

Verdana close-up.

Verdana Bold

ABCDEFGHIJKLMNOPQRSTUVWXYZ
abcdefghijklmnopqrstuvwxyz
0123456789$¢.,:;?!&

Figure 4.21

Verdana Bold.

Here is a close-up of Verdana Bold at 14 point.

Typography
Hamburgefonts

Figure 4.22

Verdana Bold close-up.

Verdana Italic

*ABCDEFGHIJKLMNOPQRSTUVWXYZ
abcdefghijklmnopqrstuvwxyz
0123456789$¢.,:;?!&*

Figure 4.23

Verdana Italic.

Here is a close-up of Verdana Italic at 14 point.

Figure 4.24

Verdana Italic close-up.

Verdana Bold Italic

Figure 4.25

Verdana Bold Italic.

Here is a close-up of Verdana Bold Italic at 14 point.

Figure 4.26

Verdana Bold Italic.

Trebuchet

Trebuchet is a sans serif design. It could be classified as a Geometric, carrying many of the same attributes as Futura—sharp edges, clean looking, a true geometric design.

ABCDEFGHIJKLMNOPQRSTUVWXYZ
abcdefghijklmnopqrstuvwxyz
0123456789$¢.,:;?!&

Figure 4.27

Trebuchet.

Here is a close-up of Trebuchet at 14 point.

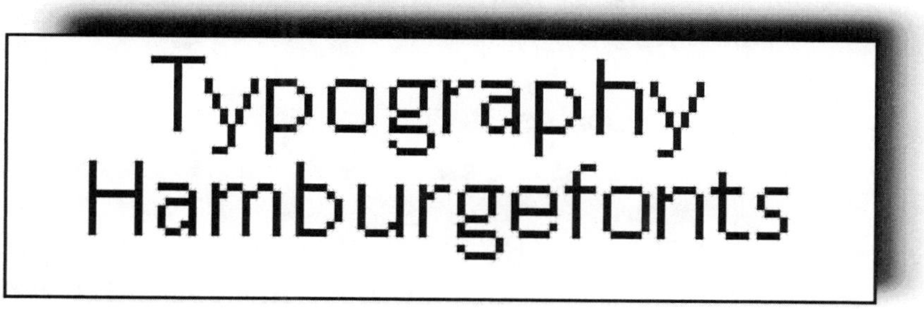

Typography
Hamburgefonts

Figure 4.28

Trebuchet close-up.

Trebuchet Bold

ABCDEFGHIJKLMNOPQRSTUVWXYZ
abcdefghijklmnopqrstuvwxyz
0123456789$¢.,:;?!&

Figure 4.29

Trebuchet Bold.

Here is a close-up of Trebuchet Bold at 14 point.

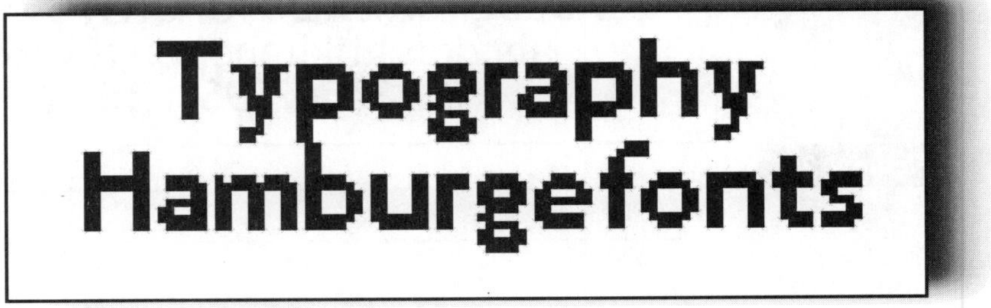
Typography
Hamburgefonts

Figure 4.30

Trebuchet Bold close-up.

Trebuchet Italic

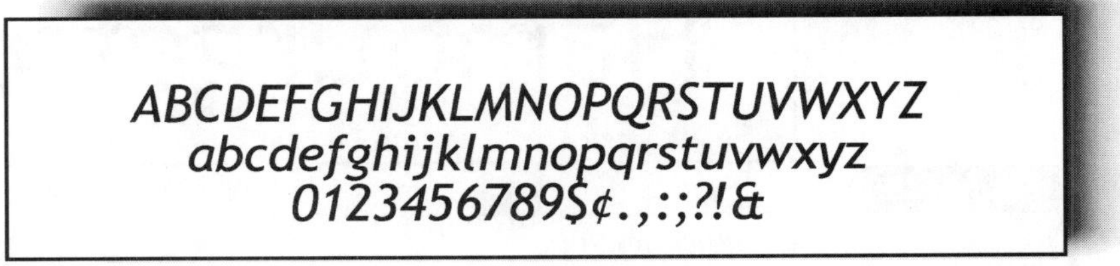
ABCDEFGHIJKLMNOPQRSTUVWXYZ
abcdefghijklmnopqrstuvwxyz
0123456789$¢.,:;?!&

Figure 4.31

Trebuchet Italic.

Here is a close-up of Trebuchet Italic at 14 point.

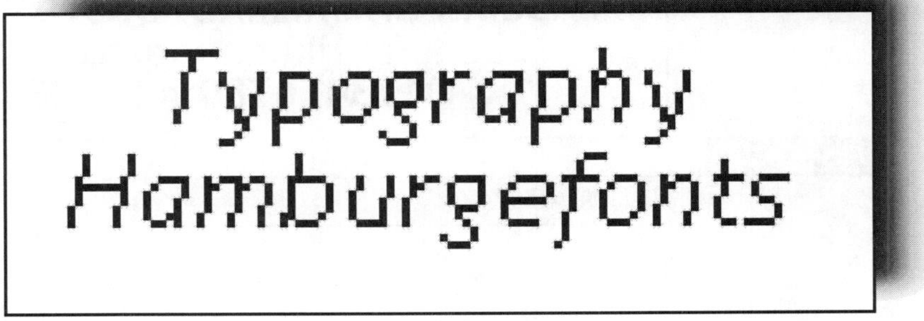
Typography
Hamburgefonts

Figure 4.32

Trebuchet Italic close-up.

Trebuchet Bold Italic

ABCDEFGHIJKLMNOPQRSTUVWXYZ
abcdefghijklmnopqrstuvwxyz
0123456789$¢.,:;?!&

Trebuchet Bold Italic.

Here is a close-up of Trebuchet Bold Italic at 14 point.

Typography
Hamburgefonts

Trebuchet Bold Italic close-up.

Galápagos Design's Baltra GD

Baltra GD is a very condensed face. It has a very classical look to it. It can be used effectively when there are large amounts of text that need to be typed into a small, defined area.

Here is a close-up of Baltra GD at 14 point.

Figure 4.35

Baltra GD close-up.

Galápagos Design's Maiandra GD

Maiandra GD is a free-flowing sans serif typeface. It reads extremely well at small screen sizes.

Here is a close-up of Maiandra GD at 14 point.

Figure 4.36

Maiandra GD close-up.

Conclusion

What we have learned in this chapter is that there are fonts being developed specifically for the Web. With the Web becoming the new media outlet and place to do business, it was only a matter of time before a strong set of Web fonts were developed and brought to the public.

It is always best to look carefully and with furrowed brow upon freeware fonts. Issues of improper character sets and the lack of functionality always seem to rear their ugly heads when mentioning freeware fonts. It is best to purchase fonts from an established font foundry or their resellers. Our discussion included ways to test any fonts you receive or purchase to ensure the font(s) work properly.

You were also introduced to a set of Web fonts from Microsoft Corporation and Galápagos Design Group. These screen examples should give you a good idea as to the quality that is available at low resolution and screen size.

The next chapter will begin an in-depth look at style sheets, including a tutorial in which you create the style sheets for a Web publication. Enjoy!

PART

2

Type on the Web

CHAPTER 5

Introduction to Style Sheets

The Web is a mess. It began as a simple, effective means of sending scientific papers across a world-wide network. It succeeded at this because it was *structured*—all you had to do was provide the text and a few little tags telling the user's program how to display the text. Make the title big and bold. Make the author's name smaller than the title. Indent this block quote. Emphasize this word. Web pages all looked like manuscripts, and they could be read on an institutional computer department's ancient VAX/VMS terminals. The people—who Web site designer David Siegel calls "Information Purists"—loved the structure of the Web. They loved (and still love) that a text-only, data-laden site loads quickly and tells them everything they need to know. They loved that structured pages can be queried by databases and converted to text. They loved that structured pages can be searched by subject, author, title, and content. This Web they invented worked great.

This Web worked *so* great, in fact, that everybody else saw the potential in it, and wanted to use it, too. Designers started asking why they couldn't change the color of the page and the type, and why they had to use the ugly preset browser typography. They wanted more control, and software companies (Netscape first, and now Microsoft) gave it to them. They wanted graphics, and they started using them. They wanted to choose *where* on a page they could put text and graphics, so Netscape invented tables, and designers started carving their pages into cells. They improved the look and usability of the Web immensely. And they complained, all the time, about the limitations of the persistently dull and structured HTML, which made it all possible—and at the same time—made typography so difficult. And the purists called the designers traitors.

Information vs. Design. The Web is at cross purposes. If the Web were a person, it would have had a nervous breakdown by now.

Even the design camp is split between competing manufacturers. Together, Netscape and Microsoft ended the browser wars, but they have started the tag wars. Anyone who has designed a site can tell you about the difficulty in designing for the competing browsers. They read the same tags differently, leading to extra prep time in testing. They have proprietary programming requirements—Netscape with its Java and JavaScript, and Microsoft with its VB-Script and ActiveX—and never the twain shall meet.

And despite all this invention, designers still complain. Typography on the Web hasn't improved hardly a whit. What the Web needs is a powerful standard that everyone—purists, designers, on any browser anywhere—can use.

CSS

The best answer so far is Cascading Style Sheets (CSS) specification, authored by Håkon Lie of the World Wide Web Consortium (W3C). CSS very cleverly rides all sides of the debate because it gives great typographical control without introducing new tags into HTML.

A Web page that uses CSS, in fact, looks in code almost exactly like a clunky first-generation Web page. This is because CSS modifies *existing, standard HTML*. Instead of headlines being big and bold, you can tell headlines to look big, bold, and red. Or big, bold, and centered. Or maybe not bold at all. Or maybe in a different font.

And the best part is that H1 stays H1. If purists look at your page on an ancient version of Lynx (a first-generation text-only browser) they'll find just what they want: structure. But if designers look at your page, they'll find what *they* want—sophisticated typography, including first-line indents, leading, drop caps, and color. CSS really is the best of both worlds.

CSS is a standard. Because it is recommended by the W3C, it is as standard as HTML. Microsoft Internet Explorer already supports much of the CSS spec, and version 4 will support all of the spec. Netscape has announced support for CSS in Navigator 4.0 and

Communicator. Because of this, CSS will probably be a reality on the Web by the time this book hits the shelves. At the time of this writing (February 1997) there are already many early adopters. CSS is a safe bet.

CSS is also easy to learn. If you've used styles before, whether in word-processing programs, desktop publishing software, or serious tools such as SGML, you'll understand CSS very quickly. It is simple and declarative, using commonsense terms such as *font-family* and *margin-left* to describe formatting.

In this chapter I'll provide an overview of CSS, including basic syntax and some of the major features, like the cascade, powerful styling features such as classes and pseudo-classes, and how to attach style sheets to your HTML.

Anatomy of CSS

CSS uses simple syntax to maintain influence over a document's layout and typography. Luckily for designers, CSS syntax is easier to understand than HTML, as it is written in fairly plain language. CSS uses some writing conventions that programmers of languages such as C++ and Java will recognize. Like a programming language, CSS uses precise terms to describe itself—those terms are defined later in this chapter. Even so, CSS is not a true programming language, but a set of layout and powerful typographic specs. In this section, I'll discuss the basic syntax and appearance of a style sheet, in addition to measurement units of color and length.

Basic Syntax

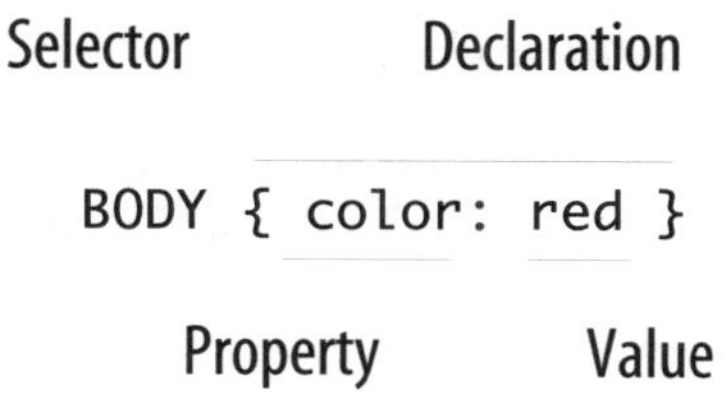

Selector   Declaration

BODY { color: red }

Property   Value

Figure 5.1

Anatomy of a CSS style.

Simple or complex, a CSS style (called a "rule") is made up of two basic parts.

➡ Selector—Any HTML element can be a selector. The selector is simply the element that the CSS style modifies.

➡ Declaration—The declaration is applied to the selector (the HTML element) to modify its appearance and layout characteristics. It is composed of two parts: the property and the property's value.

There are about 35 properties currently in CSS, divided between font properties (which choose the font's appearance), text properties (which govern alignment and spacing), color and background properties, box properties (which affect a page's layout), and classification properties (which generally organize HTML elements rather than affect their appearance). You can find a list of CSS properties later in this chapter.

Each property has a companion set of possible values—see the list of properties in Chapter 8.

For the complete specification and the latest news on CSS, see the World Wide Commission's Web site at `http://www.w3.org`.

Examples in Action

Here are a few different ways you can write CSS styles; simple or complex, all are the same to a CSS-compliant browser.

```
H1 { font: Arial }
```

The simplest kind of CSS rule. Note that the brackets { and } must be separated from their contents by a space.

Even this simplest of rules shows off the parts of CSS. This example is made up of two parts: the selector and the declaration.

It's not important to capitalize the selector, but it makes the style sheet a little easier to read.

```
H3, H5 { font-style: italic }
```

CSS rules enable you to group selectors together to save space and typing. They don't have to be related at all (as they are here, both being headers), they just have to share a declaration.

```
H3, H5 { font-style: italic; color: blue }
```

CSS rules also enable the designer to group declarations, thus enabling many modifications to the selectors. Multiple declarations must be separated by a semicolon and space. In the previous example the declarations are on the same line...

```
BODY {
  color: darkred;
  text-indent: 18px;
}
```

...and in this example they are on separate lines. Note that the second declaration is followed by a semicolon even though there is no third declaration. This is because lines in a style sheet must end with an open or close bracket or a semicolon. This last example is my preferred method of writing styles that have more than one declaration; it takes no longer to write, really, and the styles will remain readable at a glance even if they become numerous and lengthy.

Length Units in CSS

CSS has three kinds of length units: absolute, percentage, and relative. These three measurements have advantages and disadvantages for the designer. Relative units scale well from one medium to another (say from screen to print) and retain a predictable "look and feel" when one medium is flexible, as is the typical browser window (the browser window can be tall or short, wide or narrow). Relative units of measurement will expand and contract to suit the space. A useful relative measurement is the keyword measurement, such as x-large and small, which can enable type to scale to suit the reader's browser and personal preferences.

Absolute Measurements

Absolute measurements enable very precise control over the look of a document, but they are most useful only when you know the exact nature of the output medium. One example of this is measuring your page in millimeters, which CSS enables you to do. Millimeters?

If you measured in millimeters, your page would be thrown off by a screen size for which you didn't design. If you designed with a 17" monitor, your page would run off the screen when viewed with a 15" monitor (I have viewed pages like this on my 15" monitor, and it's not an effect I recommend). Millimeter, centimeter, point, and pica measurements reflect both the international intent of CSS and its flexibility; CSS is meant to work for a variety of purposes, including hard-copy printing in many languages.

Absolute units include in (inches); cm (centimeters); mm (millimeters); pt (points), a typographical and design measure, $\frac{1}{72}$ of an inch; and pc (picas)—one pica is twelve points. Again, these measures can break down in the flexible world of the online screen, but points remains the accepted standard for type measure. (I still like pixels.) Here are some examples:

```
BODY { margin-left: 1in }
```

This example gives the BODY element text a left margin of one inch—which the user may or may not see, depending on the resolution of the monitor.

```
P { font-size: 14pt }
```

This sets the text in the P element to 14-point type. In general, think a little big when you design for the screen; in most cases 14-point type will be more readable than the normal 12, especially when you are setting extended text. As a rule of thumb, (and rules are meant to be broken when they don't serve) 12-point is the minimum size you would want to use onscreen, unless you desire a specific effect that only small type can give. It all depends on the font—Verdana 12, for example, looks much bigger than Times 12.

Percentage Units

Percentage units can be considered relative units because they refer to another measurement. They work well for defining screen real estate, so that the margins look roughly the same no matter what size the user's browser window is set to. They also scale well when the user has custom style settings that push sizes up or down.

Percentage units express length in terms of another measurement (usually the font size, but not always). For example:

```
BODY {
  margin-left: 25%;
  font-size: 14pt;
  line-height: 125%;
}
```

This style sets the left margin to 25% of the browser's window size, whether the browser is narrow or wide, the screen will redraw to fit. And the line height (the leading) is 125% of the font size—that makes the body text 14/17.5 (the customary way of expressing size to leading is by separating the two with a slash—it is read aloud as "14 on 17.5"). The advantage of setting leading with this method is that if the end user has a custom style sheet that demands, say, 18-point type, the leading will still be 125%. In the case of the custom font size, that makes it 18/22.5.

Relative Units

Relative units include em, which is relative to the font size—an em in CSS is the height of the element's font; ex, also relative to the font size, based on the x-height of the font; and px, a measurement of length in pixels (this may seem like an absolute measurement, but it's not, because it is dependent on the number of pixels displayed by the user's browser—bigger browser window, more pixels). Some examples:

```
BODY {
  font-size: 12pt;
  text-indent: 1em;
}
```

In this case, the text-indent (an old-fashioned paragraph indent) will be 12 points, the same as the font size. Why not just specify the indent in points? If the user has a personal style sheet demanding that body type be 18 or even 24 points, a 12-point indent will be too small. The relative em unit allows flexibility by adapting to the current font size.

```
P {
  font-size: 12px;
  line-height: 15px;
}
```

This example specifies a font and "leading" of 12/15 pixels. In print, this could be the equivalent of specifying font and leading in points, which is familiar to anyone who has used PageMaker or QuarkXPress, or who in fact has set type using any equipment.

Warning

> The pixel measurement is discouraged in the CSS spec, because it is too dependent on the browser's window size, which the designer cannot know. For example, if you design a page with 35px left and right margins, and you are counting on someone having the browser window open to 600 pixels, you are spec'ing a 530-pixel line length (600 pixels minus the 70 pixels of left and right margins). If someone has a big monitor and has the browser open all the way, your line will be too long, because the margins will stay 35px each. Too-long lines are hard to read.
>
> But the pixel measurement has its uses. It can be used to offset a column of text to the right, leaving room for a colored bar of a set size (a very popular effect). And, as in the example above, with the px unit, you can elect to set font sizes and line spacing in pixels. Have you seen how type renders bigger in Windows than on a Mac? This is because the two computers map the traditional point-sized font values differently. Type renders larger and leading wider on Windows, because Windows applies 1.25 pixels for every Mac pixel—or the Mac applies .8 pixels for every Windows pixel. Either way, they're not the same, unless you specify the font's size and leading in pixels. Only then do you know exactly how the type will display on the user's screen.

Color Units

CSS measures color in two ways, either by a color name (like blue) or by a numerical RGB specification (like #99CCFF—hexadecimal notation for sky-blue).

Color Names

The simplest way to pick a color is to name it. The CSS spec suggests using the basic 16 color names from the Windows VGA palette: aqua, black, blue, fuchsia, gray, green, lime, maroon, navy, olive, purple, red, silver, teal, white, and yellow. These colors will also be used in HTML 3.2 (the latest proposed version at the time of this writing) and presumably into the future as well. The syntax is very straightforward:

```
BODY { color: olive; background: white }
```

RGB Values

You'll most likely want to use more than 16 colors in your Web site style sheet. CSS uses the same RGB (red-green-blue) color values that many current browsers support. At the very least, this gives you the 216 "browser-safe" colors, which are colors that display well on basic systems without grainy-looking dithering (until *everybody* is using a powerful computer with lots of video RAM, I recommend using the "browser-safe" palette). CSS can read RGB values in three ways: hexadecimal notation, numerical values, and percentages.

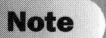 **Note**

David Siegel's book *Creating Killer Web Sites*, Tim Webster's book *Web Designer's Guide to PNG, GIF and JPEG*, and Lynda Weinman's *Designing Web Graphics* all offer excellent advice on using color on the Web.

Methods of Determining Color

Hexadecimal notation should already be familiar to Web designers—if you've ever written the code

```
<BODY BGCOLOR="FFFFFF">
```

you've used hex notation. "FFFFFF" makes the background of this BODY element white. Zero is the lowest value, and F is the highest, and so "FF0000" would, for example, turn the background red.

Examples of browser-safe colors include FF3366, 990033, and 66CC00. See the similarities? For one, the hex code is arranged in groups of two. Second, these values count up in threes—the safe values are 00, 33, 66, 99, CC, and FF. In combination, they give you the possibility of 216 combinations.

Hex notation can actually define many more than 216 colors—it can define millions. For instance, merely adding the values 11, 22, 44, 55, 77, 88, and so on gives you many more colors. (And a hex color like 12fc79 would be exceedingly subtle—it actually would be one of millions of colors—such that the viewer would need a good monitor and lots of video RAM to see it properly.)

CSS has two ways of specifying hex colors—the normal Netscape way, "rrggbb" (red-green-blue), and a simplified way, "rgb." The color white, in the first version, is notated as "FFFFFF." In the simplified notation, white would be written as "FFF." So:

```
BODY { background: #fff; color: #333300 }
```

Hex notation is by far the most common way of specifying color on the Web, but CSS also supports two more ways of selecting a color. You can specify "rgb" values in integers from 0 to 255, so that the color "red" looks like

```
H1 { color: rgb(255,0,0) }
```

And you can specify colors in percentages from 0.0% to 100.0%. In this example, red looks like

```
H1 { color: rgb(100%,0%,0%) }
```

Adding CSS to HTML Documents

You can add a style sheet to an HTML document in four different ways: embedding the style sheet in an HTML document, linking to an external style sheet, importing a style sheet, and inlining styles in the HTML code.

Embedding the Style Sheet in the HTML Document

Used this way, CSS will give you typographical control over a single HTML page. In order for the browser to "see" the CSS information, the style sheet must be contained within HTML's <style> element. The <style> element should be placed in the <head> of the page, like this:

```
<head>
<title>CSS Works!</title>
<style type="text/css">
<!--
  BODY { color: 333333 }
  STRONG { color: 000000 }
-->
</style>
```

This style sheet will make all text on this page dark grey (RGB "333333"), with the exception of the <strong> element, which will appear as black. The style sheet itself is contained in the familiar HTML comments (<!-- -->), which prevents older browsers from printing the style sheet as text on the page. Until all browsers support CSS, this is the safe way to write an embedded style sheet. Most current browsers, if they don't understand CSS, will ignore the STYLE element.

Linking to an External Style Sheet

If you want the style sheet to apply to more than one page, it's more efficient to link to a separate style sheet instead of laboriously copying each style sheet into the <head> of each page. Imagine doing this with a hundred—or thousand—page site! What if you missed one? What if you wanted to change the stylesheet? You'd have to re-open each page and make the changes by hand.

Be lazy. Remember this. It's the cardinal rule of style sheets, whether for desktop publishing programs like QuarkXPress and PageMaker, or for graphics applications like FreeHand, or for HTML Cascading Style Sheets. *Be lazy.* Let other people work hard! You've got better things to do than sit in front of a monitor, endlessly hand-keying character formatting into code. Laziness, when you do it right, will reduce stress, give you more time outside in the sun, and make you more efficient.

Here's how to do it. In this case, let's say that we've created a text file called "wombat.css," which contains the following style sheet:

```
BODY { color: 333333 }
STRONG { color: 000000 }
```

That's it—a two-line text file. Notice that it's the same as the embedded style that we discussed above. All we're doing is telling the HTML to access it differently. To link to the style sheet, place a bit of code in the <head> of the HTML document using the <link> element:

```
<head>
<title>CSS Works!</title>
<link rel=StyleSheet href="wombat.css"
 TYPE="text/css" TITLE="Wombat Style">
```

Instead of writing the style sheet in the HTML, you've provided a link to the standalone style sheet. You don't need to comment out the <link> element, because if the browser doesn't understand it, it will just ignore it. What you've done here is tell the user's browser several things: first, to link to a "Style Sheet;" second, the location and name of that style sheet, "wombat.css." Third, the format of the style sheet—in this case, "text/css," a text file containing CSS information. (There are other kinds of style sheet out there, including JavaScript, which is proprietary to Netscape). Fourth, you've given the style sheet a name, "Wombat Style," which is useful if you want to use multiple style sheets in a single document. All you have to do is refer to it afterwards by name, instead of keying in a possibly lengthy URL.

Again, this method—linking to an external style sheet—has some clear advantages for multi-page Web sites. If you want to change the look and feel of your site, all you have to do is modify one text file. This is reason *enough* to adopt style sheets! Also, that style sheet will load into the user's browser cache, and will load quickly, speeding up the display of the pages. The only disadvantage is a slight delay when the user's browser first loads the style sheet—the browser pauses before loading the rest of the HTML.

This external link can also be a full URL; in this way a web site on one server uses a style sheet on another server. For example, a large corporation could make the "look and feel" of their foreign office's Web site exactly like their domestic web site, simply by using the same style sheet. An entire international corporate identity could be modified by changing that single style sheet.

Importing a Style Sheet

Importing a style sheet is a way of combining the two methods above. Instead of providing a link to an outside style sheet, you "import" the style sheet and embed it inside the STYLE element. For example:

```
<HEAD>
<TITLE>CSS Works!</TITLE>
<STYLE TYPE="text/css">
<!--
  @import url(wombat.css);
```

```
   H1 { color: ff0000 }
-->
</style>
```

So, to a CSS–capable browser, this style sheet looks like:

```
<!--
  BODY { color: 333333 }
  STRONG { color: 000000 }
  H1 { color: ff0000 }
-->
```

With a complex style sheet, this allows some local control over the styles. Here's how it works. Let's say that you've imported (using @import) a stylesheet that, among other things, specifies that all header elements (H1, H2, H3, and so on) should appear blue. But let's say that for some reason you want H2 on this page to appear red. Here's what you would write into your HTML:

```
<style type="text/css">
<!--
  @import url(bluestyle.css);
  H2 { color: ff0000 }
-->
</style>
```

When you enter style information for H2, you countermand the previous order—in this case, you switch red for blue. CSS obeys its last command; if a CSS-capable browser came across the following style sheet

```
H2 { color: blue }
H2 { color: red }
H2 { color: yellow }
H2 { color: black }
```

the browser would render H2 elements as black. If you set up a personal style sheet that demanded that H2 be gray, then your style sheet would be the last in line, and H2 would be gray. This is actually the same as a current non-CSS browser, and is an essential feature of the Web: the user is granted final control over the look of the document (did you hear that disembodied ripping sound? That was the sound of designers across the world tearing their hair out in frustration). Even in your current browser (if you use Netscape, Internet Explorer, or even Mosaic) you can change the display font and size to one that the designer may never have intended. This is so users with poor vision or other needs can customize the Web for their own use. If, for example, you have trouble seeing the color red (just like my own father), you could set up a personal style sheet that turned any tag black—or blue, or magenta. You would be able to reject the designer's suggestions if they didn't suit you. It's very democratic.

Unfortunately, at the time of this writing, there isn't a browser in common use that properly recognizes the @import statement, or supports user-defined CSS, and therefore takes advantage of the nature of cascading style sheets. Microsoft has promised that the upcoming version of Internet Explorer (4.0) will support the layout features of CSS to the letter, but it remains to be seen if IE4 will support the cascade.

Inline Styles

The last method uses the typographic and layout abilities of CSS but avoids the style sheet form altogether. In this method, the style information is added on a case-by-case basis using a regular HTML element modified by the STYLE attribute. For example, if you wanted to set a single block quote in Verdana, colored red, you might write the following:

```
<BLOCKQUOTE STYLE="color: red; font-family: Verdana">
But you are over-blest. Plenty this day<BR>
Injures; it causeth time to stay;<BR>
The tables groane, as though this feast<BR>
Would, as the flood, destroy all fowle and beast.</BLOCKQUOTE>
```

This method is very similar to the current state of affairs, where all typographic controls must be laboriously applied by hand to each instance (artificially driving up, I'm sure, the cost of Web site development). Nevertheless, inline styles have their place; sometimes you really just want to change a single thing, and it's not worth making a whole new style (and possibly changing the organization of your style sheet) just for one or two lines.

Classes and Pseudo-Classes

Often in CSS you will find that simply altering the standard HTML elements, however powerful, isn't enough. CSS allows for even more flexibility in the application of styles by introducing classes and pseudo-classes, which extend a style sheet in very powerful ways.

Classes

A class in CSS is a set of declarations that modify one of the normal HTML elements. Classes can be specified in two ways: they are either associated with specific HTML elements (like BODY or CODE) or they are independent and can be applied to any element.

Requirements and Syntax

A independent class appears in the style sheet as a selector that begins with a period, like this:

```
.indent { text-indent: 18px }
```

A class associated with an HTML element is separated from the element by the same period:

```
BODY.indent { text-indent: 18px }
```

Except for the period, a class is functionally equivalent to a regular selector, with no restrictions on the declarations. In fact, you can make any HTML element look like any other element! For example:

```
.code { font-family: monospace }
.body { font-family: serif }
```

You could apply the ".code" class to your BODY text, and it would look like CODE. If you applied the ".body" class to the CODE element, that heading would look just like the default body text. Now, just because you can doesn't mean you should; if someone looked at your page with a non–CSS browser, it would look pretty strange, because non–CSS browsers will ignore the "class" element. But this should give you an idea of the flexibility that classes provide.

Note

In these examples I have set the classes in lowercase, but it doesn't really make a difference to CSS whether the HTML element selectors are capitalized or not, or whether the classes are lowercase. Putting classes in lowercase just makes it easier to read the style sheet.

Examples in Action

Let's say that you wanted to set the color of the CODE element to black, and then create a class that turned some of the code bold (as I have done) to highlight it. You could write a style sheet (our "wombat.css") containing:

```
BODY { color: 333333 }
STRONG { color: 000000 }
CODE { color: 000000 }
.hilite { font-weight: bold }
```

Here's an example of HTML that uses this style sheet to turn a section of programming code bold (let's assume that the style sheet has been associated with this HTML, either by linking it or embedding it). In this example, the code that the Web designer is illustrating is the beginning of a Java applet:

```
<CODE>import java.awt.*;<br>
<SPAN CLASS=hilite>public class FirstApplet extends
Applet</SPAN>
</CODE>
```

This code will turn the text "public class FirstApplet extends Applet" bold because it is contained inside the SPAN element, which has the class .hilite applied to it. The SPAN element is a new addition to HTML—it doesn't really do anything except mark some text out for modifying. For example, using the SPAN element like this:

```
<SPAN>I shall build a bridge through the air!</SPAN>
```

doesn't do anything at all. You've marked out the text, but you haven't applied a CSS class to it. Well, it *can* do something: technically, the SPAN element can be modified in the same way HTML elements like H1 and BODY are modified. So you can, for instance, put the following line in a style sheet:

```
SPAN { font-weight: bold }
```

This would cause the SPAN element to do something in addition to applying a class—it would turn everything between its tags bold.

> Even though the CSS specification doesn't discourage it, I would be careful about modifying the SPAN element. There will be times when you'll really want a transparent tag to apply to other classes.

Here are two more examples as they would appear in a style sheet; the first is associated with the element H1, and the second is independent:

```
H1.warning { color: 00ff00 }
.warning { color: 00ff00 }
```

Both of these classes will turn the text that they're applied to a bright virulent green. If this were the style sheet for a weather service, you might then use H1 like so:

```
<H1 CLASS="warning">Urban Flooding Expected Tonight</H1>
```

so that your readers would know right away to read the following article. You might also wish to point out the flood danger in another article, and so you could use the independent "warning" class like this:

```
<P>In other news, the National Weather Service has issued an
<SPAN class="warning">Emergency Flood Watch</SPAN> for Seattle,
Tacoma, and Snohomish County.</P>
```

You use these two kinds of classes (independent and associated) differently, to manage your style sheets. As with a style sheet in PageMaker, QuarkXPress, or Microsoft Word, a full style sheet can grow quite large. For instance, a style sheet for a book like the one you're reading can contain 30 or more styles—some are modifications to the body text, some are for different kinds of captions, some are headlines, and so on.

In general, the independent classes in CSS are more powerful, because they can be applied anywhere to any element. It all depends on how you organize your styles. A rule for a first paragraph in a feature story—let's say it's set in larger type with wider leading—could be called BODY.feature.first; this way you would know at a glance how the style would be used. An independent style of .first might be wrongly applied to the P element, for example. Again, it depends on how you like to organize your style sheets, and what your classes do.

Pseudo-Classes and Pseudo-Elements

Pseudo-classes and pseudo-elements look similar to regular classes and elements, but they function a little differently. Pseudo-classes, for instance, serve to differentiate between two otherwise identical elements—in the case of CSS1 (the first incarnation of CSS) the pseudo-class available is the link pseudo-class, which allows the designer to set the typographic appearance of the ANCHOR links (such as "A HREF" or "A NAME") on the page, whether unselected, active, or visited.

Pseudo-elements refer to sections of other elements. The two pseudo-elements available to the designer are first-line, which can automatically set typographical specs for the first line of text in an element, and first-letter, which is used to create initial letters such as drop caps.

Requirements and Syntax

Pseudo-classes and pseudo-elements look quite similar to class syntax, except that they are separated from the selector by a colon instead of a period.

```
A:link { color:red }
P:first-letter { font-size: 24px }
```

Examples in Action

One of the easiest ways to customize the look of your site is to change the link colors. CSS enables you to do this with the link pseudo-class. You can, for example, turn off link underlining (no more asking the reader to pry into their preferences and do it for you), which is a popular effect that helps the look of a page. We'll do that here:

In your style sheet, you would write:

```
A:link { text-decoration: none }
A:visited { text-decoration: none }
A:active { text-decoration: none }
```

Now when a CSS-capable browser hits the page associated with this style sheet, link underlining will automatically be turned off. The property text-decoration can also be set to underline, overline, or strike through the link. It will even recreate the infamous blink. The pseudo-class link can only be assigned to the A element.

One of the more difficult effects to achieve in HTML is the good old-fashioned drop cap. Drop caps are very useful—they help the reader to find the first line of text very quickly, and they can add color and life to an otherwise static page. They're a real help in the hard-to-read environment of the computer screen, but until CSS, a GIF of a letter had to be created by hand in a graphics program, saved, and set using a table in the HTML. This means that people surfing the Web with graphics off (very common nowadays) couldn't see the handmade drop cap at all.

CSS will, with the first-letter pseudo-element, automatically select and modify the first letter of a block-level element (like DIV or P) to create a drop cap. Here's what this pseudo-element might look like in action:

```
P:first-letter { font-size: 300%; float: left }
```

This would generate a drop cap 40 pixels tall; the float declaration (see the tutorial in Chapter 6 for an explanation of this powerful tool) would make the drop cap hang down from the top left corner. The rest of the text would flow around it. To get this effect, you might enter the following in the HTML page associated with the style sheet:

```
<P>Fourscore and seven years ago.... </P>
```

The first-letter pseudo-element would create a drop cap "F" that hung down three lines.

Inheritance in CSS

Inheritance is actually a simple concept that most computer users use every day. I am using it right now as I write this chapter on my word processor. If I, for example, make a few words bold, I show a basic application of inheritance. All I did was select the text with the cursor and click a single button above. The selected text turned bold, and inherited the rest of the attributes preceding it: font, Times; line spacing, single; tab stops, every half inch; color, black—you get the point. If I make a few words bold *and italic*, I demonstrate another level of inheritance. The italicized text first inherited the basic formatting, and then inherited the bold setting immediately in front of it. Here's what this second example might look like both in CSS:

```
STRONG { font-weight: 700 }
EM { font-style: italic }
```

and HTML:

```
If I make a <STRONG>few words bold <EM>and italic</EM>
</STRONG>, I demonstrate another level of inheritance.
```

Setting the STRONG font-weight to 700 is another way of specifying bold. Regular text is 400, "medium" is 500, "semibold" is 600, and so on. The lowest is 100 (ultra light) and the highest is 900 (ultra bold or "black"). The inline EM element inherits the font-weight setting from STRONG and italicizes the text.

HTML already uses inheritance, and inheritance simplifies your life as a CSS designer. Instead of having to start over completely and redo the specs for every bit of text, you just make the one change you wish to make. If things didn't inherit, the detail work would drive you insane!

In CSS, inheritance starts with the oldest ancestor. For CSS purposes, the oldest ancestor is the BODY element. All the elements that follow (called child elements) inherit formatting from it. For example, the embedded CSS style sheet and HTML document

```
<html>
<head>
<title>CSS Works!</title>
<style type="text/css">
<!—
BODY { font-family: Verdana }
—>
</STYLE>
<BODY>
<H1>This is H1</H1>
<P>And this is body text.</P>
<H2>This is H2</H2>
<P>And this is still more body text</P>
<H3>This is H3</H3>
<P>And you're getting really sick of this body text</P>
<BLOCKQUOTE>Man, this is boring body text! -
<CITE>Jane Q. End-User</CITE></BLOCKQUOTE>
</BODY>
</HTML>
```

will set elements such as BLOCKQUOTE, H1, and CITE in the free (and excellent) Microsoft screen font Verdana (see Figure 5.2), because the elements are contained inside the BODY element.

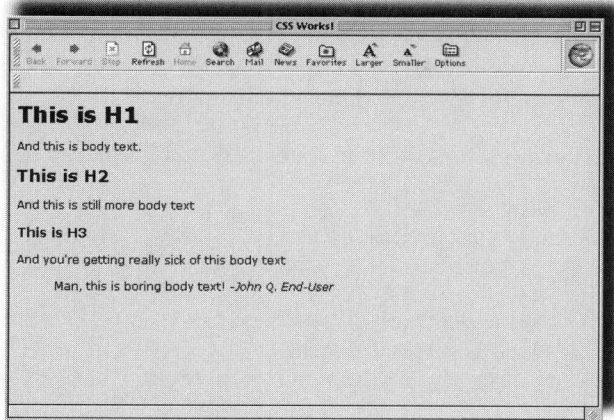

Figure 5.2

The levels of inheritance.

The Cascade

The essential feature of CSS is that style sheets cascade—that is, more than one style sheet can affect the Web presentation at the same time. "Cascade" refers to how a CSS-capable browser decides which styles to use.

There are two main reasons for the cascade. The first is that combining style sheets enables several imcomplete style sheets (one governing header elements, for example, and another the various body text classes) to function as one seamless style sheet.

HTML and CSS are also meant to empower the user, giving them veto power over designers' decisions if they are inappropriate—like my father replacing red text with black because he can't see the color red. So CSS is meant to support user-defined style sheets.

Unfortunately, Microsoft Internet Explorer 3.0—the only CSS-capable browser that most regular users are currently able to use—does not support the cascade, either by recognizing the @import statement (explained earlier in this chapter) or by allowing user-defined style sheets. It remains to be seen whether this essential feature of CSS will be supported in IE4.0. And Netscape has announced CSS support for Communicator, but again, it remains to be seen if it will be well-implemented (let's hope it will!). In any case, the cascade is basic to CSS—"cascade" is, after all, CSS's first name—so it's useful to understand how it works.

To combine several style sheets, use the @import statement:

```
<HEAD>
</TITLE>CSS Works!</TITLE>
<STYLE>
<! —
@import url(http://www.style.org/punk)
@import url(wombat.css)
H1, H2, H3, H4, H5 { color: black }
—>
</STYLE>
```

This will import the remote style sheet at "www.style.org/punk," add the local style sheet "wombat.css," and further modify those styles by specifying that headers 1–5 render in black.

But what if the style sheets "punk" and "wombat.css" conflict? What if, for instance, "punk" specifies

```
BLOCKQUOTE { font-family: Verdana }
```

and "wombat.css" specifies

```
BLOCKQUOTE { font-family: monospace }
```

Well, CSS has rules to deal with conflicting style sheets:

1. The browser starts by looking for all declarations that apply to the element in question. In other words, if there's no rule in either style sheet for the CITE element, then CITE will inherit from the BODY element its font, color, and so on. If the browser finds one rule, it uses that rule. If it finds two or more rules, it goes to the second.

2. It then sorts the multiple declarations by "explicit weight"—that is, the importance that the designer *explicitly* gives to the declaration. You can boost the weight of a declaration by marking it as !important:

```
BLOCKQUOTE { font-style: italic !important }
```

Declarations marked as !important carry more weight than unmarked declarations. Be careful with this rule—you could make your style sheets dominate by marking every rule as !important, but it's inconsiderate. What if someone with poor vision is unable to read your page because you thought 7-point type was "important"? Are they going to care how important your styles are, or are they just going to leave? Besides, marking formatting as !important could conceivably cause problems on equipment with specific formatting requirements, like library terminals. Leaving them out is very undemocratic.

If you have specific needs (you need big type, you can't see red) then the thing to do is mark your personal style sheet rules as !important—assuming, of course, that someone markets a browser that will let you do this...

3. The browser sorts by origin. The designer's style sheets (the style sheets specified in the HTML document) carry more weight than a reader's personal style sheet. This is so designers have control over their creations. If the reader has already marked her special rules as !important, then the reader wins round two. Otherwise, the designer wins.

4. Next, the browser sorts by "specificity"—more specific rules win out over general rules. It uses a points system to calculate the specificity. First, it counts the number of ID selectors (detailed earlier in this chapter). Next, it counts the number of class attributes, and counts the number of tag names in the selector. Then the browser concatenates the three numbers—it doesn't add them, it just sticks them side by side.

    For example, the selector BODY has no ID selectors, no class attributes, and one tag name. So: 0+0+1 = 001. The selector BODY EM has no ID selectors, no classes, and *two* tag names, so its specificity is 002. The selector BODY.wirestory has no ID selectors, one class, and one tag name, so: 0+1+1 = 011. So far, the last selector is the most specific; all this means is that it will retain its difference from the plain BODY tag. ID tags have the most specificity (it's almost unfair): the ID selector #f3 has one ID tag, no classes, and no tag names, so it calculates as 1+0+0 = 100! So I suppose a really winning tag might read

```
#r35 #f3.godzilla LI EM { font-style: italic !important }
```

By my calculations, this selector has a specificity of 212, not including its "important" status!

5. Lastly, the browser looks at the order in which the rules appear. Later rules (rules that appear "below" conflicting rules) win. So, for example, in the style sheet

```
BODY { color: green }
BODY { color: red }
```

Any text in the BODY element will be red.

Degradability

HTML, CSS, and the Web were originally designed to be very democratic, allowing anyone access to information, to the best of their equipment's ability. Not everyone in the world can afford a Pentium Pro or Power Mac—never mind a costly and difficult-to-manage Silicon Graphics workstation—so HTML is designed to "degrade" well for old or limited equipment. The Web should be accessible from the old terminals at public libraries, too, don't you think?

CSS has the advantage because a thoughtfully-designed style sheet degrades very gracefully. CSS uses standard HTML tags instead of propriety "tag war" elements. Netscape's font and blink tags have no place in the widely accessible world of CSS, nor do the proprietary tags currently being hawked by Microsoft—though Microsoft deserves credit for being an early adopter and advocate of CSS. And CSS is more powerful, too! Well-designed CSS pages are best viewed with *any* browser, whether that's a text-only browser on an ancient dimly glowing screen on a pitching vessel at sea, or on the latest, greatest equipment in Marc Andreesen's office at Netscape.

Examples in Action

Here I've set a poem using the following Netscape-style tags:

```
<TABLE BORDER=0 WIDTH=100%>
 <TR>
  <TD WIDTH=30%>
    
  </TD>
  <TD WIDTH=70%>
```

```
<FONT FACE=Verdana size=5>Epithalamions VIII: Feasts and
Revells</FONT><BR>
<FONT FACE=Verdana SIZE=4><I>   John
Donne</I></FONT><P>
<FONT FACE=Verdana>But you are over-blest. Plenty this day<BR>
      Injures; it causeth time to
stay;<BR>
      The tables groane, as though
this feast<BR>
Would, as the flood, destroy all fowle and beast.<BR>
      And were the doctrine new<BR>
That the earth mov'd, this day would make it true;<BR>
For every part to dance and revell goes.<BR>
They tread the ayre, and fal not where they rose.<BR>
Through six houres since, the Sunne to bed did part,<BR>
The masks and banquets will not yet impart<BR>
As to these weary eyes, A Center to this heart.
 </TD>
 </TR>
</table>
```

And Figure 5.3 shows what it looks like using up-to-date equipment (in my case, a Power Macintosh):

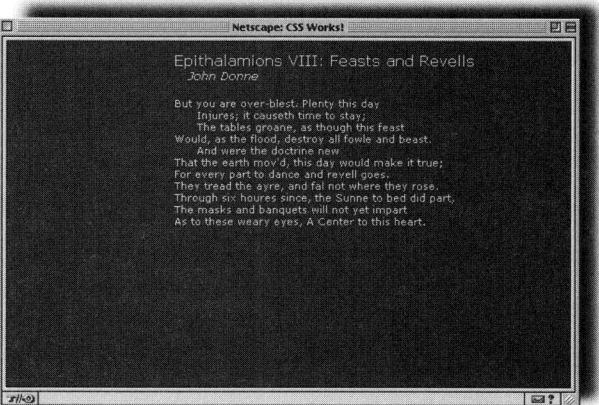

Figure 5.3

An example using Netscape-style tags.

But look what happens if it's displayed on a browser that doesn't support the latest HTML tags (I've cut out the table information, the FONT and I elements, and the   character to simulate a first-generation browser) See Figure 5.4.

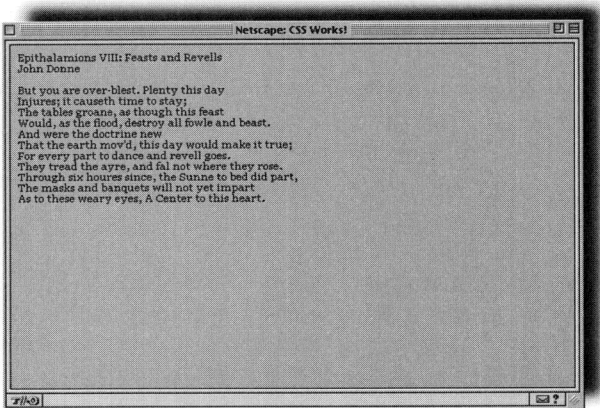

Figure 5.4

The example displayed through a browser that does not support the latest HTML tags.

Because there is no *structural* formatting, only *appearance* formatting, the look of the poem changes dramatically. And it can't be read, for example, by automatic cataloging programs, because there's no title, just a bunch of text.

Compare the performance of the Netscape-style poem with the CSS version, which uses the following style sheet and HTML:

```
BODY { color: fff;
       margin-left: 30%;
       font: 11/15 Verdana;
       }

.indent { margin-left: 34% }

H1 { font: 18/24 Verdana;
     font-weight: light }

H3 { margin-top: -7px;
     margin-left: 33%;
     font: italic 13/16 Verdana;
     font-weight: medium }
...
<BODY>

<H1>Epithalamions VIII: Feasts and Revells</H1>
<H3>John Donne</H3>
But you are over-blest. Plenty this day<BR>
<SPAN CLASS="indent">Injures; it causeth time to stay;<BR>
The tables groane, as though this feast</span><BR>
```

```
Would, as the flood, destroy all fowle and beast.<BR>
<SPAN CLASS="indent">And were the doctrine new</span><BR>
That the earth mov'd, this day would make it true;<BR>
For every part to dance and revell goes.<BR>
They tread the ayre, and fal not where they rose.<BR>
Through six houres since, the Sunne to bed did part,<BR>
The masks and banquets will not yet impart<BR>
As to these weary eyes, A Center to this heart.

</body>
```

For one, the HTML in this version is simpler, and easier to write; it contains four tags, instead of the eight tags in the Netscape version—and that's ignoring all the   codes. If you have to make many pages like this one, you'll bless your style sheet. And it looks better. I've included a little more leading in the body text, which is amazingly difficult to do in Netscape. Figure 5.5 shows how it looks in a CSS–capable browser:

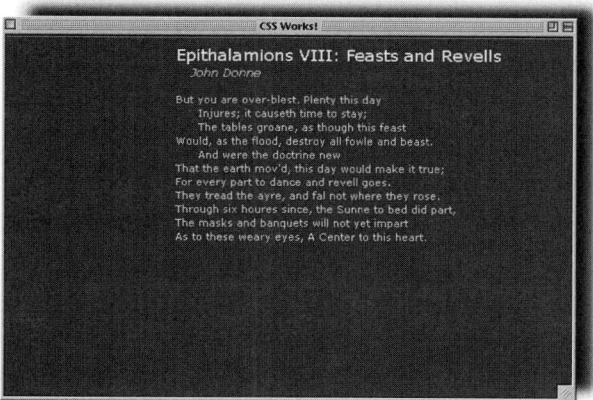

The example displayed in a CSS-capable browser.

But even more impressive is how it looks in a limited browser. Because it still contains structural HTML formatting, it keeps its heirarchy. It is machine-readable (so it can be automatically cataloged) and clear even to users logging on with ancient equipment:

In a sense, CSS restores the ideal of the world–wide electronic library by allowing all users, whether rich or poor, to use it to the best of their resources. Even machines can use it. There is (and I say this at the risk of sounding like a revolutionary) a political and economic aspect to the Web; the gulf between the information haves and have-nots is growing daily. Degradable CSS serves the haves *and* the have-nots.

In Figure 5.6, I've eliminated all the visual formatting, which is extreme. Most users are somewhere between the newest CSS-capable browser and the oldest version of Lynx. During this transition phase, when CSS isn't supported by all browsers, a safer way of implementing CSS is to use it in conjunction with formatting features like tables.

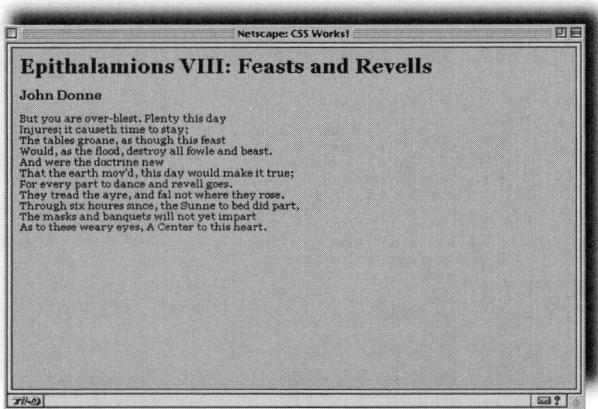

Figure 5.6

The poem displayed through a browser with no visual formatting.

For example, let's say I want to publish a version of the poem above that can be viewed well by both CSS and non-CSS browsers. First, I have to reduce the influence of CSS on the page—by using an empty table cell instead of the margin-left declaration, and by indenting lines with . I'll use a GIF for the title and Donne's name; and I'll rewrite the CSS so that it reads

```
BODY { font: 11/15 Verdana }
```

thus eliminating the color information. I'll put the color information into the BODY element. Now, with a non-CSS browser, the poem looks like this:

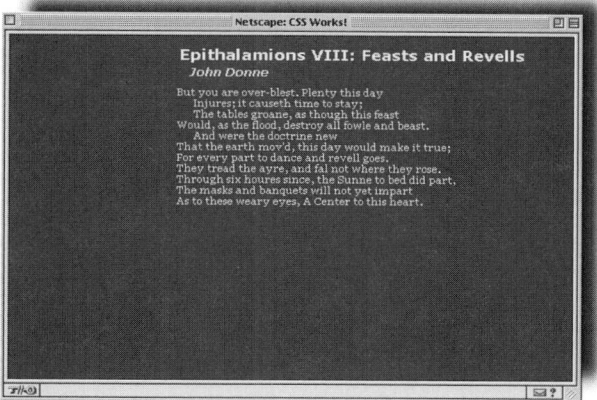

Figure 5.7

Displayed with a non-CSS browser.

And the CSS version looks like Figure 5.8:

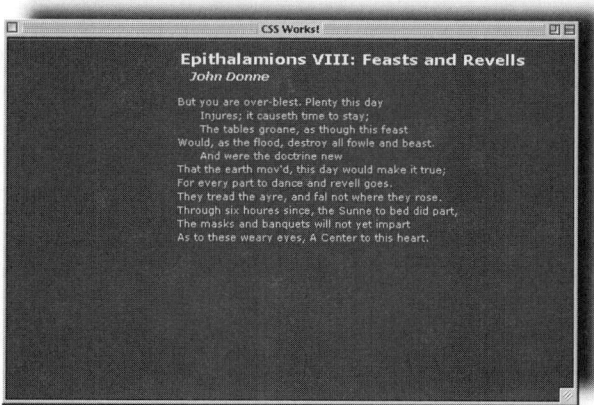

Figure 5.8

Displayed with a CSS-capable browser.

Even with the tiny style sheet, the CSS version looks a lot better, doesn't it? That's the real power of CSS. Even a minor change makes a big difference in the appearance of your pages, so don't be afraid to work CSS into your pages even in small ways.

CHAPTER 6

Using Style Sheets

I f you've ever created a style in Microsoft Word, Adobe PageMaker, or QuarkXPress, you'll find creating a style sheet for the Web very easy to understand.

If you've never worked with style sheets before, then CSS (cascading style sheets) is a great introduction. In fact, if you've ever written a simple HTML page using the regular tags such as H1, BODY, and BLOCKQUOTE, you've already used styles without knowing it.

A style is simply a set of formatting instructions. For instance, the familiar H1 tag (or element) tells most browsers to set the text in 24-point bold Times, flush left, with one line space before and after. That's a style—a short name, standing in for longer instructions, that can be repeated easily. CSS works by changing the definition of elements such as H1 from 24-point bold Times to, say, 18-point red italic Helvetica. You don't have to clutter up the HTML with excess tags anymore. A *style sheet* is a collection of styles. For instance, a style sheet might include the individual styles for H1, H2, BODY, P, and BLOCKQUOTE. Before computers revolutionized how print documents were produced, a style sheet was literally a sheet—a piece of paper with all the various head, text, and display elements defined and written out. A compositor would refer to the style sheet when setting type.

In this tutorial we'll cover simple formatting:

➡ Changing fonts using CSS

➡ Understanding inheritance

➡ Using the CSS margin

➡ Changing linespacing

➡ Adding background color

➡ Understanding the structure of an HTML page

➡ Adding CSS to a page in different ways

What You'll Need

In order to use this tutorial and the tutorial in Chapter 7, you'll need a few things:

➡ A CSS-capable Web browser. At the time of this writing the only browser in common use that supports CSS is Microsoft Internet Explorer 3.0. The W3C (the World Wide Web Commission) has written Amaya, which supports CSS, but it's only available for the Unix operating system. A version for Windows is in the works. GNUscape Emacs W3 is also CSS-capable, and is available for some of the major platforms as a beta test—many more are planned. And the Preview Release 2 of Netscape Communicator offers support (though still very buggy) for CSS.

➡ A text editor or word processor that can save to text-only format.

➡ An Internet connection to retrieve the tutorial files from `http://www.hayden.com`.

➡ Basic knowledge of HTML—in fact, you don't need to know any tricky HTML at all; the style sheet does all the complex formatting.

➡ Two of Microsoft's free Web fonts, Verdana and Georgia, available from Microsoft at `http://www.microsoft.com/truetype`.

The Basic Page

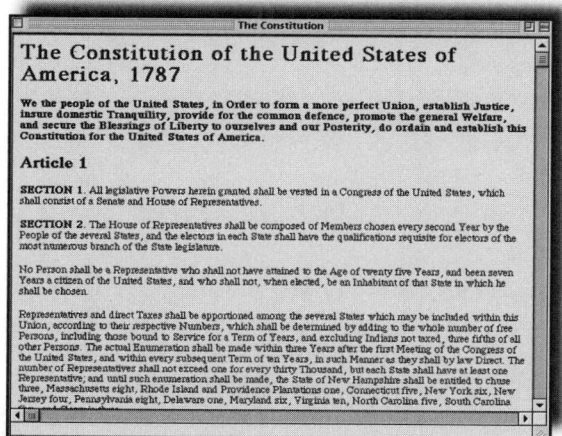

Figure 6.1

In the beginning, there was structured HTML. And it was pretty dull.

Let's look at a sample of the HTML code for this document:

```
<HTML>
<HEAD>
<TITLE>The Constitution</TITLE>
</HEAD>
<BODY>

<H1>The Constitution of the United States of America, 1787</H1>

<H4>We the people of the United States, in Order to form a more per-
fect Union, establish Justice, insure domestic Tranquility, provide
for the common defence, promote the general Welfare, and secure the
Blessings of Liberty to ourselves and our Posterity, do ordain and
establish this Constitution for the United States of America.</H4>

<H2>Article 1</H2>

<P><STRONG>SECTION 1</STRONG>.  All legislative Powers herein granted
shall be vested in a Congress of the United States, which shall con-
sist of a Senate and House of Representatives.</P>
```

```
<P><STRONG>SECTION 2</STRONG>. The House of Representatives shall be
composed of Members chosen every second Year by the People of the
several States, and the electors in each State shall have the quali-
fications requisite for electors of the most numerous branch of the
State legislature.</P>

...

</BODY>
</HTML>
```

In short, it's plain old HTML, but there are a few things to look at that will make learning CSS much easier. HTML is structured. Everything in an HTML page is defined by an element: the tags H1, H2, H4, and P are "block-level" elements contained inside the BODY (which is itself an element—that's why BODY closes at the end of the document). STRONG is an "inline" element contained inside the P element. All of these elements can be redefined by CSS.

Actually, the code inside the BODY element won't change at all throughout this tutorial. We'll just add lines of code to the document's HEAD. There are several ways to do this, but we'll start by using the new STYLE element.

First, you'll need to connect to the Web and retrieve the tutorial files from Hayden's Web site.

Adding a Style Sheet

The simplest way to add a style sheet to an HTML document is to "embed" it. This inserts a single style sheet into the beginning of an HTML document. To do this, you mark out the style information with the STYLE element. The STYLE element goes inside the document's head:

```
<HTML>
<HEAD>
<TITLE>The Constitution</TITLE>
<STYLE TYPE="text/css">
<!--
BODY { background: #ffc }
-->
</STYLE>
</HEAD>
<BODY>
```

Notice that the style is contained inside the familiar comment tags "<!--" and "-->". Until CSS browsers are commonplace, it's a good idea to "comment out" the styles. Older browsers will ignore unknown tags such as STYLE, but they will try to display the style rule as text onscreen. The TYPE attribute tells the browser what kind of style is inside the tags, in this case, "text/css" (there are also several other kinds of style sheets that the W3C has considered, and they want to keep HTML flexible).

Global Formatting with the BODY Element

Because all the displaying elements on the HTML page (in CSS, the "canvas") are contained inside the BODY element, you can change general formatting by specifying style information for BODY. Let's do that now, by inserting style information into the usconst.htm file.

The head of usconst.htm begins with:

```
<HTML>
<HEAD>
<TITLE>The Constitution</TITLE>
</HEAD>
<BODY>
```

Open usconst.htm in a text editor and insert the STYLE element into the document head, as shown here:

```
<HTML>
<HEAD>
<TITLE>The Constitution</TITLE>
<STYLE TYPE="text/css">

</STYLE>
</HEAD>
<BODY>
```

Now, this won't do anything because you haven't specified any styles—this just makes the file ready for an embedded style sheet. Be sure to save the file after you make any changes. Next, we'll add a BODY selector and some style information.

Changing the Background Color

Most browsers appear with a gray default background, which isn't particularly good for reading long text; there just isn't enough contrast. You can change this color in CSS by using the background property. Let's change the color from gray to cream; in hexadecimal notation, the code for this color is #ffc (for an explanation of the color values that CSS recognizes, see Chapter 5). Add the following lines to usconst.htm:

```
<HEAD>
<TITLE>The Constitution</TITLE>
<STYLE TYPE="text/css">
<!--
BODY { background: #ffc }
-->
</STYLE>
</HEAD>
```

Be sure to "comment out" the CSS rule, and to leave a space on either side between the brackets and the declaration. Save the file.

If you look at usconst.htm now, you'll see that the background color has changed (I haven't included an illustration because the new color won't show up in black and white).

Changing the Margins

One of the biggest problems with HTML is that it runs the text out as wide as the window will allow. People can only read about 60 or 65 characters in a line before they start to fade. Ever read a book where you have a lot of trouble getting to the end of each line? Or you have trouble finding the next line and you have to resort to using your finger to hold your place? Most people have; many times it's the result of a line that's too long. Unfortunately, most simple HTML creates very long lines. Designers have controlled the line length using tables, but it's not very intuitive—you've got to do what I call "table math," adding code to create table cells, and figuring out the width of each cell and how they interact. It takes time and patience.

CSS sets margins very simply and intuitively—you just *set* them. Let's set the margins for usconst.htm now. To do this, let's make a few changes to the BODY element. Add the following lines to the code for usconst.htm (see the results in Figure 6.2):

```
<STYLE TYPE="text/css">
<!--
BODY {
  background: #ffc;
  margin-left: 20%;
  margin-right: 20%;
  }
-->
<STYLE>
```

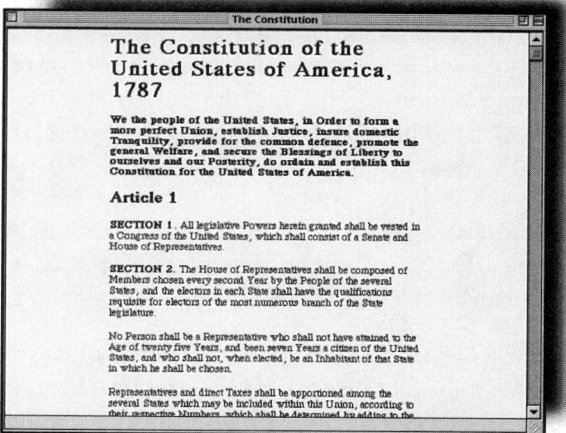

The text now includes margins.

Notice I've changed how I type out the style for BODY. I find this format organizes my styles (and if you knew me, you'd know how I need any organization I can get) and simplifies their appearance. It doesn't matter how you do it, really. All that matters is that declarations be separated by a semicolon, and that each line end with either an open or close bracket, or a semicolon. I use the previously listed format when I've got a style that uses more than one declaration.

I've set the margins in percentages because I want to control the amount of screen "real estate" that the margins take up. If the user resizes his browser window, the browser will recalculate the margins in this document to take up 20% of the window on either side of the text block. You can also set fixed widths for margins, such as

```
margin-left: 35px;
margin-right: 1in;
```

if you have background graphics or fixed-size navigational elements that you don't want the text to touch.

Changing the Font

As of this writing, OpenType, a joint proposal by Adobe and Microsoft, is still a draft document (at `http://www.microsoft.com/truetype/tt/tt.htm`). Someday OpenType promises to allow specifying any font you want by downloading it with your web page. Netscape wasn't content to wait, and has licensed a technology called Bitstream True-Doc (`http://www.bitstream.com`), which is a format for downloadable fonts. For the moment, though, the only really safe type to specify is Times or Times New Roman. I'm sick of Times (as I'm sure you are too) so I'm going to specify another type, Georgia, designed specifically for the Web, and available for free at the Microsoft Typography site (`http://www.microsoft.com/truetype`). Hopefully by the end of 1997 or early 1998 you'll be able to safely specify type like this in the real world.

Font information can be entered a number of ways in CSS, by using the font-family, font-size, font-style, and line-height properties. We're going to use the font-family property because we want to set the font but not anything else (we're going to set the other elements individually). Enter the following line into the embedded style sheet in usconst.htm:

```
<STYLE TYPE="text/css">
<!--
BODY {
  background: #ffc;
  margin-left: 20%;
  margin-right: 20%;
  font-family: Georgia, serif;
  }
-->
<STYLE>
```

In font-family you can set multiple typefaces, in descending order of importance (see Figure 6.3). In this case, you've asked the user's browser to find Georgia first, and if it's not available, to substitute the stock "serif" face—probably Times.

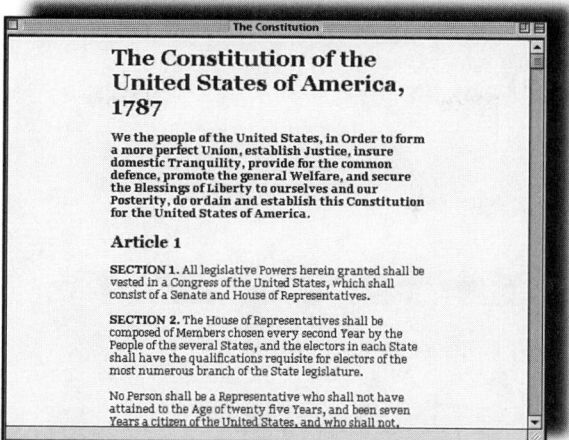

Figure 6.3

The page is now set in Microsoft's Web font, Georgia.

Notice that the H1, H2, H4, and P elements took the font and margin of BODY. This is "inheritance," as discussed in Chapter 4. Because all these elements are contained inside BODY, they "inherit" characteristics (like margin and font) unless otherwise specified.

Formatting the Header Elements

Now we're ready to make some real changes. As you already know, CSS enables you to modify individual elements, not just make global changes in the BODY element. We'll start with the header elements that make up the title, the preamble, and the section heads.

The H1 Element

Starting at the top, the stock H1 formatting—left-aligned bold 24-point type—looks pretty clunky to me. Let's center the text first. Instead of using Netscape's <CENTER> tag, we'll use the CSS text-align element (see Figure 6.4).

Write a new rule in the embedded style sheet after the BODY rule that looks like this:

```
BODY {
  background: #ffc;
```

```
    margin-left: 20%;
    margin-right: 20%;
    font-family: Georgia, serif;
    }

H1 {
    text-align: center;
    }
```

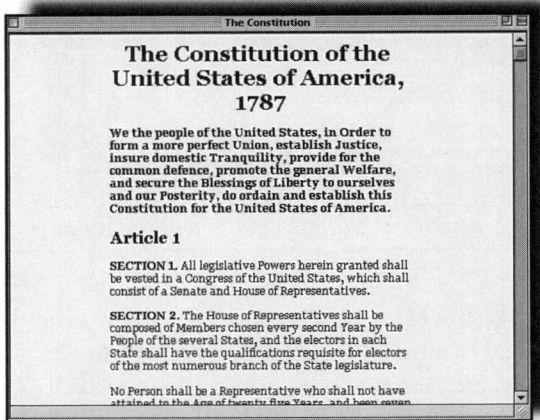

Figure 6.4

The title is now centered without the <CENTERr> tag.

To change the font style, we'll use the font property, which enables you to set many font variables with one declaration. The title is still too heavy, so let's lighten it and italicize it, as shown in Figure 6.5.

Add the following declaration to the H1 rule:

```
H1 {
  text-align: center;
  font: medium italic 24pt/30pt Georgia, serif;
  }
```

The font property has specific syntax. First you specify the weight, either by keyword (for example: light, medium, bold, black) or by number (100–900 in hundred increments; 100 is the lightest, and 400 is medium). Next, you specify font style, in this case, italic. Then you specify a size and leading, which can be in points or pixels. Lastly, you specify the font.

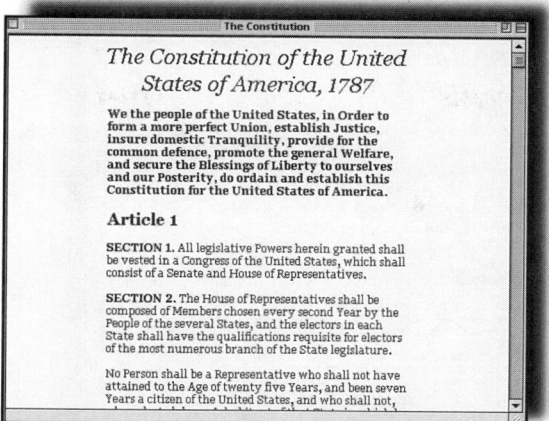

A less imposing title.

The H4 Element

The changes to H1 are quite an improvement, but now the preamble, set with the H4 element, looks too heavy. First we'll center it, then italicize it, and give it a lot of leading so that it has a decorative look (see Figure 6.6).

Add the following to the style sheet in usconst.htm:

```
H1 {
  text-align: center;
  font: medium italic 24pt/30pt Georgia, serif;
  }

H4 {
  text-align: center;
  font: medium italic 14pt/22pt Georgia;
  }
```

Now the preamble looks more elegant than ominous—in fact, the entire page is starting to look a little more dignified, isn't it?

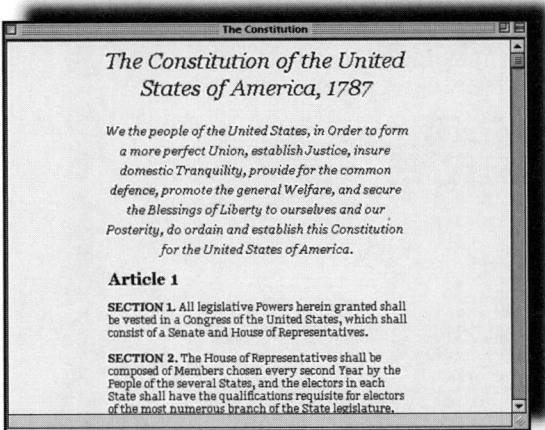

Figure 6.6

Now the preamble looks right.

The H2 Element

Now the document is looking like it wants a little light and space. Certainly the H2 head "Article 1" is too big, too bold, and too close to the preamble. Let's fix the font first and then worry about the space (see Figure 6.7).

Type a new CSS rule in the style sheet, in between H1 and H4 (I like to keep the style sheet organized like this, no matter what order the headers appear in the HTML, but you can structure your style sheets any way you like):

```
H1 { ... }

H2 {
  text-align: center;
  font: italic 13pt/15pt Georgia;
  }

H4 { ... }
```

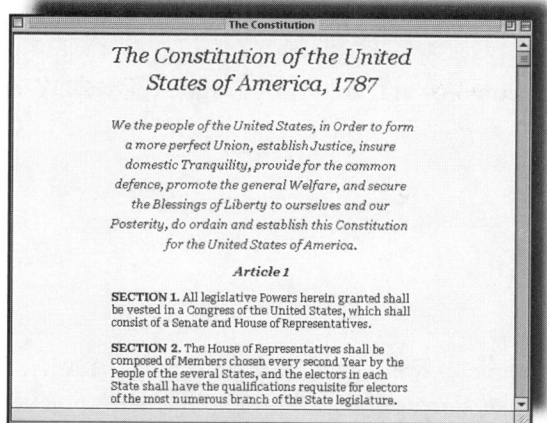

Figure 6.7

Adjusting the "Article 1" head to the proper size.

This fixes the weight of the type, but not the space. We'll add space above the H2 element by using the margin-top property.

To increase the space (see Figure 6.8), add this to your new CSS rule:

```
H2 {
   margin-top: 18pt;
   text-align: center;
   font: italic 13pt/15pt Georgia;
   }
```

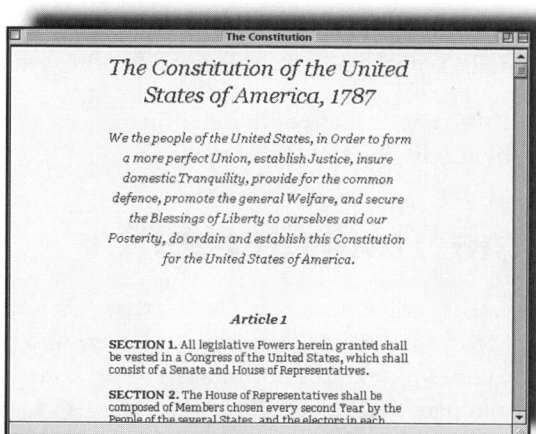

Figure 6.8

Improving the spacing between the "Article 1" head and text.

The H2 element has a top margin because of the way HTML documents are structured. Here's the structure of the tags in usconst.htm—or at least the tags inside the BODY element:

```
H1
H4
H2
P
P
P
P ...
```

These elements are stacked one on top of the other like the layers in a layer cake. Each one has right and left, and top and bottom margins. These elements can be full of ingredients themselves; the first two P elements contain an inline element called STRONG. All these elements are packed inside the BODY element (or cake, if you prefer).

Sitting on top of the BODY element is the HEAD element, which in the usconst.htm example contains two layers, TITLE and STYLE. A typical HEAD element (in the real world) could contain:

```
META
TITLE
LINK
STYLE
```

Of course, these two elements, HEAD and BODY, are themselves contained inside the HTML element. So HTML documents are like Russian dolls, with elements stuffed inside other elements.

Now that we've reformatted the document's heads, we'll redesign the text, by modifying the P element.

Formatting the Text Elements

One persistent problem with HTML is that it has been practically impossible to add spacing (known to designers and typographers as leading) to lines of text. It's not impossible, of course. If you *really had to* you could hand-break every line with the BR tag and insert transparent single-pixel GIFs set to "height=10" at the end of every line; this would push the lines apart and create leading. But that's handsetting! Who wants to do that?

The difficulty in specifying leading has led to situations like that in Figure 6.9, where the line length is fine, but the text is still difficult to read because the lines are uncomfortably close together.

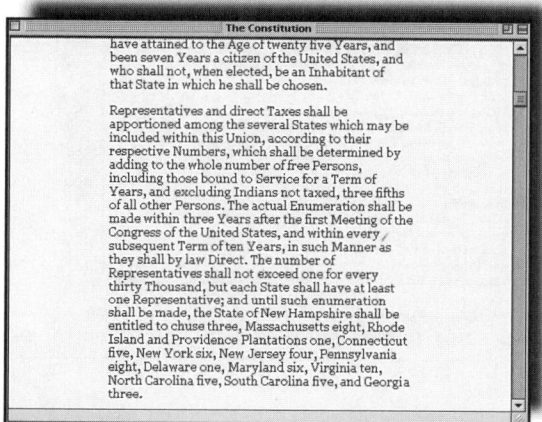

Figure 6.9

An example of not enough leading.

The P Element

As you've seen already in our formatting of the H4 element, CSS gives you control over leading. Let's do that now. We'll increase the size of the text slightly, from 12 to 13 points (in general, think big for onscreen text), and we'll give it comfortable leading, as shown in Figure 6.10.

Add a new rule to the style sheet in usconst.htm that reads:

```
BODY { ... }

P {
  font: 13pt/17pt Georgia;
  }

H1 { ... }
```

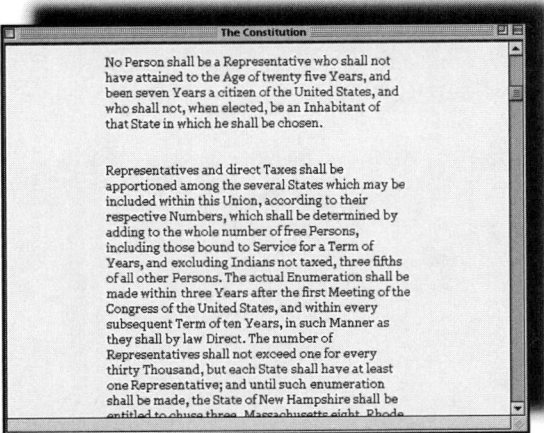

Figure 6.10

The text is easier to read, but there's too much paragraph space.

Adding leading improves the readability of the text by quite a bit, but it has an unwanted consequence: there's too much space between paragraphs. There's also too much space between the H2 element and the P element, as shown in Figure 6.11.

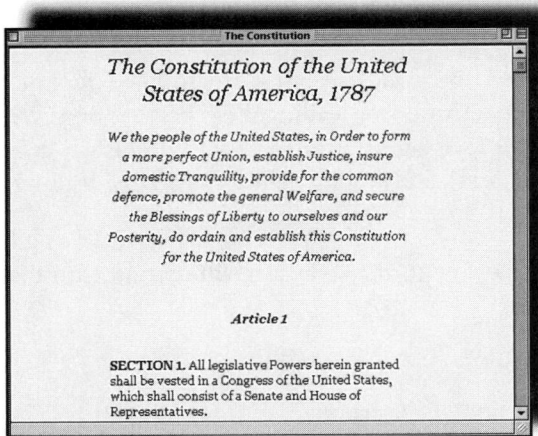

Figure 6.11

Now there's too much space between the P and H2 elements.

Fixing the paragraph space takes a little more thought, and a look at how HTML is structured. Again, the elements here are laid out like layers in the BODY cake:

```
H1
H4
H2
P
P...
```

This means that the *paragraph* spacing is really the *element* spacing—the space between H4 and H2, between H2 and P, and between P and P. Consequently the spacing is affected by two things. One, the top and bottom margins of the elements; we've already seen how H2's top margin pushes it down from the preamble set in H4. And second, the inter-element (or inter-paragraph) spacing is affected by the line spacing of the BODY element. If H1, H2, H4, and P are layers in a cake, then BODY is the frosting that binds it all together—and you can choose how much frosting to put in between the layers.

So the paragraph spacing in usconst.htm is the result of two factors: the inherently wide spacing of the P element, which by default wants an extra line afterwards; and the line spacing of the BODY element, which is pushing too much "frosting" in between the layers. To fix it, we need to reduce the BODY line spacing, and reduce the P element margins. We have to use both because if we reduce only the element's margins, the P element climbs up and overruns the H2 element.

To reduce the BODY line space, add the following line to the style sheet in usconst.htm:

```
BODY {
  background: #ffc;
  margin-left: 20%;
  margin-right: 20%;
  font-family: Georgia, serif;
      line-height: 18pt;
  }
```

As we can see in Figure 6.12, this reduces much of the space between paragraphs and moves the P element closer to the H2 element. (Why 18 points of line spacing? I wish I could tell you. I arrived at it by trial and error.)

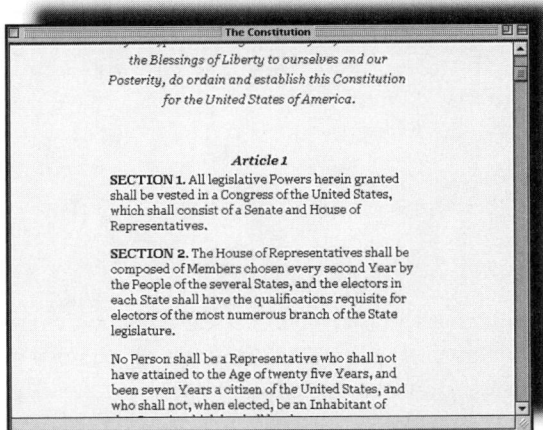

Figure 6.12.

A BODY line spacing of 18 points brings the elements closer together.

But there's still too much room between the P elements, so we'll adjust the top margin of P to fix this, as shown in Figure 6.13. Add the following to the style sheet:

```
P {
  margin-top: -10pt;
  font: 13pt/17pt Georgia;
  }
```

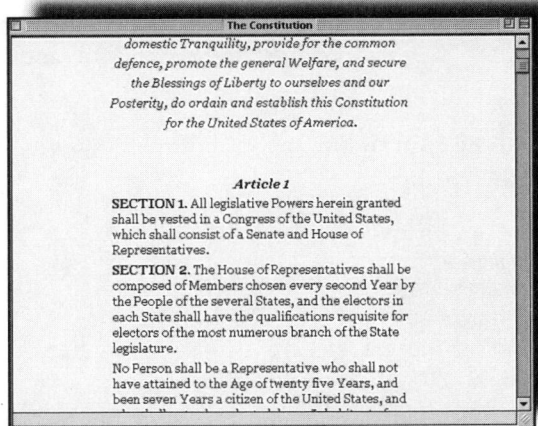

Figure 6.13

A negative top margin fixes the spacing.

CSS enables you to set negative margins, which can be used for some very creative effects—you can see some of them at Microsoft's CSS pages. Negative margins also can make up for the built-in spacing of tags such as P, which apply spacing afterwards. (We're adjusting the margin-top because of a bug in version 3.0 of Internet Explorer, which won't recognize the margin-bottom property; this problem has been fixed in version 4.0—in fact, it was fixed not long after IE3 shipped, but there wasn't time to make it part of the release.)

The STRONG Inline Element

Now we come to the easiest change of all. Notice how the words inside the STRONG element are just a bit too big and bold? Let's just reduce the size of them so they look more like small caps. Future versions of CSS browsers will let you create small caps directly, but for now we'll just reduce the size, as seen in Figure 6.14.

Add a new rule to the style sheet in usconst.htm that reads:

```
H4 { ...}

STRONG { font: 11pt/17pt Georgia }
```

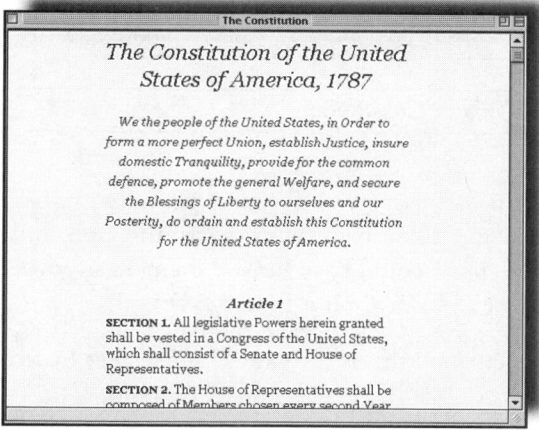

Figure 6.14.

Now the subheads "Section 1" and "Section 2" are less obtrusive.

Changing Style Sheets

Now, would you believe that the *same HTML code* that created this neoclassical-looking page can be used to create something a lot wilder? Take a look at Figure 5.15—trust me, the code is the same (okay, not completely—the words inside the STRONG tags aren't capitalized, but that's it).

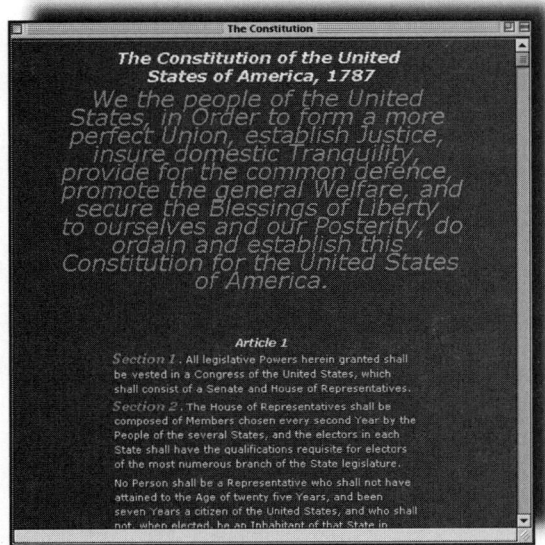

Figure 6.15

Not your father's Constitution.

In fact, I was conservative in how I played with the style sheet. All the elements are basically centered the same and in the same position—but I could have moved them all over the place *without touching the HTML markup.* Pretty exciting!

If you're curious, this is the "kewl" style sheet I used:

```
BODY {
  color: #ffc;
  margin-left: 20%;
  margin-right: 20%;
  line-height: 19pt;
  }
```

```
P
  margin-top: -10pt;
  font: 11pt/16pt Verdana;
  }

H1 {
  color: #cff;
  font: italic 18pt/20pt Verdana;
  text-align: center;
  }

H2 {
  margin-top: 18pt;
  text-align: center;
  font: italic 13pt/15pt Verdana;
  }

H4 {
  color: #f69;
  margin-left: 10%;
  margin-right: 10%;
  margin-top: -6pt;
  text-align: center;
  font: medium italic 25pt/20pt Verdana;
  }

STRONG {
  color: #f69;
  font: italic 15pt/16pt Georgia;
  }
```

Try making your own style sheets for this document—the faster the Founding Fathers spin in their graves, the better!

Conclusion

In this chapter, you've applied a style sheet to a very simply formatted HTML page. Even a simple page can be made to create very nice effects. The most important factor, though, is experimentation. Don't settle for this tutorial! Refer to the CSS declarations and syntax in Chapter 8 and write your own style sheets, so you can get used to writing the code. That's the only way to learn—so take some time and write your own style sheets. Explore any style you like, or break all the rules.

For a more advanced look at CSS, Chapter 7 will offer you a chance to create an online magazine using advanced CSS features like classes and pseudo-classes, that give you pinpoint control over a wide range of typographic styles.

Specifying Typography

In this tutorial, we'll cover more advanced type and page formatting including:

➡ Using linked, external style sheets, which save time and production effort

➡ Strategies for managing complicated style sheets so that you don't mix your styles

➡ Using classes to extend the reach of your HTML tags, giving almost unlimited possibilities for formatting

➡ Reusing styles across pages in a site so that you don't waste effort rewriting style sheets

➡ Using pseudo-classes to change the look and behavior of hypertext links

➡ Working around bugs in IE3 to get the effect you want

➡ Adding background color

What You'll Need

To use this tutorial, you'll need a few things:

➡ A CSS-capable Web browser. At the time of this writing (February 1997), the only browser in common use that supports CSS is Microsoft Internet Explorer 3.0. The W3C has written Arena, which supports CSS, but it's only available for the Unix operating system. GNUscape Emacs W3 is also CSS-capable, and it is available for the major platforms as a beta test.

Netscape Communicator—in prerelease form at the time of this writing—offers buggy support for CSS.

➡ A text editor or word processor that can save to text-only format.

➡ An Internet connection to retrieve the tutorial files from `http://www.hayden.com`.

➡ Basic knowledge of HTML—in fact, you don't need to know any tricky HTML at all; the style sheet does the complex formatting.

➡ Two of Microsoft's free Web fonts, Verdana and Georgia, available from Microsoft at `www.microsoft.com/truetype`. These fonts are in the "full installs" of Internet Explorer. These fonts are designed especially for the screen, and are very readable.

Start with Design

This tutorial may differ from a lot of CSS material you'll find on the Web. Instead of concentrating on "creative" uses of CSS, this lesson focuses on what the first version of CSS does best: formatting long texts. HTML is still a bookish sort of *structured* language—it doesn't respond well to a lot of trickery. In time, the W3 will add layout control to HTML in the same way that they've added typographic control: by extending HTML. (One of the proposals for layout control is discussed on the W3C's Web site, `www.w3.org`.) For now, though, CSS is happiest when it's formatting text like a word processor does: up and down.

With this in mind, let's say that we've just taken a job as a production designer for a literary online magazine. This magazine has features, business, opinion, and editorial articles, as well as book reviews and short fiction. Your assignment is to create text pages for this magazine.

Because the magazine is intended to be read, not just looked at, design goals to focus on might include simplicity (so the reader's eye never gets lost or dazzled), consistency (so the magazine is familiar and easy to navigate), readability, and typographic contrast and variation (so the text stays fresh, and the reader's eye can pick out the page elements, like the title and the links).

The First Story

Let's begin by designing the short fiction piece. This page will sit one level down from the table of contents. Our little magazine is just that—little—and it contains a contents page and seven or eight article pages. We're going to write the style sheet for those articles. As I mentioned before, these should be readable and load fast—they're the real heart of the magazine.

Linking the Style Sheet

Because this magazine is going to use one style sheet to format many pages, we can link the style sheet to all the pages and save ourselves a lot of typing (or cutting and pasting). Not only does this save untold amounts of production time, it allows for quick redesigns if needed.

Linked style sheets are included in the HTML by using the new LINK element, which goes into the HEAD of the document. Therefore, to link a style sheet to "fiction.htm" you would write:

```
<HTML>
<HEAD>
<TITLE>Fiction: The Sphinx without a Secret</TITLE>
<LINK REL="StyleSheet" HREF="article.css"
TYPE="text/css">
</head>
```

This tells the browser that this HTML document is "linked" to another file, in this case, a style sheet called article.css. The syntax `TYPE="text/css"` also tells the browser to interpret the style sheet as a text document containing CSS rules. It's important to include this parameter, as `"text/css"` isn't the only type of style sheet available. Netscape Communicator also recognizes JavaScript style sheets, which are similar but not interchangeable.

 **Warning**

> Microsoft Internet Explorer 3 won't recognize background colors or images from external style sheets. To get around this bug, simply write the style sheet rule for the background as an embedded style sheet. The rest of the style sheet can be linked.

Next embed the background style by entering:

```
<html>
<head>
<title>Fiction: The Sphinx without a Secret</title>
<link rel="StyleSheet" href="article.css">
  <STYLE TYPE="text/css"
  <!--
  BODY { background: #633 }
  -->
  </style>
</head>
```

In fact, embedding the background color style gives you the opportunity to enliven the site by giving each page a different color. Let's make this page a burgundy color (I find that the darker colors are much better-looking than the lighter colors—which tend to be pastel or neon—so let's commit to making this site *reversed*, that is, light text on darker backgrounds). For more information on specifying colors, see Chapter 6.

Writing the External Style Sheet

Start by changing the formatting for the BODY and P elements. Because all the other elements are contained inside it, the BODY element will change the basic formatting of the document. We'll format P because all the body text is contained inside P tags.

Open an empty page in your text editor and save it as "article.css." Then type the following:

```
BODY {
  color: #fff;
  font-family: Georgia;
  }
```

All the text in the HTML document linked to this style sheet is now white and set in the font Georgia.

Next, assign style information to the P element.

```
BODY { ... }

P {
  text-indent: 15px;
  margin-left: 30%;
  margin-right: 20%;
  margin-top: -31px;
  font: 12px/19px Georgia;
}
```

These properties should be familiar from the tutorial in Chapter 6. Measurements are in pixels, so they appear the same on all platforms, or in percentages, so they stretch and contract with the browser window. The property text–indent gives each paragraph a first line indent of 15 pixels. The left and right margins keep the column at a manageable width. The margin–top property eliminates the blank line between paragraphs, and the font has been set to 12-pixel Georgia on 19 pixels of leading. The results can be seen in Figures 7.1 and 7.2.

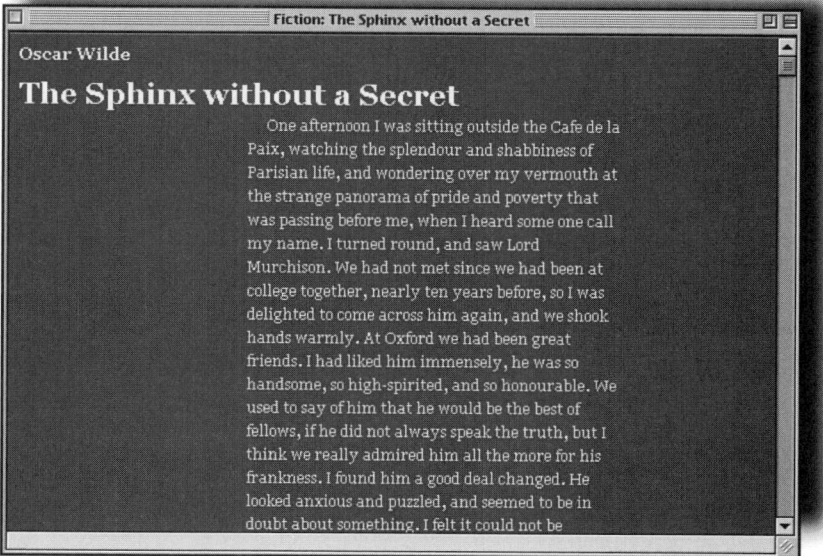

Figure 7.1

The body text after applying CSS styling to the P element.

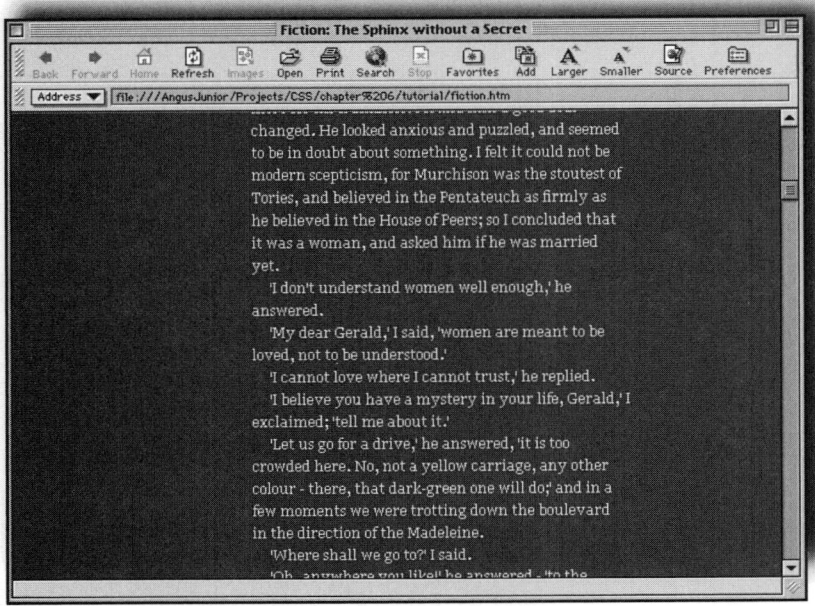

changed. He looked anxious and puzzled, and seemed
to be in doubt about something. I felt it could not be
modern scepticism, for Murchison was the stoutest of
Tories, and believed in the Pentateuch as firmly as
he believed in the House of Peers; so I concluded that
it was a woman, and asked him if he was married
yet.

'I don't understand women well enough,' he
answered.

'My dear Gerald,' I said, 'women are meant to be
loved, not to be understood.'

'I cannot love where I cannot trust,' he replied.

'I believe you have a mystery in your life, Gerald,' I
exclaimed; 'tell me about it.'

'Let us go for a drive,' he answered, 'it is too
crowded here. No, not a yellow carriage, any other
colour - there, that dark-green one will do;' and in a
few moments we were trotting down the boulevard
in the direction of the Madeleine.

'Where shall we go to?' I said.

'Oh, anywhere you like!' he answered - 'to the

Figure 7.2

*The addition of indention and leading is a subtle but marked improvement
over regular HTML text.*

The Author Class

Now style the author's name by adding a class to the author's name.
What you're doing is telling the browser to use a special type of H3
element reserved for the author listing. In CSS, this is called a class.
Classes enable you to change standard HTML elements in many
ways—you can have almost an unlimited number of H1s or H3s in
your document, all looking different, but performing the same *structural* role. This lets non-CSS browsers (which won't show the classes
or CSS typography) display the page with some typographic structure.

Scroll down in "fiction.htm" and find the code for the author's
name. Change it to read:

```
<BODY>

<H3 CLASS="author">Oscar Wilde</H3>

<H1>The Sphinx without a Secret</H1>
```

```
<P>One afternoon I was sitting outside the Cafe de la Paix, watching
the splendour and shabbiness of Parisian life, and wondering over my
vermouth at the strange panorama of pride and poverty that was pass-
ing before me, when I heard some one call my name.</P>
```

Now add a rule to the style sheet that reads:

```
P { ... }

H3.author {
  color: ff0;
  margin-left: 50%;
  font: italic 12px/18px Verdana;
  font-weight: black;
  }
```

The result is shown in Figure 7.3:

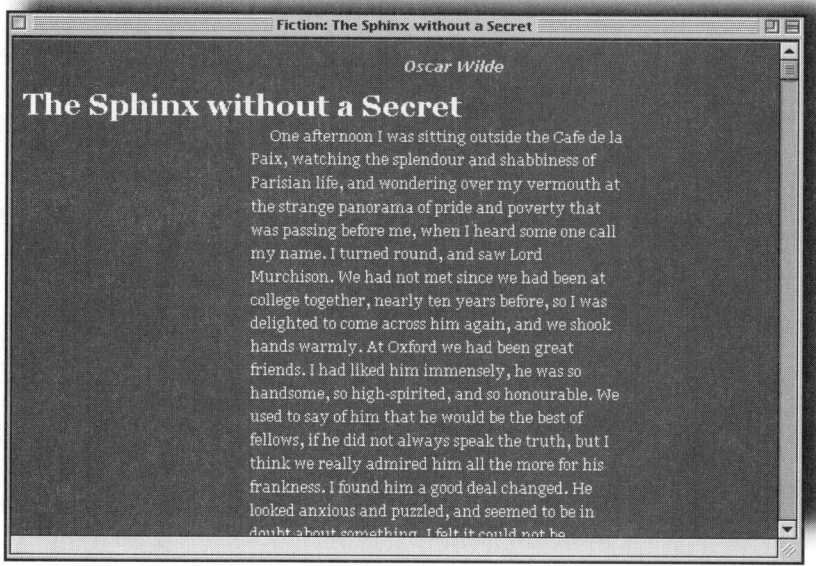

Now the author's name is styled more in keeping with the new design.

This sets up a specific "look" for the author's name, but it still lets you use the H3 element elsewhere—on the contents page, perhaps, or as a subhead in a long article.

The Article Title

Moving down the page, the next element to look at is the article's title head, set in HTML using H1. Let's create a class for the article title in the H1 element like we did for the H3 element.

In the style sheet, write the new rule:

```
P { ... }

H1.article {
  color: #aaf;
  margin-left: 30%;
  margin-right: 20%;
  font: 20px/40px Georgia;
  font-weight: medium;
  }

H3.author { ... }
```

Change the HTML to read:

```
<H1 CLASS="article">The Sphinx without a Secret</H1>
```

This creates a class associated with H1 that is to be used as an article title. If the magazine expanded to include a chat group or a bulletin board, you could create additional classes for H1, such as H1.chat or H1.bulletin. Classes give you an incredible amount of flexibility.

In many cases it's a good idea to name CSS classes after what they do, not what they look like. If you've ever worked with a big magazine or book style sheet in Quark or PageMaker, you might know this already. A class called "article" or "author" tells you how and when to use it—but a class called "mediumblue" or "boldyellow" gives you no clue. You'll save yourself (or your assistants) a lot of frustration if your classes are self-explanatory.

The new class "article" makes the page look like Figure 7.4.

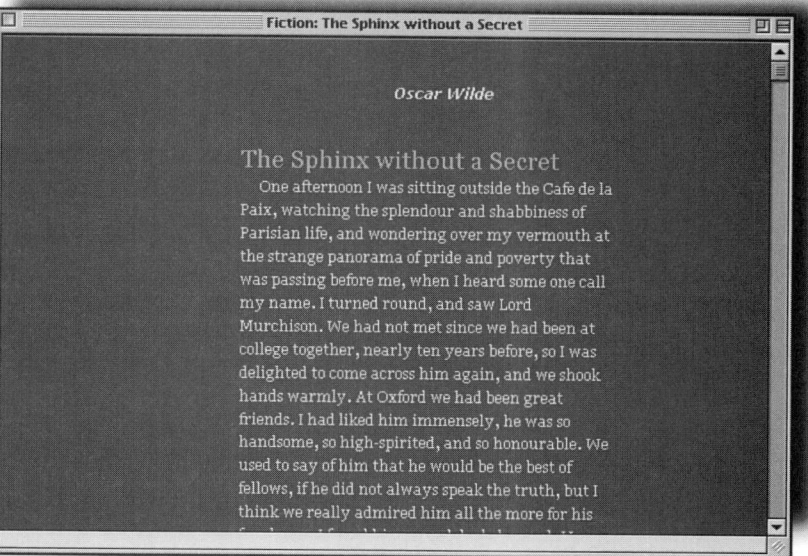

Figure 7.4

The page is beginning to take shape.

Creating an Initial Paragraph

One of the most exciting things about CSS is that it lets you create two essential typographic effects—initial caps (commonly called drop caps, except that they don't all drop) and first-line formatting (commonly seen in the major print magazines, where the first line of text is in small caps or bold).

Warning

> Internet Explorer 3.0 (which I used in creating these chapters) doesn't support the formatting commands that make CSS drop caps and first lines. This is a flaw in IE3 that has been corrected in IE4. At the time of this writing, IE4 is to enter beta testing in a few weeks. In fact, by the time you read this, Internet Explorer 4 may be in common use—it is almost fully CSS-compliant.

Instead of creating an inital letter or first line (see the warning), I'm going to suggest taking another route to help the reader. We'll create an inital paragraph instead. Generally, initial letters, lines, words, or paragraphs are helpful to the reader because they help the eye find the first line.

What we'll do is modify the first paragraph as marked in the HTML. Modify "fiction.htm" to look like this:

```
<H3 CLASS="author">Oscar Wilde</H3>

<H1 CLASS="article">The Sphinx without a Secret</H1>

<P CLASS="intro">One afternoon I was sitting outside the Cafe de la
Paix, watching the splendour and shabbiness of Parisian life, and
wondering over my vermouth...</P>
```

And now create a new rule in the style sheet "article.css" that reads:

```
P { ... }

P.intro {
  text-indent: 0px;
  margin-top: 10pt;
  font: 18px/22px Georgia;
  }

H1 { ... }
```

This gives an initial paragraph that looks like Figure 7.5.

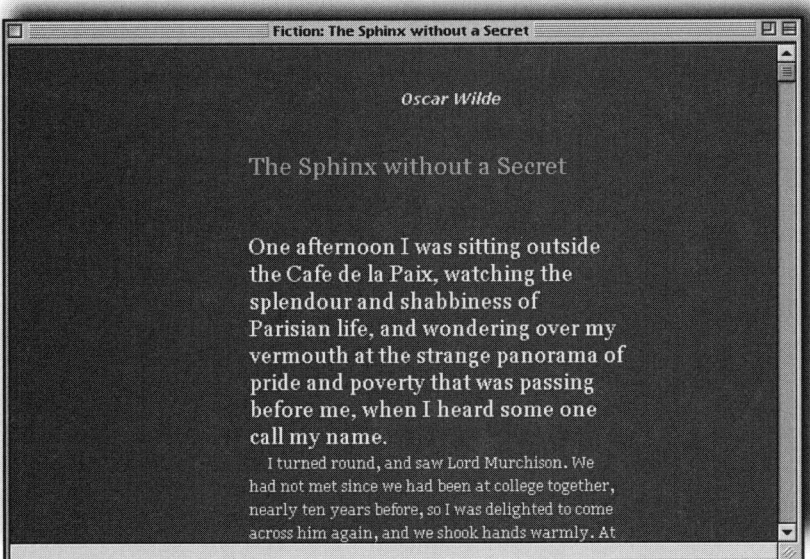

Figure 7.5

It's clear, but nothing you would want to read.

Creating a Pull Quote

Unfortunately, our layout is a little bland, not offering much incentive to start reading the story. We can help solve the problem by creating a pull quote to liven up the layout and arouse the reader's interest. We'll offset the quote a bit, and set it in bright green to contrast with the rest of the colors.

I've gone through the text and found a quote that I like (of course, if you find a better one, by all means, use it). Change the code in "fiction.htm" to read:

```
<H1 CLASS="article">The Sphinx without a Secret</H1>

<P CLASS="serifpull">He took from his pocket a little silver-clasped
morocco case, and handed it to me. I opened it</P>

<P CLASS="intro">One afternoon I was sitting outside the Cafe de la
Paix, watching the splendour and shabbiness of Parisian life, and
wondering over my vermouth...</P>
```

You'll see why I've named the new class "serifpull" in the section to follow where we format a new article. Now write a new rule in "article.css":

```
P.intro { ... }

P.serifpull {
  color: 0f0;
  text-indent: 0px;
  margin-top: -30px;
  margin-left: 36%;
  margin-right: 15%;
  font: italic 12px/20px Georgia;
  }

H1.article { ... }
```

The results are a big improvement as shown in Figure 7.6.

Creating Links with CSS

Now, if you scroll to the bottom of the page, you'll see something pretty unsightly (see Figure 7.7)—the navigational links.

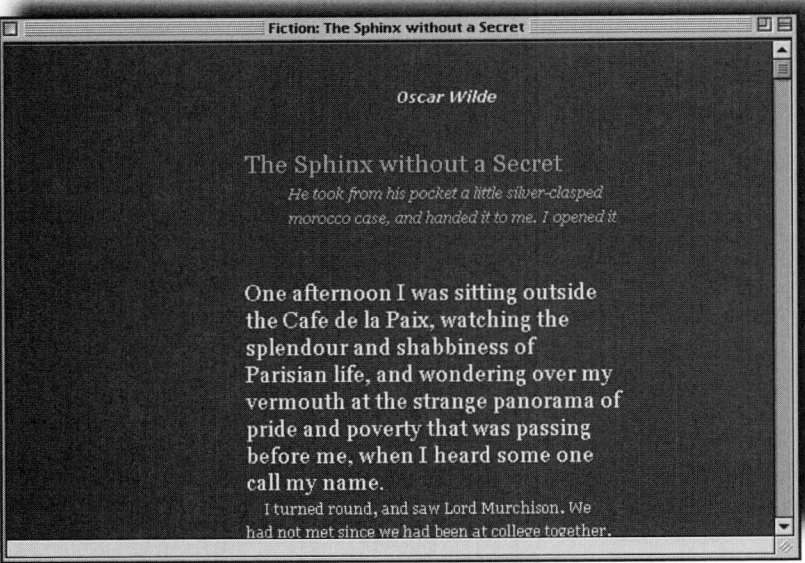

Figure 7.6

More enticing than before.

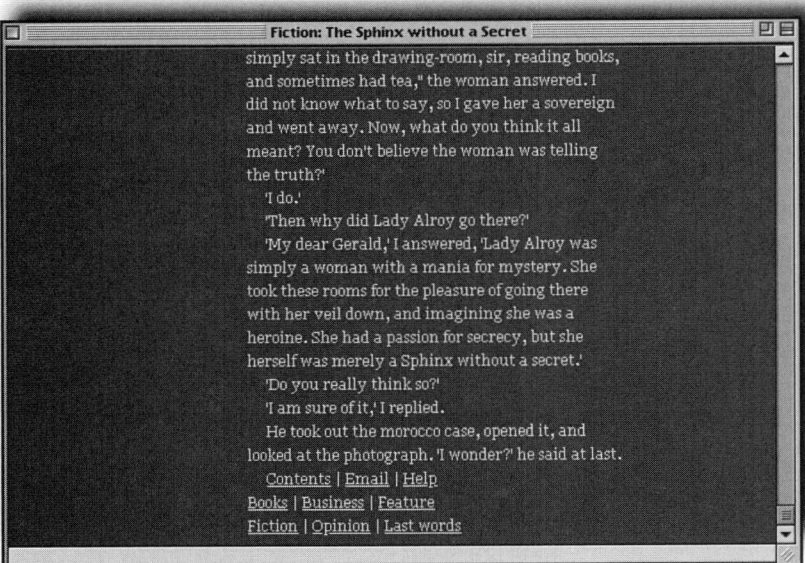

Figure 7.7

The links don't match the document and are hard to differentiate from the rest of the text.

Do two things to improve the look and functionality of these links—get rid of the underlining and change the link colors with the pseudo–classes, and set them in a different font and layout, so they don't look so much like the body text. This will make them easier to find and use.

First, let's change the font and the layout. Write the following rule into the style sheet

```
P.serifpull { ... }

P.links {
  color: #f03;
  text-indent: 0px;
  margin-top: 10px;
  font: medium 11px/15px Verdana, Arial, sans-serif;
  }

H1.article { ... }
```

and change the links section of the HTML to read:

```
<P>He took out the morocco case....</P>

<P CLASS="links">
<a href="index.htm">Contents</a> |
<a href="mail.htm">Email</a> |
<a href="help.htm">Help</a><BR>
<a href="bookrev.htm">Books</a> |
<a href="busecon.htm">Business</a> |
<a href="feature.htm">Feature</a><BR>
<a href="fiction.htm">Fiction</a> |
<a href="stanton.htm">Opinion</a> |
<a href="last.htm">Last words</a></P>

</BODY>
```

This will change the placement of the links (by putting vertical space between the links and the text), change the font to Verdana, and turn the "links" text to red, as shown in Figure 7.8.

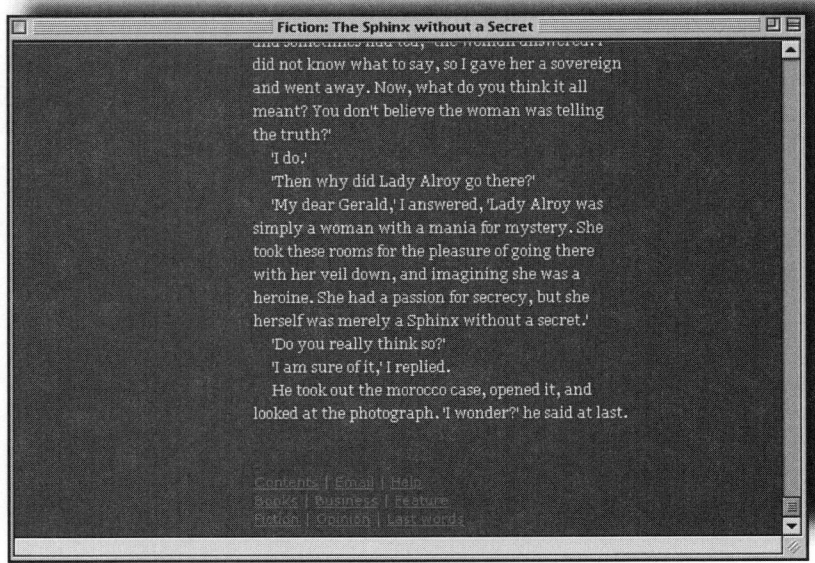

Figure 7.8

Links improved, but not so that you can tell.

Next, we'll change the appearance of the links by using the pseudo-classes. CSS has several pseudo-classes that we will use here: `A:link`, `A:active`, and `A:visited`. They are called "pseudo" because they can be set up like regular classes, but they do something rather different: they control dynamic, interactive formatting. In this case, the pseudo-classes control the color and decoration of links, showing when they've been visited or are being clicked on.

Write the following into the top of the style sheet "article.css":

```
A:link {
  color: #fff;
  text-decoration: none
  }

A:active {
  color: #f33;
  text-decoration: none
  }

A:visited {
  color: #fff;
  text-decoration: none
  }
```

This sets the colors for unvisited links and visited links to white, and currently selected links ("active") to red. It turns off link underlining by setting the text-decoration to "none."

The "links" class made all the text turn red; but now the A pseudo-classes have specified that visited and unvisited links render in white. The result is that only the horizontal bars are red, which separates the links and helps them stand out (see Figure 7.9).

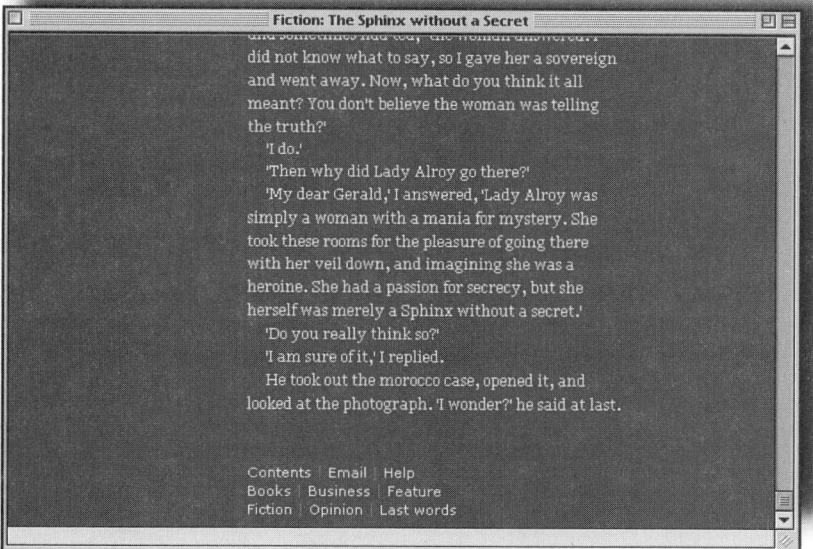

Figure 7.9

Now the links are usable.

An Opinion Piece

Now we've already built most of our style sheet. For this second kind of article, let's extend our style sheet—and the magazine's design—and create a second level of text face, by using a sans–serif body text style.

To begin, format the file "stanton.htm" to work with the style sheet "article.css." Enter the following code into the HTML:

```
<head>
<title>Opinion: Women's Rights</title>
<link rel="StyleSheet" href="text.css">
```

```
<STYLE TYPE="text/css"
<!--
BODY { background: #003 }
-->
</STYLE>
</head>
```

And add the following classes to the HTML document:

```
<BODY>

<H3 CLASS="author">Elizabeth Cady Stanton</H3>

<H1 CLASS="article">Women's Rights</H1>

<P CLASS="intro">We have met here today to discuss our rights and
wrongs, civil and political, and not, as some have supposed, to go
into the detail of social life alone. </P>
```

Now "stanton.htm" looks like Figure 7.10 when viewed in the browser.

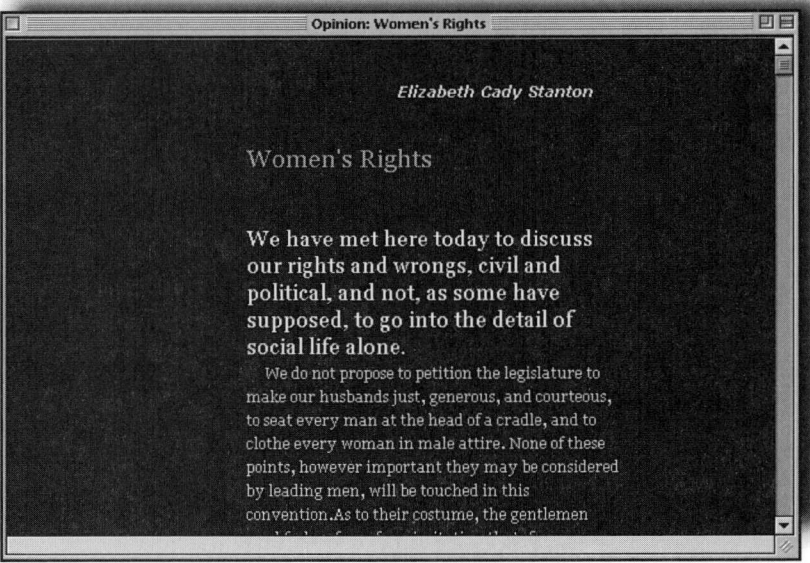

Figure 7.10

Stanton.htm after formatting the author's name, the title, and the intro paragraph.

Creating a New Pull Quote

Now create a sans-serif pull quote in sans-serif, for more variation.
Type a new class into the style sheet that reads:

```
P.serifpull { ... }

P.sanspull {
  color: 0f0;
  text-indent: 0px;
  margin-top: -30px;
  margin-left: 36%;
  margin-right: 15%;
  font: 11px/20px Verdana;
  }

P.links { ... }
```

Next, find a suitable quote for the article (or use the one I've chosen) and enter the following into the file stanton.htm:

```
<H1 CLASS="article">Women's Rights</H1>

<P CLASS="sanspull">We are assembled to protest against a form of
government existing without the consent of the governed</p>

<P CLASS="intro">We have met here today to discuss our rights and
wrongs, civil and political, and not, as some have supposed, to go
into the detail of social life alone. </P>
```

Save both files; the results should look like Figure 7.11.

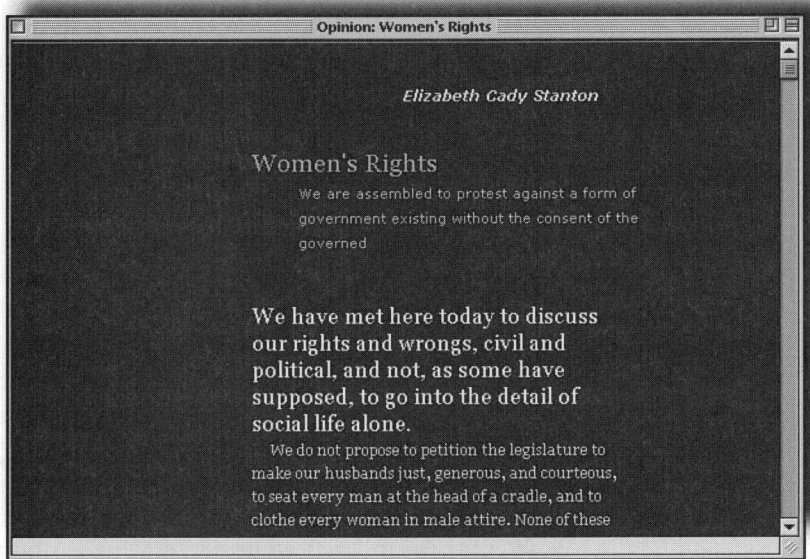

Figure 7.11

Stanton.htm after adding a pull quote.

Creating Sans Serif Text

Now we'll change the body text in this document to a sans–serif face. This is common in magazines such as *Wired*. The idea is to provide another level of typographic variation. You can set technology articles in sans serif, and long reportage in serif, for example, and the magazine stays consistent-looking, but fresh. In our case, let's put opinion pieces in the sans–serif Verdana, and everything else in serif.

Enter a new rule into the style sheet "article.css":

```
P.serifpull { ... }

P.sanstext {
  text-indent: 18px;
  margin-left: 30%;
  margin-top: -30px;
  font: 11px/18px Verdana;
  }

P.sanspull { ... }
```

This new rule for sans serif text is basically the same as the regular P text, but with a slightly different margin-top (–30 pixels instead of –31) and the different font, font size, and leading.

Now comes the ugly part. You're going to have to mark every text paragraph in stanton.htm like this:

```
<P CLASS="sanstext"> We do not propose to petition the legislature to
make our husbands just, generous, and courteous....</P>

<P CLASS="sanstext">But we are assembled to protest against a form of
government existing without the consent of the governed - to declare
our right to be free as man is free, to be represented in the govern-
ment....</P>

<P CLASS="sanstext">And, strange as it may seem to many, we now de-
mand our right to vote according to the declaration of the government
under which we live. This right no one pretends to deny...</P>
```

It is easier to format if you just cut and paste your way down the page. This is one reason why I decided to use sans serif for opinion pieces—they tend to be shorter than long features, and they'll be easier to format in sans serif. Save the results; when viewed in a browser, it should look like Figure 7.12.

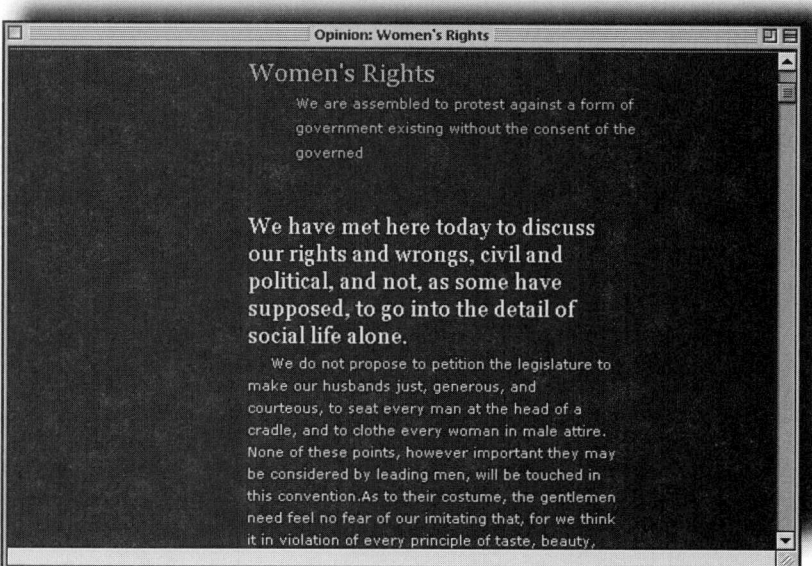

Figure 7.12

Sans serif text.

There's just one last thing to do for the text formatting. Notice the paragraph directly follows the initial paragraph? Well, it shouldn't be like that—if you remember, we split that paragraph so that the initial paragraph wouldn't be too imposing. What we need to do is make a class for that "first" paragraph. Enter this new rule into your style sheet:

```
P.sanstext { ... }

P.sansfirst {
  text-indent: 0px;
  margin-left: 30%;
  margin-top: -30px;
  font: 11px/18px Verdana
  }

P.sanspull { ... }
```

This new sansfirst rule is actually identical to sanstext except that the text-indent property is set to zero. Next, mark the paragraph in the HTML so that it reads:

```
<P CLASS="sansfirst"> We do not propose to petition the legislature to
make our husbands just, generous, and courteous....</P>
```

The results should look like Figure 7.13.

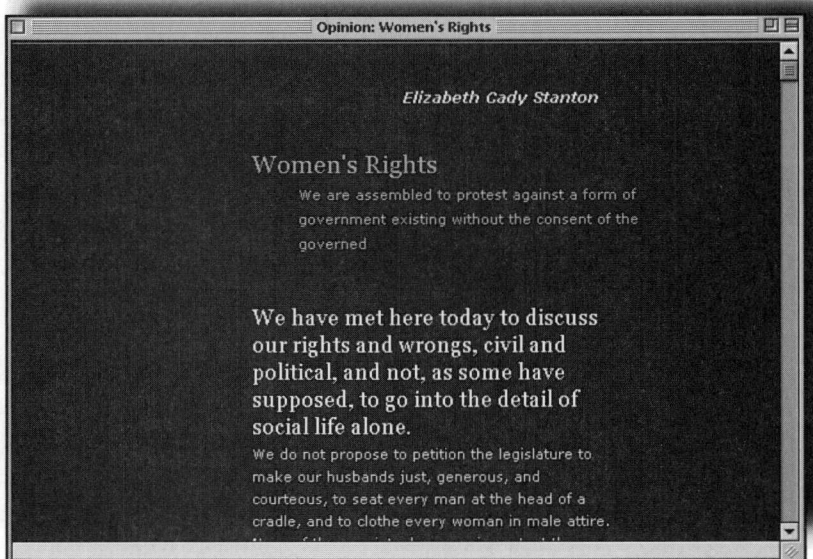

Figure 7.13

No indent for the first regular paragraph.

Correcting the Links

The last consideration is the links at the bottom of the page. Of course, now it's easy. You've already created the styles to format them (by creating the P.links and A rules), so all you have to do is specify the classes in the HTML file. Go to the bottom of stanton.htm and change the links' tag to:

```
<P CLASS="links">
<a href="index.htm">Contents</a> |
<a href="mail.htm">Email</a> |
<a href="help.htm">Help</a><BR>
<a href="bookrev.htm">Books</a> |
<a href="busecon.htm">Business</a> |
<a href="feature.htm">Feature</a><BR>
<a href="fiction.htm">Fiction</a> |
<a href="stanton.htm">Opinion</a> |
<a href="last.htm">Last words</a></P>

</BODY>
</HTML>
```

The links should now look like Figure 7.14. Easy, once you've made the styles, isn't it?

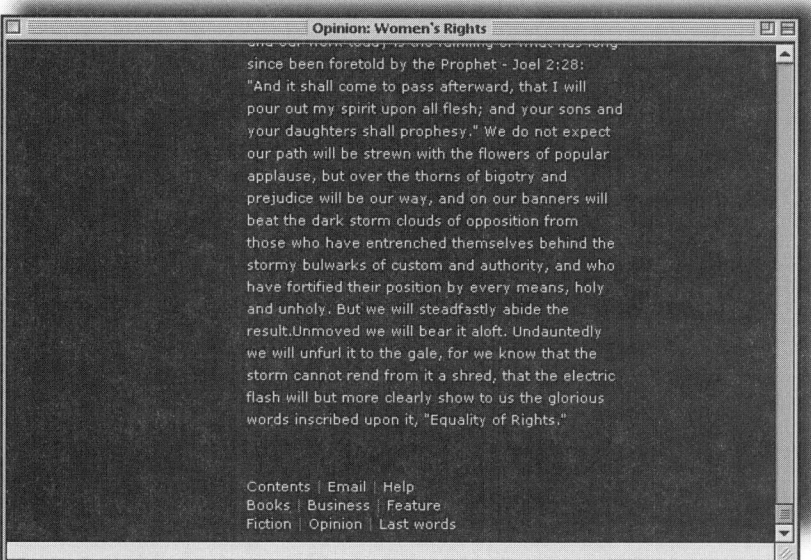

Figure 7.14

The links are easily fixed when you've already created the style sheet.

Conclusion

The layout capabilities of CSS show themselves best when used for long, complex documents. Many related pages can use a single stylesheet—this both eases the frustration of entering line after line of browser-specific codes like FONT, and reduces development time. It also reduces the chance for errors.

To see what I mean, dowload the rest of our little magazine's articles from `www.hayden.com`; they're unformatted, so just enter the classes into the code. In almost no time, you'll have formatted an entire magazine. Imagine having to write that style sheet for each page!

Also, take a look at the pages you've created in a non-CSS browser (Lynx, Mosaic, Netscape 2.0-3.0, or Internet Explorer 2.0). You'll see that the pages degrade very gracefully, allowing them to be translated into Braille, if need be, or redesigned into a book, or even translated for voice synthesis (see the next chapter for a discussion of this interesting proposal). This is the essence of HTML: the same document serves different purposes.

CSS Properties

This chapter is intended as a reference for designers writing their own style sheets. Much of this information comes from the CSS-1 specification, "Cascading Style Sheets, level 1" a document available at `http://www.w3.org/pub/WWW/TR/REC-CSS1`. The World Wide Web Consortium's site is, in fact, the best resource for keeping abreast of many changes on the Web, and I recommend that you bookmark it and visit it regularly.

Not all browsers are fully CSS–compliant. Microsoft IE3 is one of them. But because IE3 is the only browser in common use that supports CSS, I have mentioned in each property whether that feature is supported by IE3. This way you can design for IE3—it will still be used for some time.

Netscape Communicator (Navigator 4) supports both CSS and Java-Script Accessible Style Sheets, but at the time of this writing, that support is very buggy. Since Navigator 4 is in Public Release 2 (a beta release), I haven't included the numerous errors.

Font Properties

Setting font properties will probably be the most popular use of CSS. CSS defines the properties "font-family," "font-style," "font-variant," "font-weight," "font-size," and "font" (this last one combines the values of all the rest).

Font-Family

Value: \<family-name\>, \<generic-name\>
Initial: browser's default
Applies to: all elements
Inherited: yes
Percentage value: N/A
Example:

```
P { font-family: Verdana, Arial, Helvetica, sans-serif }
```

This property is a prioritized list of font names, either specific family names, like "Verdana" or "Palatino," or generic ones. CSS browsers go down the list, using the first font they can find. If the user's computer lacked Verdana, for example, then Arial would be substituted. Family names containing spaces should be enclosed in quotes, as in

```
H2 { font-family: "Century Schoolbook", Times, serif }
```

CSS recognizes the following generic names:

- ➡ "serif," as in Times

- ➡ "sans-serif," as in Helvetica

- ➡ "cursive," as in Zapf Chancery

- ➡ "fantasy," as in Western

- ➡ "monospace," as in Courier

Microsoft Internet Explorer 3 does not support the "cursive" or "fantasy" generic family names.

Font-Style

Value: normal | italic | oblique
Initial: normal
Applies to: all elements
Inherited: yes
Percentage value: N/A
Example:

```
H3.author { font-style: italic }
```

The "normal" value selects the "upright" or "roman" style of a font. A value of "oblique" selects the oblique style (for example, Helvetica

Oblique) while the value of "italic" first looks for an italic style; if italic is not available, it uses "oblique."

Font-Variant

Value: normal | small–caps
Initial: normal
Applies to: all elements
Inherited: yes
Percentage value: N/A
Example:

```
EM { font-variant: small-caps }
```

When you specify small caps, CSS first tries to find the small–caps version of the font—if, for example, you write

```
P { font-family: Georgia }
EM { font-variant: small-caps }
```

```
<P>That, dad, is an <EM>australopithecus afarensis</EM>.</P>
```

the browser will first look for a small-caps font of Georgia, and, not finding it, will capitalize the text inside the EM element and scale it down slightly.

This would work perfectly, except that even in cases where the typeface has true small caps (like Adobe Caslon), there is currently no standard way for the browser to find them. In the case of Adobe Caslon, the small caps are contained in an expert set. In the case of a typeface like Tiro Typeworks' Manticore, the small caps are included in the font. Until font formats are standardized, <font-variant> will always capitalize and scale down. The joint proposal by Adobe and Microsoft of "OpenType" is one example of a common font format. You can find the OpenType specification at `http://www.microsoft.com/truetype`. In any case, IE3 does not support this declaration (by reducing the font size to simulate small caps), though IE4 should.

Font-Weight

Value: normal | bold | bolder | lighter | 100 | 200 | 300 | 400 | 500 | 600 | 700 | 800 | 900

Initial: normal
Applies to: all elements
Inherited: yes
Percentage value: N/A
Example:

```
P { font-weight: 400 }

STRONG { font-weight: bolder }
```

The numerical value of "400" is equal to "normal" and the value of "700" is equal to "bold." CSS thus gives a wide range of weights that can be specified. Someday, when it is possible to specify a typeface like Franklin Gothic in a Web presentation, designers will have access to Franklin Gothic's full range of weights, from light to ultra bold and black.

CSS "fills in the holes" if it uses a typeface that has fewer than nine values. For example, if the Web presentation uses a face that has three values, "normal," "bold," and "black," CSS assigns numbers 100–500 to "normal," 600 and 700 to "bold," and 800 and 900 to "black." This keeps the browser from coming across an unassigned number and getting confused.

Font-Size

Value: <absolute-size> | <relative-size> | <length> | <percentage>
Initial: medium
Applies to: all elements
Inherited: yes
Percentage values: relative to parent element's font size
Examples:

```
P { font-size: 12pt; }

BLOCKQUOTE { font-size: larger }

EM { font-size: 150% }

EM { font-size: 1.5em }
```

"Absolute size" is a keyword to an index of font sizes known by the Web browser. They are "xx-small," "x-small," "small," "medium," "large," "x-large," and "xx-large."

Font

Value: <font-style> <font-variant> <font-weight> <font-size> / <line-height> <font-family>

Initial: not defined
Applies to: all elements
Inherited: yes
Percentage values: allowed on <font-size> and <line-height>
Examples:

```
P { font: 12pt/14pt sans-serif }

P { font: 80% sans-serif }

P { font: x-large/110% "new century schoolbook", serif }

P { font: bold italic large Palatino, serif }

P { font: normal small-caps 120%/120% fantasy }
```

The <font> declaration is really a "shorthand" way of writing all the font declarations in a single rule.

Color and Background Properties

These properties define foreground (or text) colors, and background colors and images. When used, they reduce the amount of code you must write by a tremendous amount. For instance, you only have to specify a color once with a stylesheet, as opposed to writing it multiple times using Netscape tags.

Color

Value: <color>
Initial: determined by Web browser
Applies to: all elements
Inherited: yes
Percentage values: N/A
Examples:

```
EM { color: red }

EM { color: #f00 }
```

This color describes the text color of the element. Color can be specified in the ways detailed in Chapter 5, "Introduction to Style Sheets."

background-color

Value: <color> | transparent
Initial: transparent
Applies to: all elements
Inherited: no
Percentage values: N/A
Example:

```
BODY { background-color: #F00 }
```

This describes the background color of the element. In this example, it will turn the background of the Web page to red.

This declaration currently works in IE3 only when the style sheet is embedded into the HTML page using the STYLE element, not when the style sheet is linked. If you try to suggest background colors or elements from a linked style sheet, it won't work—no color, no background. This will be fixed for IE4.

background-image

Value: <url> | none
Initial: none
Applies to: all elements
Inherited: no
Percentage values: N/A
Examples:

```
BODY { background-image: url(marble.gif) }
```

```
P { background-image: none }
```

This sets the background image of a document to a graphic that you specify. It's a good idea to also specify a background color in case the graphic fails to load, or the user is looking at your page with graphics turned off. Pick a color like your graphic.

Like "background-color," this must be embedded as a style sheet into the HTML head for IE3 to recognize it.

background-repeat

Value: repeat | repeat-x | repeat-y | no–repeat
Initial: repeat
Applies to: all elements
Inherited: no
Percentage values: N/A
Examples:

```
BODY {
  background: red url(pendant.gif);
  background-repeat: repeat-y;
  }
```

This declaration changes how the background pattern tiles. By default it tiles up and down, filling out the background of the page. However, you can also tell the image to only repeat across the top of the page, or down the side. In the example above, the graphic "pendant.gif" will only tile down the side in a horizontal bar.

background-attachment

Value: fixed | scroll
Initial: scroll
Applies to: all elements
Inherited: no
Percentage values: N/A
Examples:

```
BODY {
  background: white url(logo.gif);
  background-repeat: repeat-y;
  background-attachment: scroll;
  }cx
```

In the examples above, "background-attachment" decides whether the background image stays fixed on the HTML page as presented, or follows the scroll downwards. In this example, the graphic "logo.gif" is set to appear always in the top left-hand corner (the default location), no matter where the user is in the document.

background-position

Value: percentage | length (or) top | center | bottom (and) left | center | right
Initial: 0% 0% (or top left)
Applies to: block-level and replaced elements
Inherited: no
Percentage values: refer to the size of the element itself
Examples:

```
P.newitem {
  background-image: url(starburst.gif);
  background-attachment: scroll;
  background-position: center left;
  }
```

If a background image has been specified, "background-position" determines its inital placement. In the example above, the graphic "starburst.gif" would appear behind the first letter of every P element marked with the class "newitem," (because it is centered horizontally, and placed to the left). This element would scroll with the "new item" no matter where it flowed in the document. The same location "center left" would be written in percentages as "50%, 0%."

background

Value: <background-color> | <background-image> | <background-repeat> | <background-attachment> | <background-position>

Initial: repeat
Applies to: all elements
Inherited: no
Percentage values: N/A
Example:

```
BODY { background: url(paper.png) gray 50% repeat fixed }
```

The "background" property is shorthand for all the background properties. Putting all these properties in a single declaration—if you have many background declarations, like the example above—reduces the size of your style sheet. Your style sheet will download faster. And you'll save yourself some typing.

Text Properties

These properties define how text blocks are formatted. They adjust the space between words, lines and letters. They also orient the text vertically (super or subscript) and horizontally (left, right, center and justified).

word-spacing

Value: normal | <length>
Initial: normal
Applies to: all elements
Inherited: yes
Percentage values: N/A
Example:

```
H1 { word-spacing: 0.4em }
```

This declaration adjusts the space between words, but it is not supported by IE3. Negative values (compressing the space between words) are allowed.

letter-spacing

Value: normal | <length>
Initial: normal
Applies to: all elements
Inherited: yes
Percentage values: N/A
Example:

```
H4 { letter-spacing: 0.2em }
```

This declaration adjusts the space between letters; it is very useful for small caps and headings. Not currently supported by IE3, letter-spacing should be available with IE4.

When "letter-spacing" is set to "normal," the CSS browser will adjust the spacing as needed if the text is also justified. If "letter-spacing" is explicitly set, the browser won't adjust the space.

text-decoration

Value: none | <underline> | <overline> | <line-through> | <blink>
Initial: none
Applies to: all elements
Inherited: no
Percentage values: N/A
Example:

```
A:link, A:visited { text-decoration: none }
```

The example above turns link underlining off for unclicked and visited links, but it leaves the underlining on when the link is clicked. CSS even supports the BLINK value, useful occasionally to draw attention to an item, but hated by many. A value of "underline" could be used instead of italicization when the text face is set to Courier, thus giving the effect of a typewritten page. "Overline" draws a line over the text. The value "line-through" isn't supported by IE3.

vertical-align

Value: baseline | sub | super | top | text-top | middle | bottom | text-bottom | <percentage>
Initial: baseline
Applies to: inline elements
Inherited: no
Percentage values: refer to the <line-height> of the element
Examples:

```
.super { vertical-align: super }

.image { vertical-align: middle }
```

The first example is an independent class that superscripts the selected text. You might write, for example,

```
According to the Johnson papers<SPAN CLASS="super">3</SPAN>...
```

The keywords are defined as:

➡   "baseline" aligns the baseline of the element with the baseline of the parent

- ➡ "sub" makes the element subscript

- ➡ "super" makes the element superscript

- ➡ "middle" aligns the vertical midpoint of the element with a point midway between the baseline and x-height of the parent—used primarily with inline graphics

- ➡ "text-top" aligns the top of the element with the top of the parent element's font

- ➡ "text-bottom" aligns the bottom of the element with the bottom of the parent element's font

- ➡ "top" aligns the top of the element with the tallest element on the line

- ➡ "bottom" aligns the bottom of the element with the lowest element on the line

Percentage values raise or lower the baseline of the element above or below the baseline of the parent. For example,

```
.authorpic { vertical-align: -100% }
```

will drop the bottom of an author's picture to the baseline of the line beneath. "-50%" will take it halfway down, and "50%" elevates it off the current line. This is very useful for aligning images. It is not supported in IE3.

text-transform

Value: capitalize | uppercase | lowercase | none
Initial: none
Applies to: all elements
Inherited: yes
Percentage values: N/A
Example:

```
H1 { text-transform: capitalize }
```

This example capitalizes the first letter of each word, so that all H1-formatted text would look like a proper title. The value "uppercase" changes the text to all caps, and lowercase changes the text to all lowercase. "Text-transform" is not supported in IE3.

text-align

Value: left | right | center | justify
Initial: determined by Web browser, but usually left
Applies to: block–level elements
Inherited: yes
Percentage values: N/A
Example:

```
H3.crosshead { text-align: center }
```

In CSS, use this syntax instead of Netscape's <center> tag. In some cases, the "justify" element will specify settings other than flush left and right edges. For HTML pages in Hebrew, for example, "justify" will set the text flush right, because Hebrew is read right to left. The "justify" value is not supported in IE3.

text-indent

Value: <percentage> | <length>
Initial: 0
Applies to: block–level elements
Inherited: yes
Percentage values: refer to parent element's width
Example:

```
P { text-indent: 1em }
```

This declaration will indent the first line of the P element (a paragraph) one em—the height of the font. Negative values "outdent" the paragraph. Paragraph identing is an essential typographic element—without it, many readers find it difficult to find the first line of a new paragraph. Indentation is very important for long–distance reading.

line-height

Value: normal | <length> | <number> | <percentage>
Initial: normal
Applies to: all elements
Inherited: yes
Percentage values: relative to the font size of the element

Examples:

```
P { line-height: 1.5em; font-size: 10pt }

P { line-height: 1.5; font-size: 10pt }

P ( line-height: 15pt; font-size: 10pt }

P { line-height: 150%; font-size: 10pt }
```

All these examples will produce the same result. Experienced desk-top publishers may feel tempted to use hard-coded sizes like the third example—I am partial to measurements in pixels because they render identically on Mac and Windows browsers—but the authors of CSS recommend against it. When you use relative measurements (examples one, two, and four) the line spacing remains correct when the font size is increased or reduced—and changing the font size is the prerogative of the user.

Box Properties

Box properties define the "boxes" that make up HTML/CSS elements. "Boxes" are simply the spaces defined by the <open> and <close> tags in HTML. For example, this HTML code is made up of three boxes:

```
<H1>Dealer Says, Sell Your House Now</H1>
<H3>by Jane Q. Author</H3>
<P>Despite rumors to the contrary, the housing market...</P>
```

Actually, it's made up of four boxes; we're not counting the BODY box. These three elements, H1, H3, and P, all sit inside the BODY box, and inherit properties (like margins) from the BODY element.

Boxes behave somewhat like Netscape table cells: they have borders you can set (to draw a box around your text, say) and padding (which goes in between the text and the border). They also have margins, which behave very much like the margins in word processing programs. Margins simply insert blank space around the boxes.

margin-top, margin-right, margin-bottom, margin-left

Value: <length> | <percentage> | auto
Initial: 0
Applies to: all elements
Inherited: no
Percentage values: refer to parent element's width
Examples:

```
P { margin-top: 1.5em }

P { margin-right: 10% }

P ( margin-bottom: 25px }

P { margin-left: 10% }
```

These declarations set the the space around each side of the element. For instance, to set the left margin of the page to 100 pixels (perhaps to leave room for a navigation bar) you would write:

```
BODY { margin-left: 100px }
```

"Margin–bottom" doesn't work in IE3, but works in IE4.

margin

Value: <length> | <percentage> | auto (for each side)
Initial: not defined
Applies to: all elements
Inherited: no
Percentage values: refer to parent element's width
Examples:

```
BODY { margin: 2em }

BODY { margin: 1em 2em }

BODY { margin: 1em 2em 3em }
```

This sets all four margins using one declaration. If there is one value given, then all four margins take that measurement. If there are four, then each has its own. If there are two or three values, then the missing values are take from the opposite side—top and bottom will share, or right and left. In the first example, all margins are set to 2em. In the second, top & bottom=1em, right & left=2em. In the third, the top margin=1em, right=2em, bottom=3em, and the left margin, borrowing from the opposite, is 2em.

Tip

> Advice about using the "margin" declaration? Don't bother with the "opposites share" values at first; set them all the same by using one value, or type each side's margin individually. Sometimes it's more efficient to type three characters than to spend time thinking about which side borrows from what.

padding-top, padding-right, padding-bottom, padding-left

Value: <length> | <percentage>
Initial: 0
Applies to: all elements
Inherited: no
Percentage values: refer to parent element's width
Examples:

```
BLOCKQUOTE { padding-top: 1.5em }

BLOCKQUOTE { padding-right: 10% }

BLOCKQUOTE { padding-bottom: 1.5em }

BLOCKQUOTE { padding-left: 10% }
```

These declarations set the the space inside the element's border. In CSS, all elements have borders, rather like the cells in a Netscape table. You can adjust the margin outside the border, and the padding inside. Padding is useful for adding colored blocks that contain text—the padding prevents the text from hitting the side of the box. Padding values cannot be negative. Padding is not supported by IE3.

padding

Value: <length> | <percentage> | auto (for each side)
Initial: not defined
Applies to: all elements
Inherited: no
Percentage values: refer to parent element's width
Examples:

```
BODY { padding: 2em }

BODY { padding: 1em 2em }

BODY { padding: 1em 2em 3em }
```

The "padding" declaration follows the same rules as "margin," above.

border-top-width, border-right-width, border-bottom-width, border-left-width

Value: thin | medium | thick | <length>
Initial: medium
Applies to: all elements
Inherited: no
Percentage values: N/A
Examples:

```
P.sidebar { border-top-width: 1.5em }
P.masthead { border-right-width: thin }
```

The border is the outline of an element's "box." These declarations set the width of that border. You can choose either keywords like "thin," "medium," or "thick," or exact amounts.

border-width

Value: thin | medium | thick | <length> (for each side)
Initial: not defined
Applies to: all elements
Inherited: no

Percentage values: refer to parent element's width
Examples:

```
BODY { border-width: thin }

BODY { border-width: thick 2em }

BODY { border-width: thin 2em thin }
```

This is shorthand for setting all the border values with a single declaration. When specifying multiple values, it follows the same rules as "margin" and "border" (above).

border-color

Value: <color> (for each side)
Initial: same as <color>
Applies to: all elements
Inherited: no
Percentage values: refer to parent element's width
Examples:

```
BODY { border-color: #003 }

BODY { border-width: red blue }
```

"Border-color" can set all four sides' colors individually, as with the shorthand declarations "margin" and "padding." If no color is specified, then "border-color" reverts to the "color" value.

border-style

Value: none | dotted | dashed | solid | double | groove | ridge | inset | outset
Initial: none
Applies to: all elements
Inherited: no
Percentage values: N/A
Example:

```
P.sidebar { border-style: solid dotted }
```

"Border-style" is shorthand for setting all four sides—the example above sets the top and bottom borders solid, and the sides dotted (see the entry and my tip for "margin," above, to understand why). With some browsers all these options may appear as solid; displaying all these values isn't a required part of the CSS spec, and it's up to the programmers.

border-top, border-right, border-bottom, border-left

Value: <border–top–width> <border-style> <color>
Initial: not defined
Applies to: all elements
Inherited: no
Percentage values: N/A
Example:

```
P.newswire { border-bottom: thin dotted red }
```

This declaration is shorthand for "border-top–width," "-right–width," "-bottom–width" and "-left width," plus "border-style," and "color." The example above would set the bottom border of the P element, class "newswire," to a thin dotted red line—perhaps to draw a short rule between short news stories in a column.

border

Value: <border–width> <border-style> <color>
Initial: not defined
Applies to: all elements
Inherited: no
Percentage values: N/A
Example:

```
P.box { border: thin groove }
```

Whereas the property above is shorthand for only one side of the box at a time, this shorthand property sets the four sides the same.

width

Value: <length> | <percentage> | auto
Initial: auto
Applies to: block-level and replaced elements
Inherited: no
Percentage values: refer to parent element's width
Example:

```
IMG.mugshot { width: 100px }
```

This property sets the width, in most cases, of an image—very similar to the WIDTH statement in HTML. This helps the page load faster, because the browser doesn't stop to draw the graphic. It can be used for text blocks, but isn't available in IE3.

height

Value: <length> | <percentage> | auto
Initial: auto
Applies to: block-level and replaced elements
Inherited: no
Percentage values: refer to parent element's width
Example:

```
IMG.mugshot { width: 100px; height: 125px }
```

Similar to "width," above, but sets the height of an element. Also not supported by IE3.

float

Value: left | right | none
Initial: none
Applies to: all elements
Inherited: no
Percentage values: N/A
Example:

```
IMG.mugshot {
  float: right;
  margin-left: 0px;
  }
```

This property sets an image or text block to the right or left, or leaves it where it is, and wraps surrounding text around it. In the example above, IMG elements of class "mugshot" will move to the right of the text block, and the text will wrap around to the left and bottom. This is a great new feature for HTML—that isn't supported yet by IE3, but will appear in IE4.

clear

Value: none | left | right | both
Initial: none
Applies to: all elements
Inherited: no
Percentage values: N/A
Example:

```
P { clear: right }
```

In this example, text in the P element will jump below any left-floated elements (like IMG.mugshot, above) and will not text-wrap. With this property set to "both," text will not wrap at all—good for setting off a picture with white space. Set to "none," text wraps around images and elements on both sides. This is very similar to setting the text wrap in PageMaker or Quark.

Classification Properties

These properties organize HTML elements into categories rather than affecting specific visual effects, with the exception of the list properties, which can change bullets and numbering.

display

Value: block | inline | list-item | none
Initial: block
Applies to: all elements
Inherited: no
Percentage values: N/A
Examples:

```
P { display: block }
```

```
EM { display: inline }

LI { display: list-item }

IMG { display: none }
```

This property sets how elements are represented on the web page. Block items open a new box, with border, padding, and margins. P, BLOCKQUOTE, and H1 are examples of block elements. Inline elements, like EM and STRONG, open an "inline" box, which assumes the dimensions of whatever's between the tags—maybe one word, or a hundred lines. Inline elements can have their own backgrounds, margins, and padding. List-items are similar to block elements, but with the addition of a bullet or other marker at the beginning of each line.

"None" keeps the element from being displayed—in the fourth example above, graphics are set not to display at all.

white-space

Value: normal | pre | nowrap
Initial: normal
Applies to: block–level elements
Inherited: yes
Percentage values: N/A
Examples:

```
PRE { white-space: pre }

P.example { white-space: nowrap }
```

"White–space" tells the browser whether to collapse empty spaces down to one (the default) or to render them as they appear in the HTML markup (like the current PRE element). This property also recreates the current NOWRAP tags, by forcing lines to be broken only by the <BR> tag.

list-style-type

Value: disc | circle | square | decimal | lower–roman | upper–roman | lower–alpha | upper–alpha | none
Initial: disc
Applies to: elements with the display value "list–item"
Inherited: yes
Percentage values: N/A
Examples:

```
OL { list-style-type: decimal }
```

```
OL { list-style-type: lower-roman }
```

The first example, "decimal," sets ordered list numbers to 1., 2., 3., 4., and so on. The second example sets list numbers to lowercase roman numerals (I., ii., iii., iv., and so on).

For unordered (UL) lists, CSS provides "disk," "circle," and "square" values.

list-style-image

Value: <url> | none
Initial: none
Applies to: elements with the display value "list–item"
Inherited: yes
Percentage values: N/A
Example:

```
OL { list-style-image: url(../images/smiley.gif) }
```

This property references an image file to be used instead of the markers specified by "list–style–type," above.

list-style-position

Value: inside | outside
Initial: inside
Applies to: elements with the display value "list–item"
Inherited: yes
Percentage values: N/A

Example:

```
UL { list-style-position: inside }
```

This property specifies whether the list marker (a bullet, for example) has text wrapped around it, or sits outside.

* This list-style-position
  is inside

* This list-style-position
  is outside

This property isn't supported in IE3.

list-style

Value: <keyword> <position> <url>
Initial: not defined
Applies to: elements with the display value "list–item"
Inherited: yes
Percentage values: N/A
Examples:

```
UL { list-style: outside url(../images/smiley.gif) }

OL LI { list-style: inside lower-alpha }
```

This is shorthand for all the the "list–style" properties.

Conclusion

CSS is, essentially, a work in progress, like HTML. CSS is currently in "level one," that is, the first version that has been approved as a standard. Look for changes soon, as the W3C is considering proposals that extend CSS. One proposal enables x-, y-, and z- positioning (syntax that allows you to put an object exactly where you want it, including the "stack order" of a layer). And soon the W3C should start to consider proposals for "dynamic" CSS—that is, style sheets that are activated by scripting languages like JavaScript. A dynamic style sheet can find out, for example, the size of your reader's browser window, and choose an appropriate style sheet: perhaps a style sheet with one, two, or three columns. In any case, CSS enjoys wide support in the Web community, and should be a major player in Web design soon, simplifying page coding, and improving typography across the Web.

PART

3

Type as Image

CHAPTER 9

Introduction to Type as Image

When determining the text typestyle for your Web documents, your decisions should be subtle. You are determining which style will project your voice best, allowing the text to flow so that the reader's eye does not tire. These decisions are vastly different from determining which display fonts should be used within your Web documents.

Display fonts, as discussed previously, deliver content that needs to be expressed more vividly. Display fonts have a graphical nature to them. When the decision is to attract, provoke, shock, or surprise, the display typestyle will meet the task. There are thousands of display fonts designed by reputable font foundries that will serve the purpose of your document. These display fonts are more likely to deliver dominant, overarching messages to your audience. The text style is far too subtle to affect the reader as a display font does.

Fonts that are used in movie posters, storefront signs at your neighborhood mall—these are places where display fonts are used all the time. If these designs were used at small sizes onscreen or for long passages of text, they would become fairly readable. But as a title or heading, they make for fascinating viewing.

When graphic images (that consist of typographic letterforms) are used for downloading to the Web instead of downloading an actual font file, there can be a few drawbacks. Many times the image files must be large to accommodate the level of detail, which leads to slower download times. File formats can also present browser compatibility problems. For more on file formats, see Chapter 12.

There are circumstances in which you may want to manipulate or alter typographic images so that their appearance is even more outrageous. This is where image or type manipulation tools come into play.

HTML-based Typography

HTML–based typography has some advantages over image–based typography. Memory and download time required for using real text instead of images is much smaller. If your Web site requires lengthy text passages, HTML–based text is the only way to go.

The following is an example of declaring text via HTML tags. Figure 9.1 shows the results of the HTML tags:

```
</html>
<head>
<H2>This is HTML-based text.</H2>
<H3>This is HTML-based text.</H3>
<H4>This is HTML-based text.</H4>
</head>
</html>
```

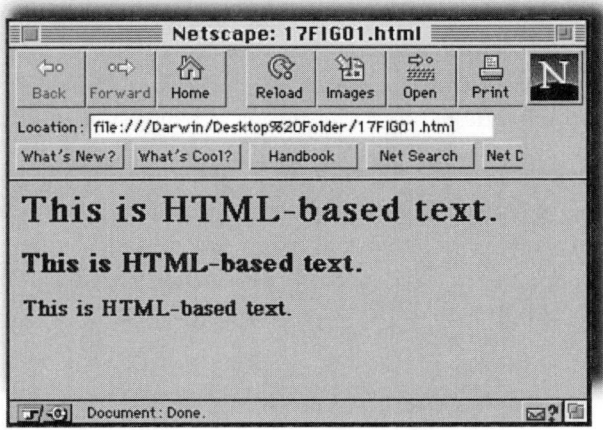

The results of the above HTML declarations.

HTML–based typography does enable some font style changes. Two of these features include making a font style bold and italic. The following are the HTML tag declarations for emboldening a font (see Figure 9.2) and italicizing a font (see Figure 9.3).

The <b> tags declare that the text within them is bold in weight.

`Take this <b>SERIOUSLY!</b><p>`

The results of the bold HTML declarations.

The <i> tags declare that the text within them is italicized.

`This is an <i> italicized version of Times Roman.</i><p>`

You can also adjust the point size of a font in HTML by using the <font=#> tag. The following is an HTML example of this, followed by the results of these tags (shown in Figure 9.4).

`What a <font size=6>great</font> game that was!`

In this declaration, the size of the font is described with a numerical value. The available numbers are from 1 through 6 with 1 being the smallest size fonts and 6 being the largest. Number 3 is the default size if none is declared.

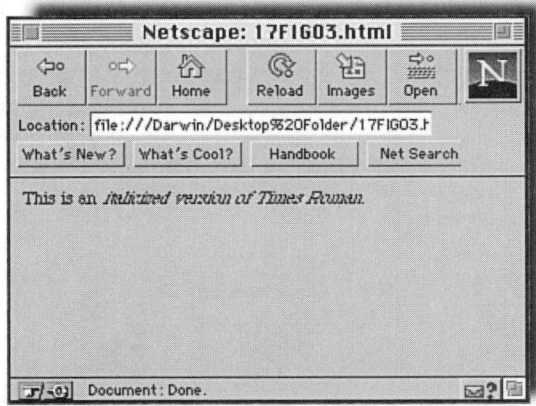

Figure 9.3

The results of the italic HTML declarations.

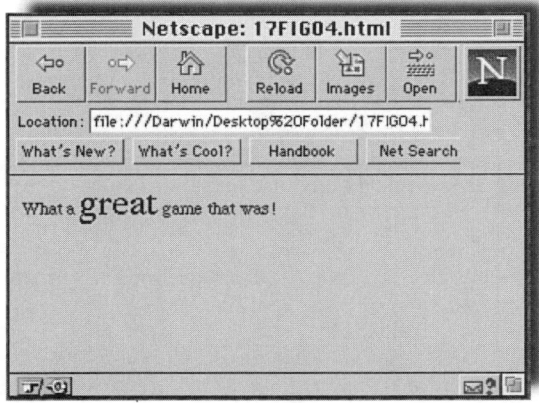

Figure 9.4

The results of the font size HTML declaration.

HTML Limitations

Previously, there was no way to show the audience your body text in any font other than the default font, which is usually Times Roman. Web designers were handcuffed, not being able to describe their text with other font styles. This problem has been addressed to a great degree with the advent of cascading style sheets. Within the style sheet language, a Web designer has the freedom to determine which fonts are available to describe his pages. As we all know (having read the section on style sheets), the reader must possess the font styles that the designer is declaring within his style sheets. Microsoft Corporation is one developer who is releasing "Web core fonts," a select group of fonts that cover a broad range of styles. As these types of fonts make their way into computer systems, they will greatly broaden our capabilities to use real font files that can be declared at any size (being format-, size-, and resolution-independent), without degradation to the design.

Image-based Typography

Using graphic images for your text provides a greater opportunity to show off. You will be able to use any font you want, without the worry of whether your audience has the font resident on their system. Because it is a graphic image (a bitmap) and not an actual font file (an outline), it shows up on your reader's system like any other graphic. The real advantage to using image-based typography is that you can manipulate the type to the desired effect. Some of the effects that can be used with image-based typography are transparency, color, drop shadows, blurs, distortions, swirls, neon, and many more. Adobe Photoshop is the premiere image manipulation application and has a robust set of tools for altering your type.

Following are three effects (as seen in Figures 9.5-9.7) that were developed within Photoshop and applied to type. In each case, the Type tool was selected and then the text was entered and deselected. Some of the effects took additional input into the option boxes that are called up as the menu commands are chosen.

Figure 9.5

The BLUR effect: Filter > Blur > Blur More.

Try using your blurred text with unblurred text. It provides good contrast.

Figure 9.6

The SHATTERED effect: Filter > Distort > Displace > select shatter map.

This effect splinters the characters.

Figure 9.7

The UNDERWATER effect: Filter > Distort > Wave.

This effect gives the feeling of wave movement.

To place your typographic images into your HTML documents, you use the <img src> tag. Here is an example of declaring an image within your HTML:

```
<html>
<img src="example.GIF">
</html>
```

Image Limitations

One of the drawbacks to using image-based typography over real type is file size. Images are much larger in size than actual text. As you manipulate your text with filters and other effects (as we did with Photoshop), you continue to add size to the file. As your file size grows, so too will the time it takes your reader to download these images and the memory required to bring these images to the screen. Just be aware of this. It is really not an alternative to stop using image-based typography. The special effects and creativity that image-based typography provides is a great asset in designing for the Web. Just keep in mind how the image is to be used.

Design Considerations

The great advantage to image-based typography is the wide scope of design possibilities. When a font is "filtered" to appear rough, blurry, shattered, or as if underwater (as in the earlier examples), it opens the door of possible uses. A blurred font image can look like it has been spray-painted onto a background. With a background simulating water, our "wave-filtered" image can easily fit into the theme. As Web documents become as dynamic as the television screen, our use of type has to become more dynamic as well. Image-based typography goes a long way in addressing that issue.

File Formats

An important consideration that must be made when creating image-based typography is the file format the image will be saved as. Depending on the type of image you are developing, one graphics file format may be more effective in rendering your images.

Photoshop, and other image editing applications, enable you to export your images into several image file formats. The latest version of Photoshop supports the following Web file formats:

➡ **GIF** Graphics Interchange Format: This format provides for "transparency" (only the image itself is visible, the area surrounding is clear) and "interlacing" (enabling the image to appear in stages onscreen). There is also a GIF89a plug-in.

➡ **JPEG** Joint Photographic Experts Group: This format provides for the Progressive JPEG format (enabling the image to appear in stages onscreen).

➡ **PNG** Portable Network Graphics: This is a new RGB format, similar to GIF. Unlike the GIF format, it does support 8-bit transparency. At the present time, PNG is supported via plug-ins in browsers.

We will discuss these and other Web file formats in detail in Chapter 12.

Conclusion

This chapter covered the use of type as an image file to be used in your Web documents. We also discussed the use of actual fonts declared through HTML. It was important to shed light on both choices for using type on the Web so that some comparisons may be drawn.

In our discussion on image-based typography, we provided several examples of graphics effects that can be used on type before it is converted to a graphic image. Photoshop is a powerful tool that can export to several different graphics file formats. A more in-depth discussion of Photoshop and how to use it to make typographic images is covered in Chapter 10.

Tools for Type Manipulation

Adobe Illustrator, currently in version 6.0, and Macromedia FreeHand, currently in version 7.0, are the two applications we will be focusing on in this chapter for type manipulation.

There are several applications that can help you create type effects for display on the Web. Obviously, some applications are more suited for specific tasks, and some have an array of strengths. TypeCaster from Xaos, for example, creates 3D type from any application supporting Photoshop plug-ins. Or you can maximize control of type with a program such as Macromedia Fontographer, which enables you to modify existing type or create your own.

This chapter delves into two of the main programs used in the industry today. Though you don't necessarily need to be an expert in the applications to go through the examples, it is helpful if you are familiar with the tools of the programs. Go through the individual application's documentation and brush up on the type, resizing, and rotating capabilities.

Drawing programs, however, continue to be the predominant tool for getting display/graphic type from concept to bitmap to the Web page. The two undisputed drawing program leaders in the industry are Illustrator and FreeHand. Adobe Photoshop (version 4.0), a pixel-based graphic program, is basically the industry standard for importing vector-based graphics/type to be exported as (.gif) files for the Web. It should also be noted that another application, DeBabelizer from Equilibrium, has gained strength in image conversion, file compression, and batch processing as explained in Chapter 12, "File Formats." In general, both Photoshop and DeBabelizer are great tools for importing graphics and image enhancing. Because of their limitations in kerning and leading, however, these applications would be a poor choice for type manipulation.

Vector- versus Pixel-based graphics

Vector-based graphics are the work of applications such as Illustrator and FreeHand, whereas pixel-based graphics are the work of Photoshop, or Claris MacPaint several years ago.

The major difference here is that vector-based images are based on lines or vectors you can control using anchor points. Pixel-based graphics are made from the tiny dots that form the image. Think of a simple line. In the vector-based world, the line is drawn from the two points of each end called anchor points. Those two points determine whether it's a straight or curved line, also known as the bézier curve. (Bézier curves can lead us into a whole new conversation.) In the pixel-based world, a line is made up of a series of little bits of squares or pixels (as shown in Figure 10.1). Pixel-based graphics are also known as bitmapped images.

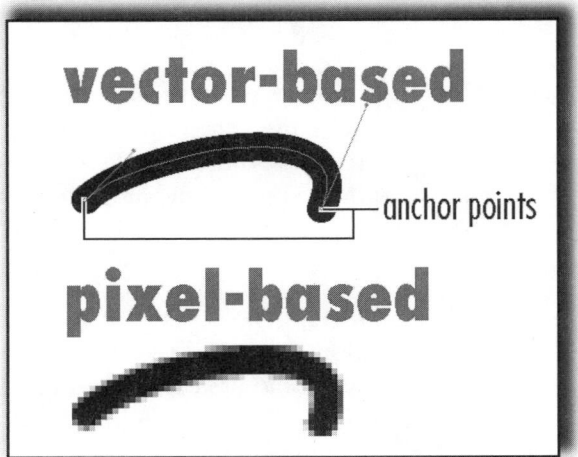

Figure 10.1

The difference between vector-based and pixel-based graphics.

The latest version of Illustrator enables you to rasterize your vector-based images into pixel-based images right on the same document.

Illustrator also enables you to rasterize to RGB, CMYK, Grayscale, or Bitmapped images. Resolution settings, as well as anti-aliasing and creating masks are all available in the Rasterizing dialog box.

The advantage of vector-based graphics is their resizing capabilities Regardless of output resolution or resolution, you can resize the lines in this graphic format and not have to worry about losing quality of the image because of the bézier curve calculations that are done for you.

Most graphics, however, found on the Web today are based on bitmapped or pixel-based images. This is why we eventually have to rasterize vector-based graphics in Illustrator or FreeHand or import these graphics into applications such as Photoshop or DeBabelizer to save or export them as GIFs or JPEGs.

Illustrator and FreeHand can perform an array of type techniques and formats. Because this chapter is focused on type on the Web, however, we'll concentrate on graphic or headline type. Any large body of text should really be treated in HTML code, as demonstrated in the earlier style sheet chapters, and not as a graphic. Therefore, our review of how to get type on the Web focuses on graphic type; we won't get bogged down too much on paragraph or tracking/ kerning attributes, although we will go over some quick steps for each program.

Illustrator

Illustrator product information can be found at http://www.adobe.com. The Adobe Web site also offers the latest patches for their applications, feature stories, and step–by–step graphic techniques.

Although Illustrator is an illustration-savvy program with the power to create realistic images, it is often used initially to develop and manipulate type. Many users may argue that type can easily be entered and altered in Photoshop alone. This may be true for a straight, simple "headline" type, but for complete kerning and leading control, as well as type manipulation, Illustrator is the way to go. FreeHand, similarly to Illustrator, can also give you complete kerning, leading, and manipulation control; however, I personally enjoy the easy file transitions between Illustrator and Photoshop since they are both made from Adobe.

The importance of total control of type on the Web page is obvious when you compare a graphic type set in Illustrator to type treatment using HTML as shown in Figure 10.2.

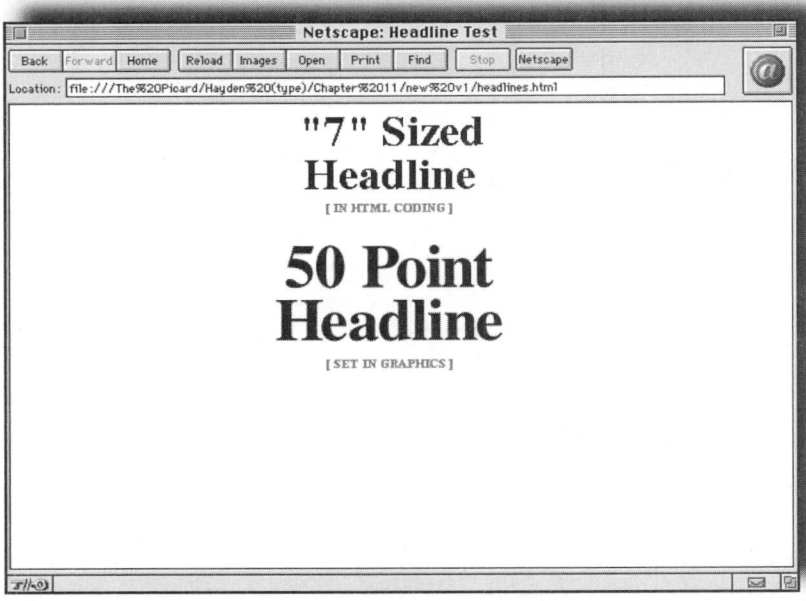

Figure 10.2

Comparing headline treatments in HTML coding and as a graphic.

As illustrated, a headline in GIF format displays better onscreen than in HTML coding. HTML does not enable you to display any type larger than the specified size="7". Creating type in the GIF format obviously does not limit you. The smooth imaging of the GIF type is also attractive compared to the jagged edges created by the HTML. But most importantly, the HTML example is from a Macintosh screen. PC screens display differently (usually the HTML runs a little larger). A word of caution, however: HTML coding downloads faster than GIFs, so use graphic headlines sparingly in your pages.

The Type and Font Menus

On 12-inch or larger-sized monitors, the Illustrator menu bar has the Font menu and the Type menu at the top of your screen. From the Type menu, you can control all of your type attributes, including size, leading, alignment, tracking/kerning, and spacing (see Figure 10.3). Note that Illustrator also enables you to link blocks of type, wrap type, check your spelling, and control type rows and columns. Here we focus on enhacing headlines and graphic type, but don't forget that Illustrator enables you to do many things with type. The Font menu and enables you to choose one of the fonts installed on your system.

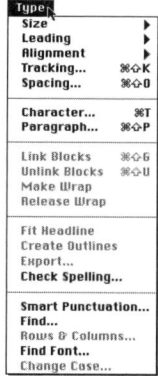

Figure 10.3

The Type menu gives you full control.

The Character Palette

Although the Type menu enables full control over type, most of the control I use can be achieved with the Character Option (see Figure 10.4). Pressing (Command-T)[Control-T] causes the Character palette to appear and disappear from the screen. This palette displays the font, styles, size, and leading available. To see more attributes, simply click the small flag to the right. The beauty of the Character palette is that it displays the attributes of the current type while giving you the option to change these attributes. We'll discuss each of these attributes later as we build a simple type graphic.

Character Palette

Figure 10.4

The Character palette provides you with information as well as options to change.

The Type Tool

The "T" icon in the Tool palette is the Type tool. Selecting the icon brings up different cursors that enable you to place a new type or modify an existing type on your canvas. If you click and hold on the icon, two other options pop-up to the right of the icon: the Area Type tool and the Path Type tool (see Figure 10.5).

The Type tool ———

Figure 10.5

The Area Type and Path Type tool are to the right of the Type tool.

The Different Types of Type

There are basically four different type areas that can be created using Illustrator: point type, area type, rectangle type, and path type. The straightforward point type is drawn by the default Type tool that Illustrator displays on start up. By clicking your canvas with the default Type tool, the point type area enables you to type on a horizontal line until you enter a soft return. A rectangle type area can also be defined with the default Type tool by clicking and dragging from your desired beginning point to the ending point of your rectangular text area. This rectangular area becomes your text area. Similar to this idea is area type, which enables you to enter a body of text in any form that you draw, be it a circle, square, triangle, or any polygon you have created using the Pen tool. Finally, there's the path type area that enables you to type on any line you have established using the Pen tool. To summarize visually, here's an example of point type, area type, and path type. The rectangular type is basically an area type, so we won't get into it here.

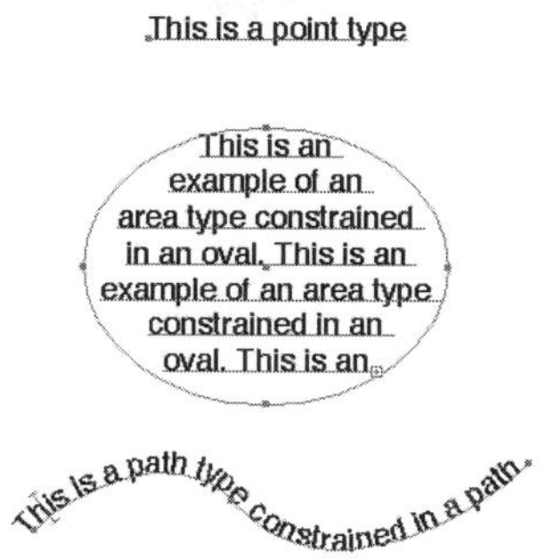

This is a point type

This is an
example of an
area type constrained
in an oval. This is an
example of an area type
constrained in an
oval. This is an

This is a path type constrained in a path.

Figure 10.6

Point type, area type, and path type.

Although I have demonstrated the area type, I rarely use it for Web design. Sure, there are times when controlling the justification of the body type would be nice, but you are also forcing the user to wait for body type in graphic form to download when they can read it in HTML, set off in TABLE or STYLE SHEET tags. As I mentioned in the introduction of this chapter, any large body of type should be implemented with HTML tags for user-friendly downloads. My rule of thumb is an eight-word limit. If the type block contains more than eight words, you should display it in HTML tags to save the user download time.

Reviewing Type Attributes

Before we dive into our exercise, let's review type attributes and how we change them using Illustrator. You can change these attributes using shortcut key commands (I'll mention each key command at each tool). To get information and to modify these increments, go to General Preferences. For now, let's revisit the areas in which we can change these attributes: the Character palette and the Type menu.

Font Style

In the Character palette, the first option is Font and Font Style. When you first open the Character palette, the Font option is highlighted by default. Here you can view which font you have selected. The default is Helvetica Regular. To change the font, click and hold on the down arrow near the Style box. Now choose from the menu of fonts installed on the system. Of course, this can also be done with the Font menu. The shortcut to a particular font is to start typing the name of the font while the cursor is in the font field.

Font Size

Another option is font size. One of the greatest challenges when moving from print design to Web designer is the different world of sizes, which I call "From Picas to Pixels." As a print designer, I learned the smallest type size to use for a particular font to retain legibility. Pixel sizes, at first, threw me way off when trying to apply what I learned in print. But after several attempts and mistakes, I learned to use higher minimal standards for type sizes. Whereas 6 or 7 point was about the smallest I would dare to go in newspaper print design, 13 and 14 points is safest for onscreen display. I would encourage smaller type if you need it, but I would also encourage testing the size. Even at 12 point, I found that increasing the tracking/kerning between letters/words and using all caps helps screen readability. To change the size in increments, select the desired type and press (Command-Shift->)[Control-Shift->] to increase the size and (Command-Shift-<)[Control-Shift-<] to decrease.

Leading

Leading is the distance between the baseline of one line of type and the baseline of the next or previous line of type (see Figure 10.7). Leading can also be increased or decreased with keyboard shortcuts Highlight the desired text and press (Option-Up Arrow)[Alt-Up Arrow] to increase and (Option-Down Arrow)[Alt-Down Arrow] to decrease leading. To achieve the recommended leading for a particular type and size, check the Auto leading checkbox to the right of the leading field.

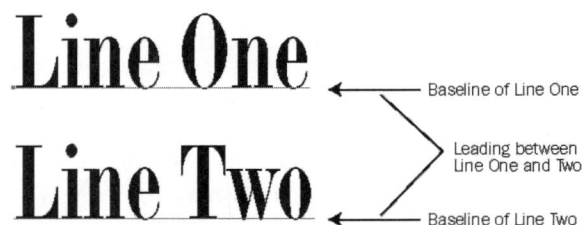

Figure 10.7

Leading made easy.

Speaking of baselines, the next option in the Character palette is the baseline shift. You can modify a type's baseline by increasing or decreasing the points. The only instance where I want to modify the baseline individually by character is when I want to create a fraction or a power-to number (see Figure 10.8) or create superscript or subscript type. Of course, this technique also involves changing the size of some of the characters. The keyboard shortcut for changing the baseline shift is similar to changing the leading; press (Option-Shift-Up Arrow)[Alt-Shift-Up Arrow] to increase and (Option-Shift-Down Arrow)[Alt-Shift-Down Arrow] to decrease.

← Baseline

Figure 10.8

Fraction control using baseline shift.

Tracking/Kerning

Next, let's examine the tracking/kerning field in the Character palette. This field name varies according to the type of selection you have set in your type area. Tracking is the amount of space between all currently selected letters. Kerning is the amount of space between two specific letters. If your cursor has highlighted one or more characters in a text area, the field name is tracking. If your insertion point is between two characters, the field name is kerning. The tracking/kerning field is one of my favorite strengths of Illustrator. The ability to kern and track characters with precision is one of the reasons why I do my graphic type in Illustrator rather than Photoshop where you would have to move pixels to achieve the same results. Figure 10.9 shows how kerning improves a graphic type.

•Typed using using default 0 tracking

•Typed using kerning control

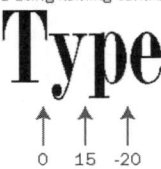

↑   ↑   ↑
0   15 -20

Figure 10.9

Kerning enhances graphic type.

Kerning between specific letters is usually set by typeface designers. Checking the Auto kerning checkbox from the Character palette usually conforms to the "experts" presets that are presented by most Adobe typefaces. There are, however, hundreds of presets established between each pair of characters that vary according to typefaces, weight, and style. As you may notice from the palette, kerning and tracking are based on em spaces, which basically is the width of two numbers. The limit of em spaces is -1000 and 10,000, with -1000 making each character display on top of one another, and 10,000 being, in all praciticality, too much space.

Honestly, I rarely set this on auto pilot. Call me old-fashioned, I continue to find myself readjusting the kerning, depending on the typeface used, even when I have auto kerning on. Let's take Agaramond Semibold as shown in Figure 10.10, for example. The first example shows Typed Headline with auto kerning off. Let's compare that with the same type with auto kerning on. There are obvious differences between the "T" and "y" and generally the whole headline looks pretty good. But visually, there are still holes in some of the type, for example the "p" and "e." But between the "H" and "e" and the "n" and "e," I might argue that I can drive a Mac truck through there. I made a third example of how I would manually kern the type within "Type Headline."

Using a drawing program to set type onscreen for export to Web display comes much closer to WYSIWYG (What You See Is What You Get) than a printer. Most, if not all, of the typefaces available today are made for printed display. The auto kerning set for these typefaces was made for printed pieces, not for screen display.

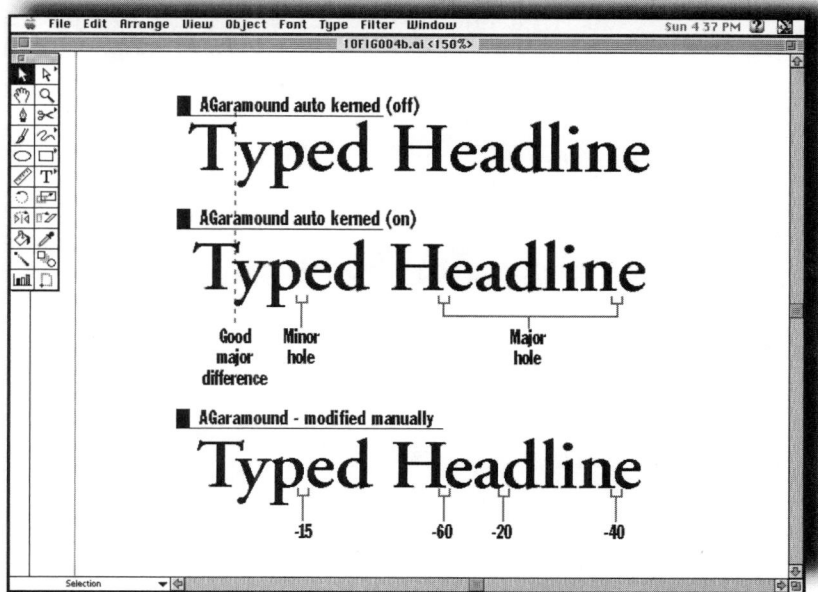

Figure 10.10

You can enhance your type by manually controlling your kerning.

Auto-kerning is quick and acceptable in most cases, but I would stick to my eyes anyday and kern my type when the needed.

Horizontal Scaling

The last, but not final, attribute in the Character palette is horizontal scaling, which controls the width of the type—causing it to expand or condense according to percentage. You can enter values from 1% to 1000%, with 100% as its original state. In good design, however, avoid the use of horizontal scaling. Typeface designers usually create whole families of type that already expand or condense type and have considered the visual consistency and nuances that horizontal scaling may take for granted.

Let's take Figure 10.11, for example, which uses Futura, a type family that has a large number of fonts. Look at the first example, Regular at 100%, as a standard. Then compare the second example, which displays Futura Regular at 200% to Futura Extra Bold at 100%. The effect is obviously different, but both "FS" carry the same weight. When type is stretched out of its norm, however, notice the width difference between the vertical line of the "F" and the horizontal line. It's a little thicker and the nuances may not be appropriate to your needs and attention to detail. Also, note that the kerning between the "FS" in the 200% horizontally scaled version has also visually increased.

By no means am I saying that horizontal scaling is bad. Just as much as I respect photographers when I am "enhancing" images in Photoshop, however, there's a certain amount of respect I give to type designers when using their typefaces.

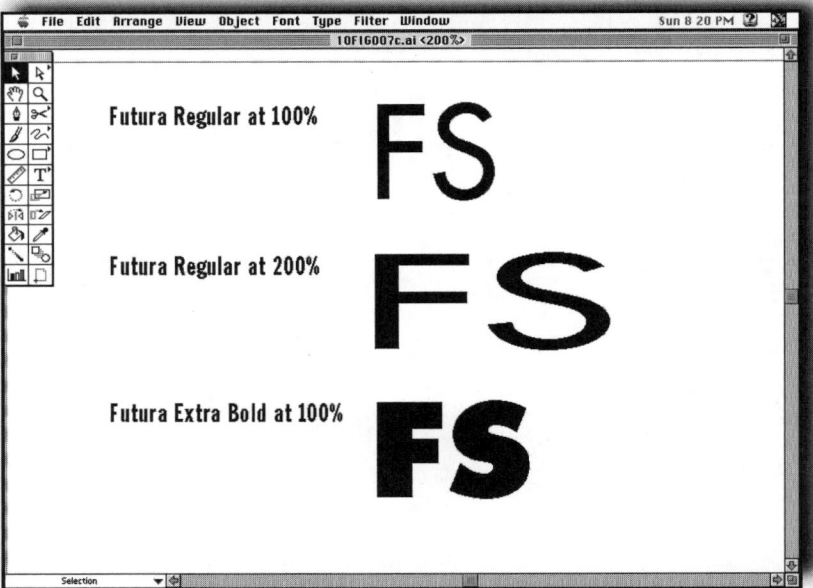

The differences that horizontal scaling causes at 200% are obvious.

Selecting Type

The baseline is the only place where you can select a point type and path type in Illustrator. In trying to move type around with your pointer, you can either click right on the baseline or click and drag over the desired type. Most people who are new to Illustrator assume that they can select the type by clicking it. Unfortunately, Illustrator makes the user click the baseline to select the type, which does have its good points and its bad points for selection. In area type, you can click the constraining polygon of the type as well as the baseline. See Figure 10.12.

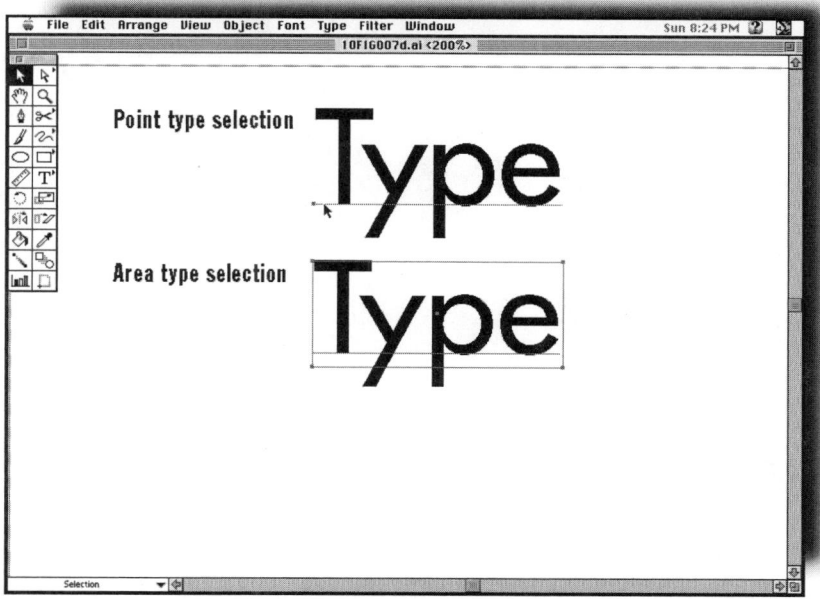

Figure 10.12

There are two kinds of type selection in Illustrator.

Layering Type for Thickness Effect

Now that we've covered some of the basics of type control in Illustrator and its attributes in the Character palette, let's give it a try and have some fun.

In the next three exercises, we eventually create type for display on the Web. The final outcome will look like Figure 10.13. For illustrative purposes in the following example, I've used the Torino and Franklin Gothic typefaces (which I've found to be great typefaces for screen resolution). The focus is on a logotype graphic. You can use any typeface or word that you want.

Figure 10.13

A preview of the final project.

1. Type Design onto your canvas. In this illustration, I used a 90–point type. Kern your letters to taste. Again, different typefaces may kern in different ways.

2. In the Paint Style palette ((Command-I)[Control-I]) fill the type with 40% black. Stroke the outline of the type with a weight of 5 at 40% black as well (see Figure 10.14).

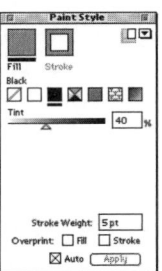

Figure 10.14

Gray type with a stroke weight of 5 points.

3. With the Design type selected, choose Edit ➡ Copy (Command-C)[Control-C] and then Edit ➡ Paste In Front (Command-F)[Control-F]. The image appears unchanged because you duplicated the type on top of itself. The selection, however, has changed to the top item.

4. With the top item selected, change its Paint Style to create a white fill type with a white stroke weight of 2 (see Figure 10.15).

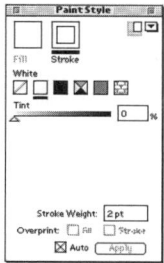

Figure 10.15

Create white type with a stroke weight of 2 pts.

5. Now repeat Step 3 to duplicate of the text on top of the now white Design type. This time, because you have a selection of the top-most Design type, give this a fill of 100% black.

Figure 10.16 illustrates three-dimensionally what Illustrator is doing with the layered effect and the appropriate fill and stroke combination on the type.

• Fill: 100% black; Stroke: none
• Fill: white; Stroke: white at 2 pts.
• Fill: 40% black; Stroke: 40% black at 5 pts.

Figure 10.16

A 3-D perspective view on the Design type.

At this point, save the working file where you can find it later. Name it "Design 1" for consistency purposes. You might be satisfied with what you have now, and in many cases this would be ready for prime-time on the Web. But for the fun of it, let's enhance what we have and implement the Type on Path technique.

Setting Type on Shapes

1. If you haven't done so already, open your Design 1 exercise.

2. With the Oval tool, draw an oval the height of the Design type but slightly more narrow.

3. Click the top line of the oval with the Path Type tool. If done correctly, you will notice a blinking cursor has appeared in place of the black semi-oval. If this did not happen, make sure that the cursor is right over the path. Notice that the cursor will change as it gets nearer to the path. Type "MAKING TYPE" in all caps and in a smaller sans serif face. (I used Franklin Gothic Extra Condensed at 20 points). As you type, the letters may be upside down or are inside the oval. We don't want this; it can be easily remedied by choosing the Selection tool (black arrow), and clicking and dragging the I-beam next to your text onto the exterior of the oval (see Figure 10.17). Although you do have full control of the cursor, you can also drag it slightly over-centered to the right.

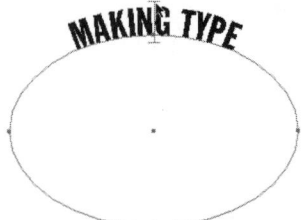

Figure 10.17

Selecting the I-Beam.

4. Now do the same with the botton half and drag MAKING TYPE onto the lower portion of the oval while holding down the (Option)[Alt] key. This essentially duplicates the type as well as your oval as you move it. Change the type on the bottom to read "IN STYLE."

5. Move the I-beam on both text areas slightly off-center. Adjust the baseline shift so that the baseline of the type is at the center (see Figure 10.18).

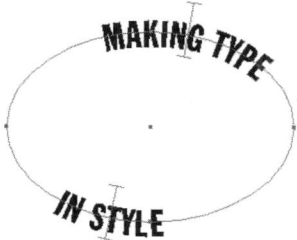

Figure 10.18

Adjusting for the baseline shift.

6. Draw another oval that duplicates the same oval shape as the text paths. Increase the width of the new circle to 25 points at 60% black and set the fill to 0. Using the Arrange menu, send the new gray outlined oval to the back and paint the type white. Group the three ovals together and send it all to the back. Skew the group oval slightly and then adjust the kerning between the MAKING TYPE and IN STYLE to fit to the screen.

Figure 10.19 demonstrates how it looks in preview mode as opposed to artwork mode.

Figure 10.19

Preview vs. artwork mode.

Exporting Type as a Web-Ready GIF

To easily export a GIF into an Illustrator file, you can download the latest GIF89a Format 1.1b3 plug-in for Illustrator at http://www.adobe.com/supportservice/custsupport/LIBRARY/3426.htm. The plug-in rasterizes only elements on visible layers, so that, as in Photoshop, the GIF89a 1.1b3 plug-in does not include elements on invisible layers in the exported GIF file.

1. Make sure that you want everything in your Illustrator file made into a GIF file.

2. File ➡ Save As your document and choose GIF89a as your format. (see Figure 10.20)

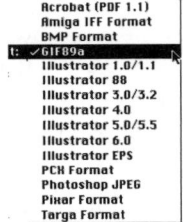

Figure 10.20

Export GIF89a format.

3. A Save dialog box appears with several options to choose from (see Figure 10.21). Choose one and you're ready for the Web prime-time.

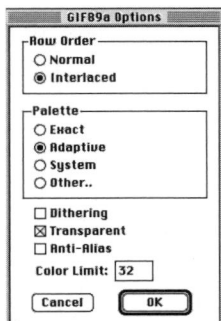

Figure 10.21

The GIF89a dialog box.

Whenever type is exported as a GIF as straight type, white space above the ascenders and below the descenders appears. As you might guess, this is not a solution for tight graphics. To avoid the undesirable white space, you must first outline the type that you want to export. To outline type, go to Type ➡ Create Outlines after you have highlighted the text.Then, voilà, instant outlined graphics. Again, make sure that all items visible are hidden or deleted from the file. Then do the same from Step 2 on. When exporting the outlined type as a GIF, you will notice the difference in height values (see Figure 10.22).

Figure 10.22

Outlined versus non-outlined fonts.

FreeHand Type Techniques

In this section, we won't necessarily create the same effects step by step, but I will point out when when tools and techniques are different between Illustrator and FreeHand. One of the differences between the two programs is the palette treatment.The palettes are similar, but the look and the feel are a little diverse (see Figure 10.23).

The FreeHand palettes.

1. Let's start off like we did in Illustrator by typing the word Design and kern between the letters to close the gaps. Luckily, FreeHand and Illustrator have the same shortcut keys for this technique: (Command-Left Arrow)[Control-Left Arrow] for narrower kerning and (Command-Right Arrow)[Control-Right Arrow] for wider kerning. Also note in Figure 10.26 that the individual kerning is also displayed.

2. To apply different size strokes to the type, as we did in Illustrator, we must first convert the type to paths. Click the Convert to Paths tool on the Text menu (see Figure 10.24). Converting type to paths changes the type into polygons. You cannot edit the type after you convert to paths.

The Convert to Paths tool.

3. Now we can apply the three levels of texture treatment as we did in Illustrator. For the bottom-most layer of the Design type, give a fill of 40% black as well as a stroke of 40% at 5 points.

4. We want to copy the object right on top of the other by choosing Edit ➡ Clone or (Command-=)[Control-=]. This step is much easier than in Illustrator where you have to copy and then do a Paste in Front. With your new cloned version, give the object a white fill with a white stroke at 2 points.

5. Create a third object by cloning the second one. With the third and top-most object, however we want to give the word Design a fill of 100% black and no stroke (a stroke weight of 0).

6. Type MAKING TYPE and IN STYLE in two separate text blocks, both in Franklin Gothic Condensed at 21 points as shown in Figure 10.25.

Figure 10.25

The Design type and the FreeHand Character palette.

7. Draw two circles; place one of on top of the Design type. You can easily duplicate another circle by holding down the (Option)[Alt] key while dragging the new one to the desired location. Now select both the first circle and the text block MAKING TYPE, then select Text ➥ Attach to Path (see Figure 10.26).

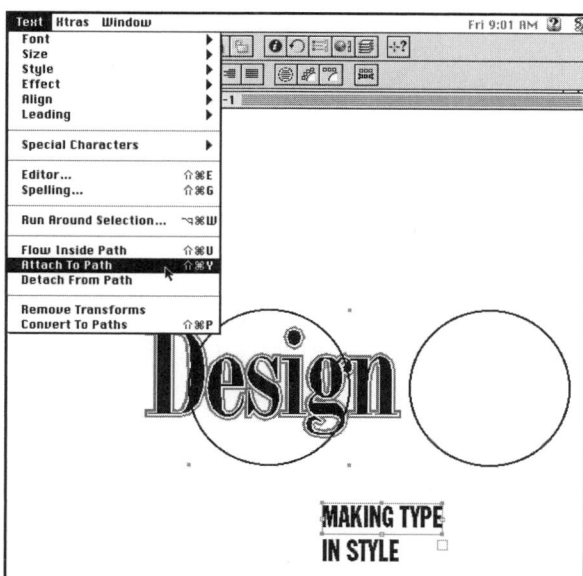

Figure 10.26

Attaching text to a path.

8. Now do the same with the second circle and the IN STYLE text block. Notice that they arrive in the same position. To get IN STYLE in the correct position, put your cursor right before the "I" and hit return. This brings the type below the circle.

9. Rotate both text blocks slightly and skew to taste. Fill both type blocks with white and no stroke. Place a 20 point 40% black stroke behind both text blocks to create the inverse. Then send all three objects to the back behind the Design type. What you get eventually is what you see in Figure 10.27.

Figure 10.27

The FreeHand version of our logo.

10. Taking the image to the Web is simple, thanks to the Macromedia plug-in that saves this file to either GIF or JPEG. Unlike Illustrator, exporting to GIF is preinstalled in the latest version of FreeHand. Go to File ➤ Export As and select the format type shown in Figure 10.28.

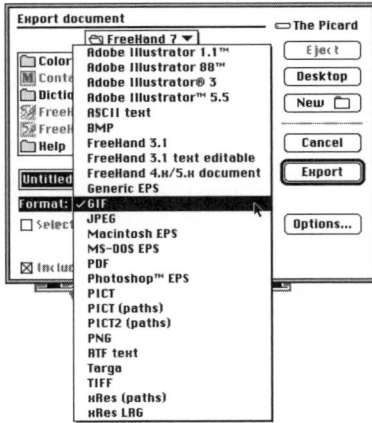

Figure 10.28

Exporting an image as a GIF is simple in FreeHand.

After selecting GIF, you can choose more options by clicking on the Options button. As you can see in Figure 10.29, FreeHand enables a handful of options when exporting your GIF including resolution settings, anti-aliasing, interlacing, and transparency.

Just as in Illustrator, exporting type as a GIF generates white space above the ascenders and below the decenders of the type. To avoid this, we have to create outlines of our type before exporting it as a GIF. Doing so eliminates the unnecessary white space.

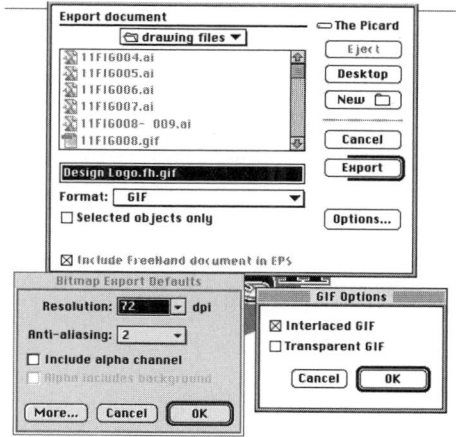

Figure 10.30

Export as GIF options in FreeHand.

Conclusion

We've just done the basics of putting type on the Web from Illustrator and FreeHand and exporting it as a GIF. I would encourage picking up additional books and tutorials on improving on each of these applications in more detail.

Keep in mind, however, that these applications are just tools. Choose which tools work for you to get the job done to your standards. Hopefully, this chapter helped make your decision on which tool to use easier.

CHAPTER 11

Font Creation

Creating a font can be a very complex task. It takes a type design er's skill in understanding the form and function of the letter-form. It also takes a quality set of tools (software) to assist the designer in the creation of these digital letterforms. Some font foundries have their own proprietary software that has been developed in house for use only by their designers. For the independent designer who does not have access to such proprietary tools, they need to use retail software to make their digital fonts.

This chapter will cover, in detail, one retail product called Fontographer. Fontographer is a very helpful tool for the beginning artist as well as affording the skilled type designer a set of tools to make high-quality designs. Macromedia Fontographer and Pyrus Software's FontLab are user-friendly tools that give extensive support for the making of fonts for multiple platforms (Mac and PC) and multiple formats (PostScript and TrueType). If these tools have an Achilles heel, it would be in their inability to make the highest quality level of TrueType for screen use (small point sizes at low resolution). Future versions of each of these tools are addressing this very issue. So without further ado, the Tools (applause)!

Proprietary Tools

Several of the well-known type foundries and other font design studios use proprietary tools to develop their typefaces. Such tools range from design systems that develop for the PostScript and TrueType format to bitmap editors. These tools and related software are usually developed in-house and are made available only to the designers who work for that company. With teams of engineers to support and continually upgrade them, they have always been much more advanced in their application and development than retail type design products. Rarely will you find proprietary tools available for purchase by independent designers. It is quite commonplace for a font foundry to keep close to the vest their suite of design tools, as their as competition within the industry to provide the best quality font possible.

Fortunately, the type tools being developed and upgraded in today's retail market are becoming so advanced that they are rivaling the proprietary software. Products such as Macromedia's Fontographer and Pyrus Software's FontLab are being used by more and more designers to develop and customize their type designs. Both products have similar procedures in creating letterforms. They have graphical user interfaces (GUIs) that are easy to understand and helpful in providing technical information about each letterform as you work on them. Fontographer has a larger base of users, having been one of the first makers of type design software. One of the reasons I like using the tool is that it has been upgraded several times, using the input of type designers like myself in upgrading certain features of the product. And now, Fontographer and its basic tool suite.

Note

> Note: For more information regarding Fontographer, visit the following URL on the Web:
>
> `http://www.macromedia.com/software/fontographer`

Fontographer

Developed in 1986, Macromedia's Fontographer has become a standard for creating fonts. It works on both the Mac and PC platforms. Before Fontographer, few options (aside from proprietary tools) existed for developing digital typefaces.

Fontographer enables a designer to generate type for several font formats—PostScript Type 1, PostScript Type 3, TrueType, and Encapsulated PostScript. It also allows for the importing and developing of font metrics to assist spacing and kerning. Font metrics are mathematical information stored within a font such as a character's set width (the width of the character as well as the white space to the left and right of it), height and weight data, and kerning pairs.

Fontographer enables the designer to import valuable metric information. You can import kerning tables from Adobe Font Metrics files (.AFM) and bitmap files. You can also import graphics files from illustration applications such as Adobe Illustrator and Macromedia FreeHand.

Although Fontographer exports fonts in varying formats, there are a few things that must take place before a font can be used on the Web. If you wish to use the actual font (and not a graphic image of the text) for the text in your Web document, your audience MUST have the same font installed on his system to view it in their browser. Without the font on their system, the reader is going to view the page's text using a system font, probably Times Roman or Helvetica.

OpenType, a font format being developed by both Microsoft and Adobe Systems, builds upon the existing PostScript and TrueType formats and will allow for the actual downloading of a font file (only those characters used in the text) to the Web for viewing without the reader needing to have the font themselves AND without the risk of the font data being tampered with or stolen. Built-in encoding and security software will flag the file as corrupt if a naughty Web surfer decides to steal or manipulate the font file.

Until OpenType is introduced, the alternative and most common solution is to convert your text into a graphic image. This can be done in any number of illustration or paint programs.

The graphic image is then uploaded to the Web server, where your Web documents are stored and will reside until a Web reader clicks your page. Once they do, your Web page containing the graphic representation would then be downloaded to your reader's browser and voila! You have text in any typestyle and there is no threat of font violation.

Unfortunately, in delivering type to the Web this way, graphic files tend to be large and can slow the download time of your page. Keep in mind the size of any graphic file and test it first to see how long it takes to represent itself in the browser.

The Font Window

The Font window in Fontographer (as seen in Figure 11.1) displays all of the characters in the font. The Font window is opened by selecting "New" or "Open" from under the File menu. Above each character cell is a description of that character. This description may be one of several attributes:

Figure 11.1

Characters are being viewed by their Character attribute.

→ A small image of the character itself

→ The keystroke typed on the keyboard to call upon the character

→ The character's unicode value

→ The character's decimal value

→ The character's hexidecimal value

→ The character's octal value

→ The character's width

→ The left sidebearing

→ The right sidebearing

It is from this window that you choose which character to bring to the screen. When applying fontwide attributes to a font (in other words, autospacing, autohinting), you choose "Select All" from the Edit menu. Autospacing and autohinting are attributes that, when selected, allow the program to make global (font-wide) decisions about the font and then "space" it or "hint" it automatically.

The Character Window

To open the Character window (as seen in Figure 11.2), simply double-click a character image in the Font window.

It is in the Character window that you can create or alter an image; the toolbox (as seen in Figure 11.3) provides everything you need.

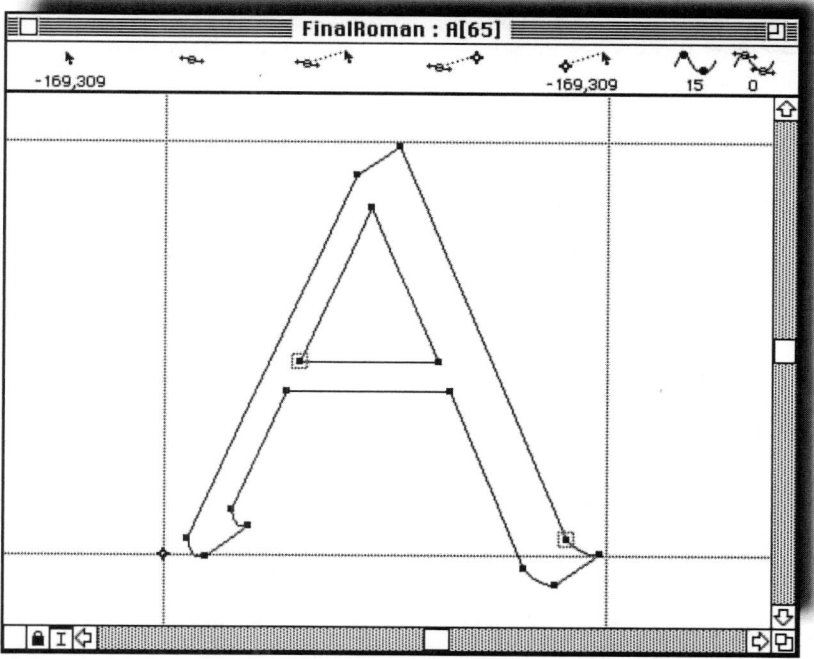

Figure 11.2

The Character window.

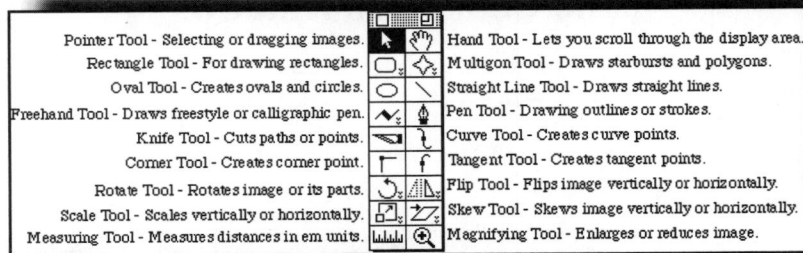

Figure 11.3

The Character window toolbox.

In the Character window, you can display a character in one of several layers. The Outline Layer (seen in Figure 11.4) is where you create and edit your images. Choosing the Outline Layer box selects that layer. Highlighting the Outline Layer line activates its attributes (such as the points on the image).

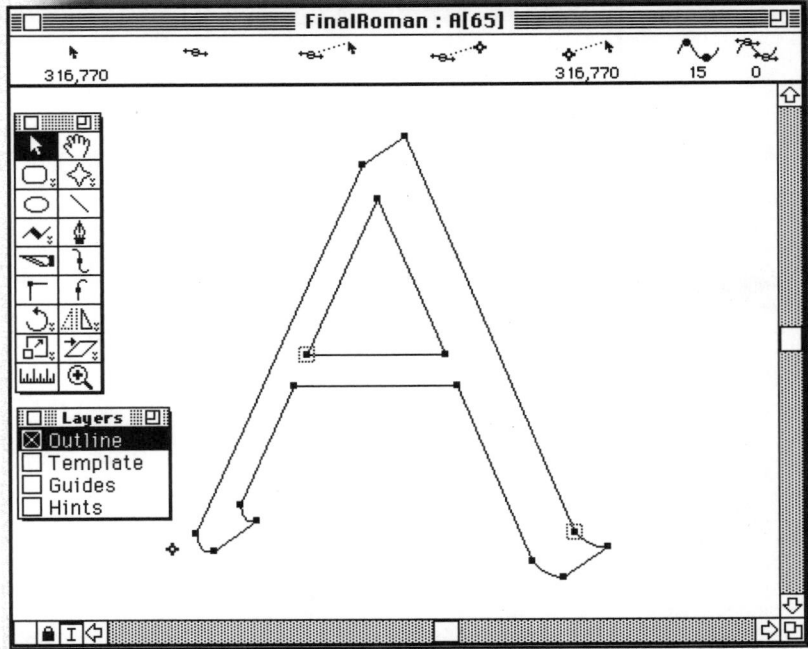

Figure 11.4

The Character window in Outline Layer.

The Template Layer (seen in Figure 11.5) is for placing an image you wish to use as a template. Points drawn in this layer will show as gray and are not part of the image. You can paste PICT images into this layer. Checking the box selects this layer. Highlighting the Template Layer line enables you to work within it.

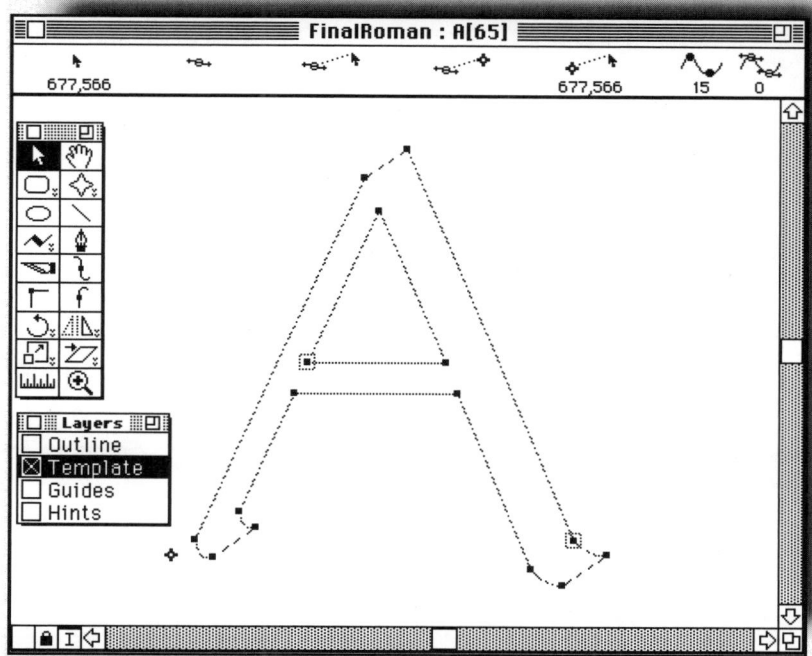

Figure 11.5

The Character window in the Template Layer.

The Guides Layer (seen in Figure 11.6) is where you place your alignment and set width lines. These guidelines assist the designer when drawing each character. Checking the box selects this layer. Highlighting the Guides Layer line enables you to work within it.

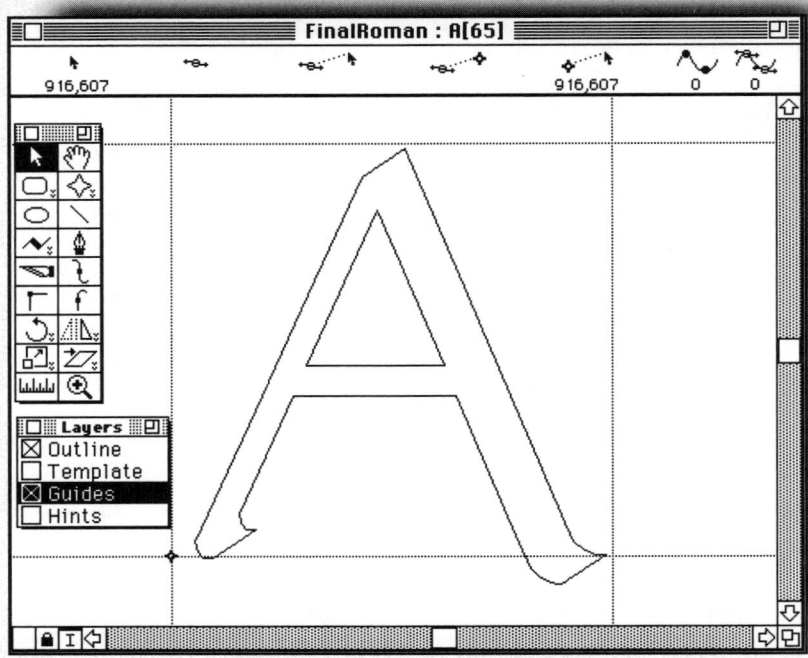

Figure 11.6

The Character window in the Guides Layer.

The Hints Layer (seen in Figure 11.7) shows the hints that are applied to features like stems, hairlines, serifs, and character heights. Checking the box selects this layer. Highlighting the Hints Layer line enables you to edit and create hints.

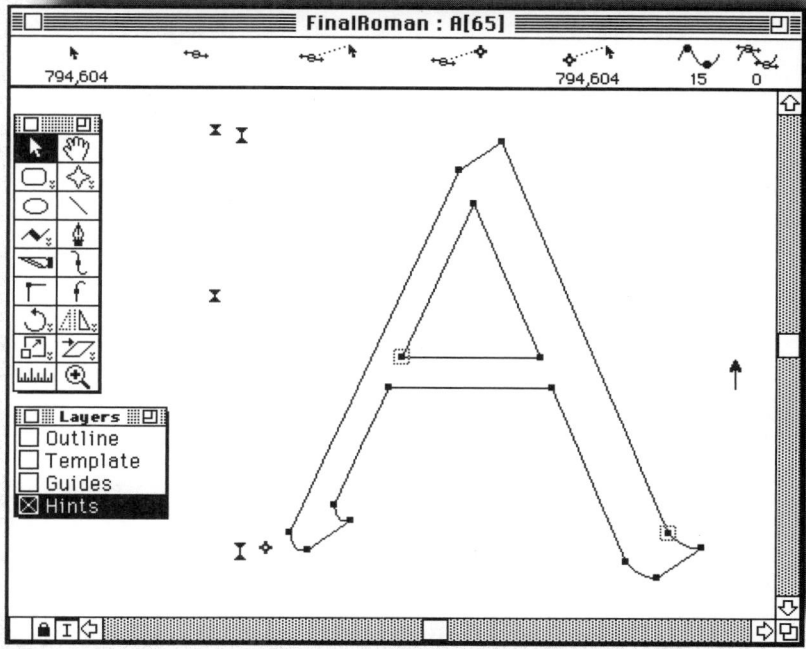

Figure 11.7

The Character window in the Hints Layer.

Creating Digital Characters

To create a new font, the type designer will spend a great portion of his time designing his letterforms and shapes with pencil and paper. Whether you are working with existing images or creating letterforms with pencil and paper, you will need to import these images into Fontographer in order to convert them into digital letterforms. To do this, you must first scan the images using a digital scanner. Save the scanned images in PICT or other bitmap format.

A type designer will work over the basic shapes and features he wants his typestyle to possess. This can be done on any type of paper with pencil, but some designers prefer to use tracing paper to work up their ideas. I find this to be a preferable way to work. This allows the designer to overlay the letterforms as subtle changes are being made and compare the shapes to see if he is achieving the desired result.

The letterforms can be drawn at almost any size. I find it preferable to draw my lowercase characters somewhere between two and three inches in height. This gives me a letterform that is large enough to scan or digitize (using a digitizing tablet and pressure sensitive pen).

This size character also fits nicely onto your computer screen as you view it within your design program. The design program will scale your image to fit within its "em square" (the area desinated as the available space, both vertically and horizontally, for a character). Most type design tools provide sample fonts, which are a good starting point for some learning to design.

Note

> Wacom makes a great tablet—for more information about their graphics tablets, check out their Web site:
>
> http://www.wacom.com/productinfo/showcase.html

Importing Images into Fontographer

To import a scanned image into Fontographer:

1. Place your bitmap image into your scrapbook or clipboard.

2. In Fontographer, copy the image and paste it into the Outline window.

3. The image will show up as gray in color, in the Template Layer. Any image that is imported to the Template Layer is scaled to fit within its "em square."

4. To reposition your image, click the Template Layer box, click image (gray box will appear), and drag cursor on image to reposition.

5. Now that you have the image where you want it, trace it and bring the resulting digital outline to the Outline Layer.

AutoTracing Images in Fontographer

AutoTrace gives the designer the option of performing this task using the "easy" or "advanced" mode. The advanced mode enables the designer to be much more specific in determining his autotrace options. To autotrace an image in Fontographer (using the easy mode):

1. Highlight and select the Outline Layer in the Character window.

2. Click the Elements menu and select AutoTrace. An AutoTrace box will appear.

3. Select the easy mode. It will give you a good idea of how the tracing tool outlines an image.

4. The curve fir bar sets the looseness or tightness of the curve fit. The tighter the fit, the more points that are added to describe an image. Leave this setting at five, which is the default.

5. Click on Trace. Now you have a digital image, which you can edit.

Editing Digital Characters

The editing process is a decision-making one. You are introduced to the basic elements that make up a digital outline character. The successful manipulation of these elements will determine the look and feel of your typestyle. Though there are only three types of points (corner, tangent, curve) that make up the outline, these points can be manipulated to give you very exacting results.

Outline Window

Within Fontographer's Outline window, you can alter an image several different ways. Points on an outline can be moved, duplicated, merged, inserted, or deleted. It is with these points that the designer can mold and shape the image.

Points

There are three different point types: curve, tangent, and corner.

Curve points (as seen in Figure 11.8) define the curved part of a line. They own "control handles," which are features that appear to the right and left of the curve point. These handles can be adjusted to smooth out a curve. Curve points are displayed as circles on the character outline. The circle is hollowed out to indicate it has been selected.

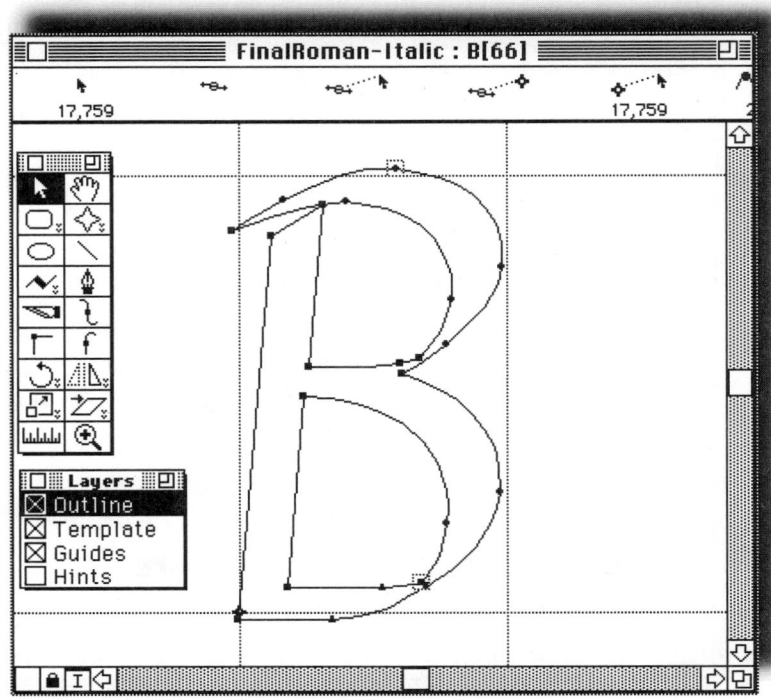

Figure 11.8

Curve points selected.

Tangent points (as seen in Figure 11.9) define the point at which a smooth curve line segment connects with a straight line segment. Tangents have control handles like the curve point. They can be adjusted to smooth the transition from curve to straight. These tangents are displayed as triangles on the character outline. The tangent is hollowed out to indicate it has been selected.

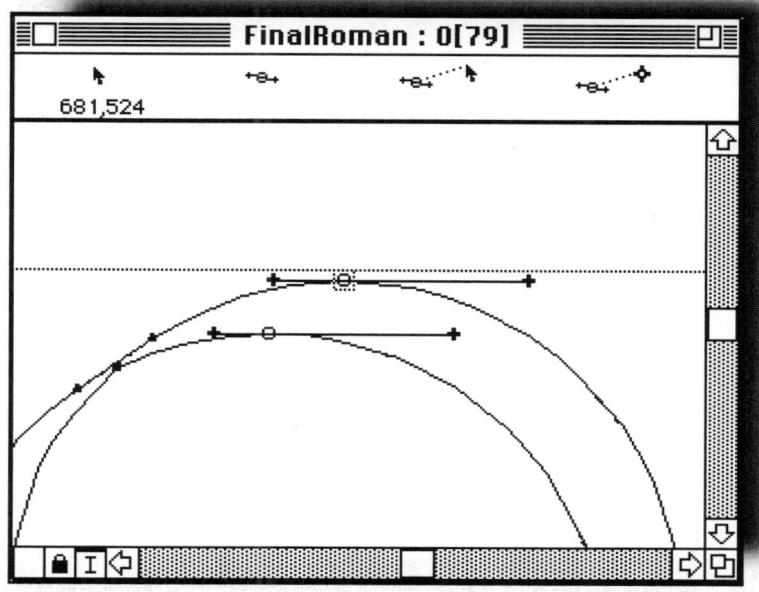

Figure 11.9

Tangent points selected.

Corner points (as seen in Figure 11.10) define the point at which a smooth curve line segment or a straight line segment connects with a straight line segment. Corner points also have control handles like the curve point, but they are pulled in toward the point itself. By pulling the handles out from the point, the corner point acts like a curve point. These corner points are displayed as squares on the character outline. The square is hollowed out to indicate it has been selected.

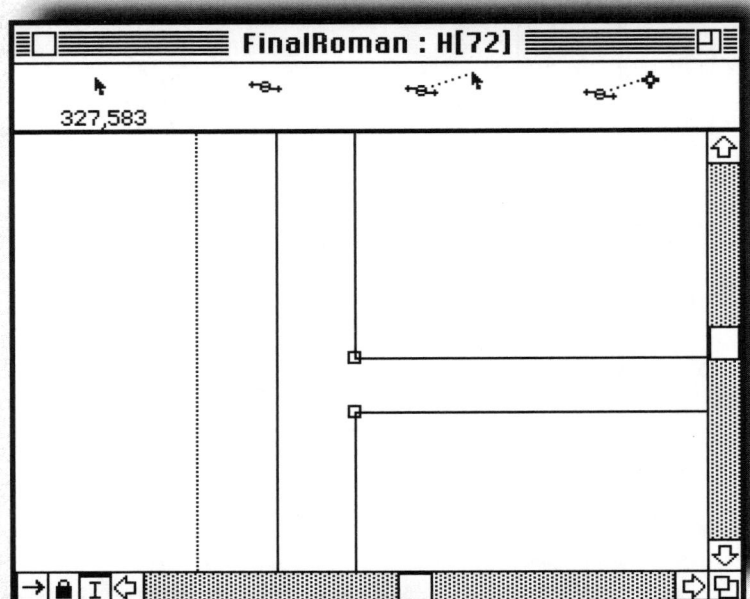

Figure 11.10

Corner points selected.

Practice creating and moving the points on your image to get a better feel for how each point type and its control handles affect the smoothness and straightness of the lines.

Introducing a New Character

To create a new character:

1. Select an open character cell from within the Font window.

2. With the Character window open, select one of the three point type tools from within the toolbox.

3. Begin by clicking within the window and continuing through the image, placing points on both the extreme edges of a character and at those places where you think the image may need some support and/or alteration. Figure 11.11 shows a straight edge character being drawn in the Character window.

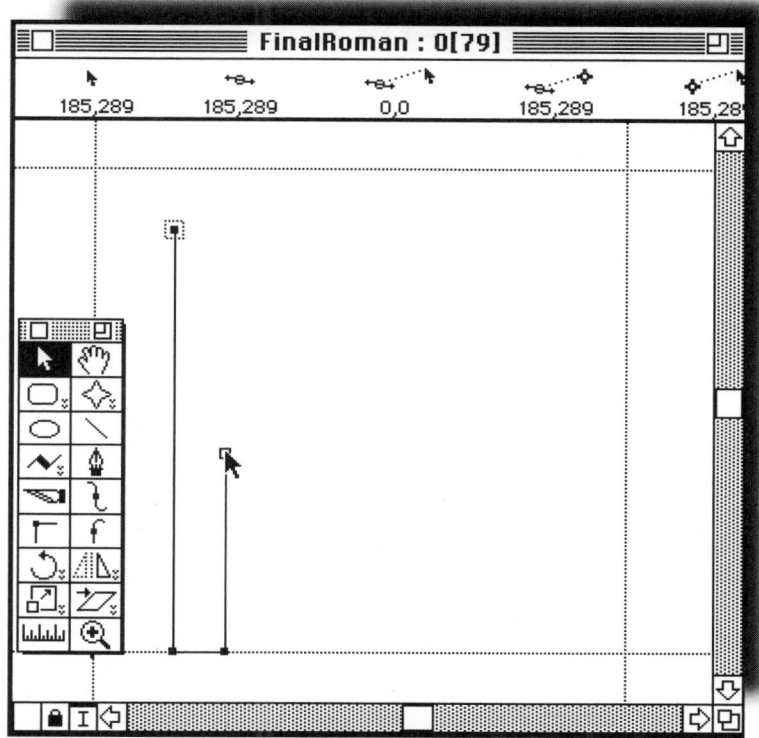

Figure 11.11

Character being drawn.

You can preview your characters as they would appear on a page, as black images. While in the Character window, and with your character displayed onscreen, select "preview" from within the View menu.

Metrics Window

The Metrics window (seen in Figure 11.12) enables the designer to view characters together onscreen. Most metric concerns involve the relationship between two or more characters. It is within this window that you can check "letterspacing" as well as "kerning." If you are designing a text typeface, letterspacing and kerning are critical to the success of the font. If you are designing a logo or similar graphic image, spacing may not be as much of concern.

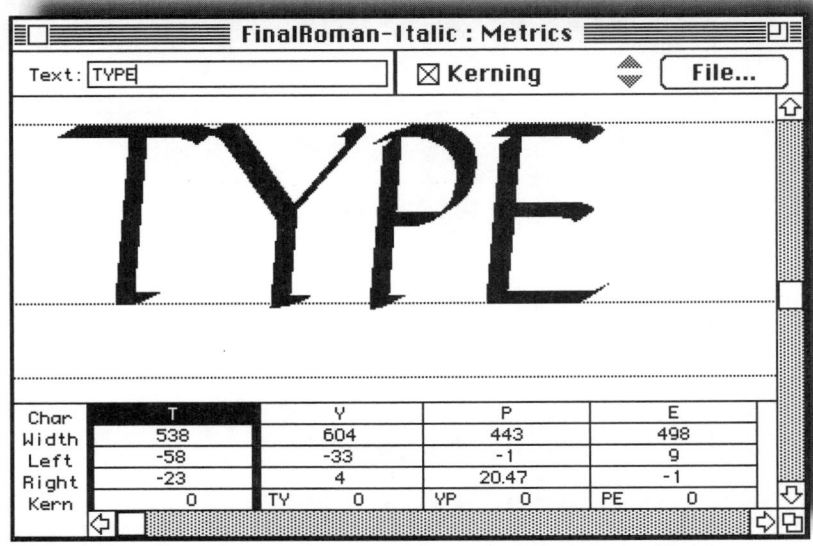

Figure 11.12

Metrics window.

It takes a well-trained eye to correctly space and kern a typeface. Fontographer provides two tools to deal with these processes. There is an "autotracing" tool that adjusts the letterspacing across the entire font. There is also an "autokern" tool that creates kerning pairs automatically. Kerning pairs are two-character pairs that are problems when they are placed next to each other (such as AV, Ty).

Autospacing a Font

Fontographer has a unique feature called Autospacing. The program examines the entire character set and gives every letterform what it believes to be the best spacing possible. It can save the designer a great deal of time attempting to space each character individually. To use Autospacing, do the following:

1. From within the Metrics window, select AutoSpace. A dialog box (as seen in Figure 11.13) will appear.

2. Click "easy" mode. Become familiar with the results of this mode before selecting the "advanced" mode.

3. Enter a spacing value.

4. Click Space.

5. Check the results of the autospacing by typing characters in the Metrics window.

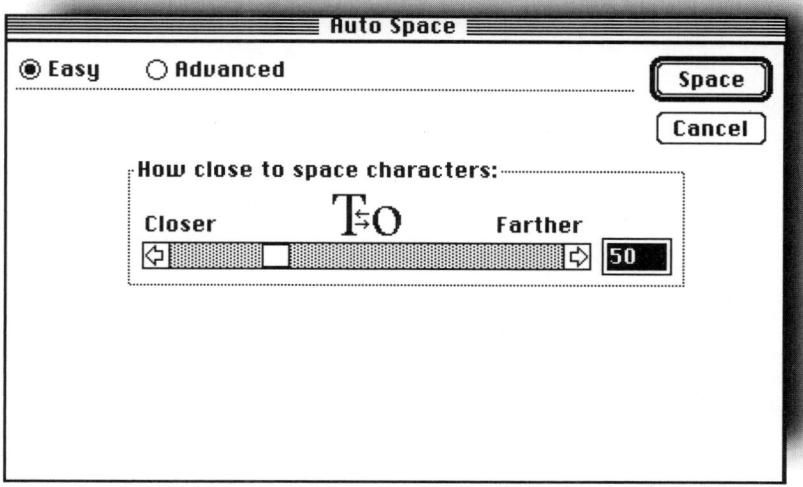

Figure 11.13

The Auto Space dialog box.

Autokerning a Font

Autokerning is a feature that, when applied, examines the letterforms of a font and creates kerning pairs automatically.

1. From within the Metrics window, select AutoKern. A dialog box (as seen in Figure 11.14) will appear.

2. Decide how many kerning pairs you want and enter the value (500 is not only the default choice, but it is a good starting place). More advanced type designers use up to and more than 1000 kerning pairs.

3. Choose a "tightness" setting. This determines the closeness of the kerning.

4. If you have imported a font that was previously created and it contains kerning pairs already, you can change or keep those pairs by selecting (or deselecting) the "existing kerning pairs" box.

5. Check the results of the autokerning by typing characters in the Metrics window.

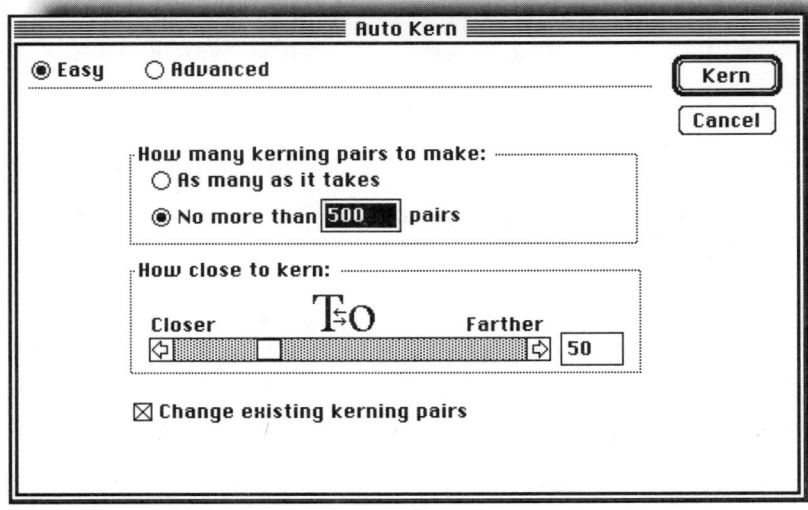

Figure 11.14

The Auto Kern dialog box.

Hinting

Fontographer has tools that develop "hints," advanced mathematical algorithms that help construct a character's shape and alignment when it is being converted from an outline to a bitmap. Because of Fontographer's Graphical User Interface (GUI), you can apply these hints graphically, rather than having to learn the high-level hinting language.However, to apply hints to a typeface, you must have extensive knowledge of type design and how hints affect the look of a font. Fontographer provides an Autohint feature that will hint the entire font automatically so that you can output a PostScript or TrueType font.

Autohinting a Font

Hinting a fonts should happen after all of your editing is completed.

1. At the Font window, choose Select All from within the Edit menu. This will highlight all of the characters within the font.

2. Within the Window menu, select Hint Parameters. Within this window (as seen in Figure 11.15), you can make a number of hint choices. If you are a beginner, make sure that the you use the default settings, which are as follows:

➡ "Hints to include" section has all boxes checked.

➡ "Hint order" for horizontal and vertical are set to "Most Frequent."

➡ "Hint Direction" is set to "Toward Center."

➡ Click "Recalc" and the program will then examine the font and find the most common stem (horizontal) weight and hairline (vertical) weight.

➡ Click "OK."

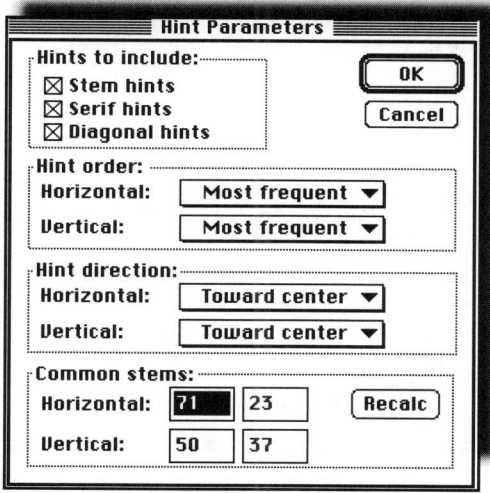

Figure 11.15

The Hint Parameters window.

Next, you will want to set the alignment criteria for the letterforms in the font.

1. Within the Window menu, select Vertical Alignment Zones (as seen in Figure 11.16). This is where height (ascent and descent) alignments are set.

2. Click "Recompute." This will recalculate the heights of control characters, whose alignments may have changes because of edits you made.

3. Click OK.

4. From the same Windows menu, select "Autohint." The program will apply hints to the characters' shapes.

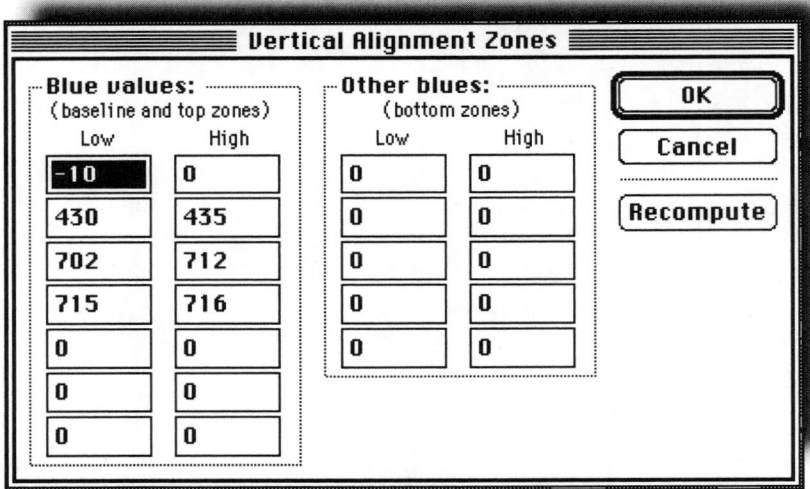

Figure 11.16

The Vertical Alignment Zones window.

Making Bitmap Characters

Bitmap characters are comprised of pixels—square dots that make up a representation of your outline character. If you are producing Mac TrueType fonts, you will need to produce bitmaps to accompany the outline font file.

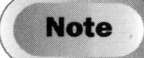

> TrueType fonts developed in Fontographer do not render well at sizes below 12 point.

Bitmaps can be hand–edited in Fontographer to provide more recognizable and readable characters. The first step is to produce the bitmaps. They should be created after you have adjusted all your metrics and your hints are in place.

To create bitmaps:

1. Within the Window menu, click Open Bitmap window.

2. If bitmaps had not yet been made, Fontographer will ask you if you would like them to be created. Click yes.

3. Enter the point sizes of the bitmaps you wish to create. Click OK.

Bitmap Window

After entering the point sizes of the bitmaps you wish to create, Fontographer produces the bitmaps at the sizes you entered. If you have a Character window open while it is generating the bitmaps, it will open the Bitmap window to that character when it has finished.

The Bitmap window contains information about the character it is displaying. It contains:

➡ The "ascent"—the total number of pixels above the baseline

➡ The "descent"—the total number of pixels below the baseline

➡ The "offset"—the distance from the left sidebearing to left side of character

➡ The "width"—the distance from left sidebearing to right sidebearing

The Bitmap window has a toolbox (as seen in Figure 11.17) that differs from the one in the Character window:

➡ The Line tool draws an entire line of pixels by clicking and dragging the cursor.

➡ The Hand tool repositions the image in your Bitmap window.

➡ The Pencil tool turns a pixel on or off by clicking it.

➡ The Eraser tool erases those pixels it crosses when moved over a character.

➡ The Marquee tool selects a group of pixels by lassoing them. The selected pixels can then be deleted by using the Delete key on your keyboard.

➡ The Selection tool moves the bitmap image around its em square.

➡ The Magnifying tool is used to zoom in and out when viewing an image.

➡ The Measuring tool counts the pixels by clicking and dragging the cursor from one pixel to another.

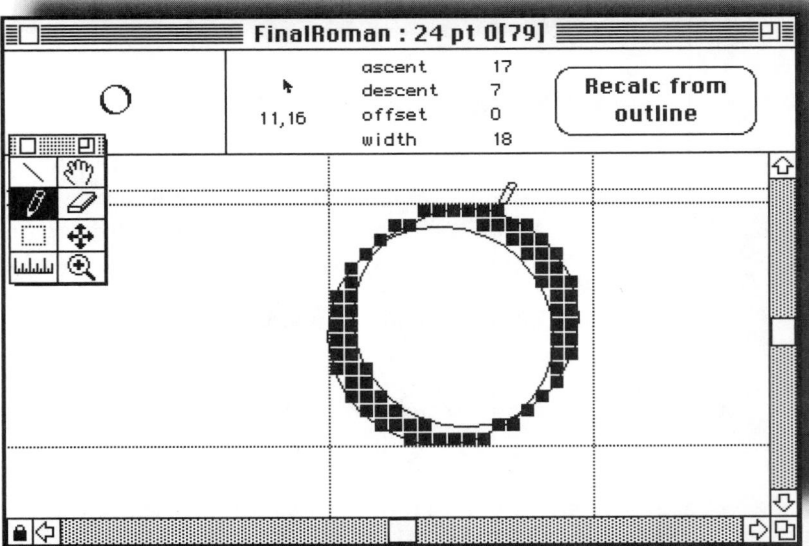

Figure 11.17

The Bitmap toolbox.

Figure 11.17 shows an upppercase O having been bitmapped at 24 point. Most characters are quite readable at this size. However, when you have very thin hairlines, pixels can drop out (disappear) and the transition areas (from thin to thick) can suffer. This character at 24 point gives us more pixels than if it were a 12-point character; it enables you to see (more dramatically) how pixel pattern can affect a letter appearance.

Figure 11.18 shows that editing (clicking on and off those pixels you wish to affect) the bitmap character creates a much more readable image and one that supports the actual design of the outline better.

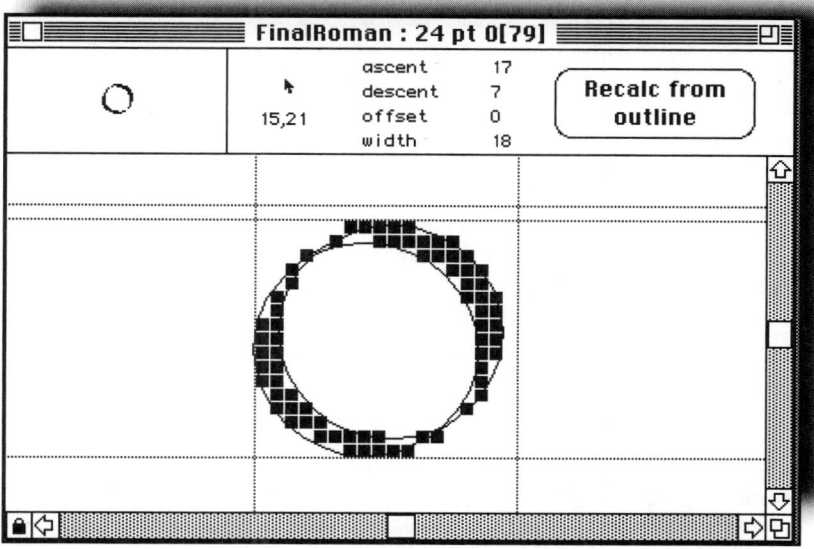

Figure 11.18

Bitmap character edited.

Font Information Window

The Font Information Window (as seen in Figure 11.19) enables the designer to set some global information within the font. From this window you can:

➡ Enter the name of your font.

➡ Determine the encoding, which is based on the platform you wish to format your fonts—this is usually selected as Macintosh or Windows.

➡ Set the additional global font metrics (Ascent, Descent, Em Square, Leading, Underline position, Underline width, Retaining path coordinates when changing em square, and Automatically computing the em square from the ascent + descent). You will want to set most of these metrics before hinting, bitmapping, and generating font formats.

➡Add a notice or copyright to your font.

➡Determine the amount of characters in your font.

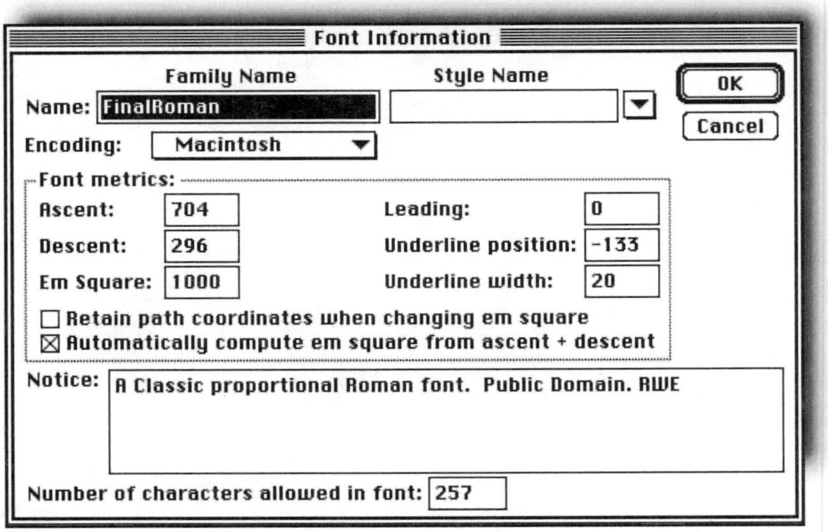

Figure 11.19

The Font Information window.

Font Format/Platform Generation

After you have designed the font, adjusted it, set the font metrics and hinted your font, it is now time to generate your digital typeface into one of several font formats for the computer platform of your choice. This is done in the Generate Font Files window (as seen in Figure 11.20).

To generate a font to a specific font format (PostScript or TrueType):

1. While you are in the Font window, select Select All from the Edit menu.

2. There are two choices for generating fonts: easy and advanced. You will need to become familiar with this process before using the advanced mode. Let's choose the easy mode.

3. Choose the computer platform you want your font to work on.

4. Choose which font format you want your font to be. The most common are PostScript and TrueType.

5. Select bitmap sizes if you need to create them. If you are generating PostScript fonts for the Mac and you will be using Adobe Type Manager (ATM), you do not need bitmaps. If you are not using ATM, you will need bitmaps for those screen point sizes you think you will be using. If you are generating PostScript fonts for the PC, you do not need bitmaps. If you are generating TrueType for the Mac, you will need to generate bitmaps for those screen sizes you think you will be using. If you are generating TrueType for the PC, you do not need bitmaps.

6. Choose where you want the generated fonts to go on your computer system, once they are made.

7. Click Generate.

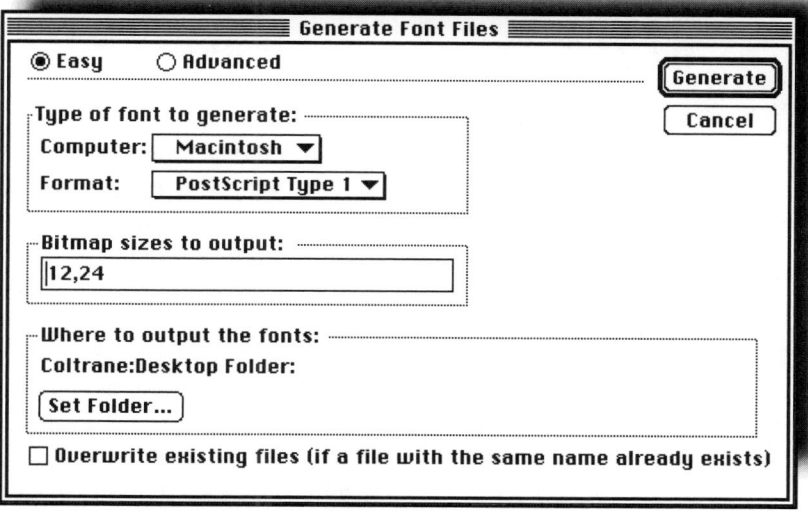

Figure 11.20

The Generate Font Files window in easy mode.

Conclusion

Here are the resulting files you will have once you have generated your font(s):

A Macintosh platform/PostScript format font:

➡ An outline file

➡ A font suitcase that contains the bitmap files

A PC platform/PostScript format font:

➡ A printer file (.pfb)

➡ Adobe Font Metrics File (,afm)

➡ Information file (.inf)

➡ PostScript Font Metrics file (.pfm)

A Macintosh platform/TrueType format font:

➡ A TrueType suitcase which encases the outline file

➡ A bitmap suitcase which encases the sizes you selected

A PC platform/TrueType format font:

➡ TrueType file (.ttf)

Now you have a PostScript or TrueType format font, a Mac or PC font. How do we use our new typestyle within a Web page? As we mentioned earlier in this chapter, there are a few solutions. Presently, if you wish to display your text in a Web document using your font, your audience will need to have that same typestyle already installed onto their computer system. If this situation is not possible (and it does seem very unlikely that you would give your font away to a large audience just for viewing purposes), then you must convert your text into a graphic image (bitmap), via an illustration program such as Adobe Illustrator or Macromedia Freehand, or a paint program such as Adobe Photoshop. Your graphic image must be in a format that is understandable to the Web. If it is an illustration, it should be converted to GIF format. This GIF file would then be uploaded to your Web server and when your Web page is retrieved, the graphics file will be downloaded as well.

The future of fonts on the Web is OpenType, discussed in detail later in the book. OpenType will provide a font format that can be downloaded to the Web, does not require that the reader have it installed on her system, and provides the designer of that fontstyle some security that the letterforms will not be copied, stolen, or manipulated.

CHAPTER **12**

File Formats

JPEG, GIF, and PNG are the basic file formats for putting images
on the Web. The first question one might have is why use the
different file formats at all? The underlying reason for the development of these formats are different for each, but ultimately the reason for creating these formats are:

➡ Cross-platform capabilities: The image's capability to be displayed on the Web regardless if the user is viewing it through
a browser on a Windows, Macintosh, or Unix system.

➡ File size reduction: The image's capability to reduce its file size
through compression or image quality reduction. The way this
reduction is achieved is through an encoding and decoding
process. When you save a file as JPEG, GIF, or PNG, what
you are really doing is encoding the image to make it smaller.
A browser will then know the algorithm for decoding these
images to be displayed onscreen. That is why older browsers
will not read recent advancements in image compression.
For example, Netscape 1.0 could not read progressive JPEGs
(explained later in this chapter) and only Netscape 5.0 and IE
4.0 and above can read the new PNG file format (again, explained later in this chapter).

➡ Image quality: Depending on the setting you give your image
file format, the common strength of these formats is their
ability to display the image at close to its original quality.

Obviously, the last two reasons are dependent on each other.
Retaining original image quality also creates a large file size, whereas
reducing file sizes will result in a poor image quality.

File Formats and Compression

Ultimately, smaller files mean faster downloads and more space for archiving. Some argue that a page should not be larger than 30K or the accumulation of text and graphics shouldn't exceed 30K. But in today's Web pages, the average has exceeded this standard. On a test of a range of pages on one particular day, for example, these results came out for total Web page sizes: c|net (www.cnet.com) was 62K, Mercury Center (www.sjmercury.com) was 104K, *The Chicago Tribune* (www.chicago. tribune.com) was 96K and Excite! (www.excite.com) was 28K. Obviously, smaller file size is better. However, some sites may exceed to display as much content and navigation options in the first screen, which may ultimately take it over 30K.

As traffic increases on the Internet and as Web pages increase in total file size, image compression becomes not only a necessity but also an art. Sure, as broader bandwidth and satellite transmission become reality, file sizes may seem less of an issue. But as the pipe gets bigger, our pages get bigger. Also consider that total download size on the page will include the HTML type, graphics, JavaScript type, Java applets, and plug-ins such as Shockwave, FutureSplash, and RealAudio. And as soon as our connection gets so wide that video downloads become more common, there will be a need for better MPEG (the standard for motion picture) compression technology. So the understanding and practice of compressing images to smaller file sizes will benefit you as well as the user downloading your pages.

Other advantages often overlooked in file compression are storage and archiving. Because stories and supporting graphics are usually forever stored on the server you upload to the Web, minimizing file sizes would be in your best interest. Creating a backup of files you've uploaded to the Web is also critical in any computer system. Therefore, archiving for the purposes of backup or later use would also be beneficial to you if the files are small. When the files compressed and transmitted across the Net are small, they are also taking up less space on your server. Now let's take a look at the two most common image file formats today, JPEGs and GIFs, as well as other future alternatives.

Joint Photographic Expert Group

JPEG, or the Joint Photographic Expert Group, is the original name of the committee that wrote the standard for image compression mechanism. Basically, JPEG compression makes your files smaller and retains a 24–bit-per-pixel color depth or millions of color.

JPEG was developed for compressing images, both full-color or grayscale, of photographic or natural artwork quality. A detailed discussion of how an image uses mathematical scheme is beyond the scope of the book and is basically unnecessary to understand how to get the best use of the technology. It might be enough to say that JPEG technology reduces the size of the file by using a "lossy" compression algorithm that actually redraws the details of an image.

Ray-traced images are graphics created using 3D programs such as Infi-D, Stratavision 3D, and Mac Renderman. For example, the frames in the Disney animated movie *Toy Story* were created using ray-tracing technology. The more realistic the image appears, the more you might be leaning on compressing it in JPEG. Basically, images with any continuous variation in tones and color are best compressed in JPEG format. However, JPEG does not compress graphics such as lettering, line drawings, or cartoons well. For such images, GIFs (Graphics Interchange Format) should be used.

JPEG Compression

One of JPEGs strengths is its capability to adjust the amount of compression you allow in an image. Of course, adjusting compression parameters is inversely related to the amount of quality you retain in the image. In other words, the smaller the file size, the poorer the quality of detail you retain in the image.

Photoshop's JPEG Compression

Let's compare the difference between higher compression/low quality versus smaller compression/high quality using Photoshop 4.0. We take an image and run it through the four major compression ratios set in the Image Options: Maximum, 8; High, 6; Medium, 3; Low, 1. (The JPEG Options dialog box can be found when you Save As an RGB file and select JPEG as its file format in the Save As dialog box). Precise compression ranging from 0 to 10 is also available through the Photoshop's JPEG file format as shown in Figure 12.1. Some say a range between 3–4 is acceptable for Web images. I tend to set mine to 5 (or higher depending on the image) to retain quality in the image.

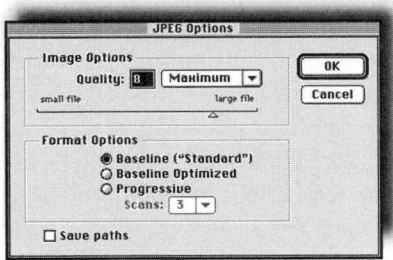

Figure 12.1

JPEG file format options.

There are three format options available in the JPEG Options dialog box. Let's take a look at them:

➡ Baseline ("standard") redraws your image on the Web from top to bottom.

➡ Baseline Optimized uses Hoffman coding, a data compression technique that achieves about 25 percent savings. For Web display, use Optimized when using Baseline format.

➡ Progressive JPEGs define the image's ability to display a lower quality "scan" of the final image as data is gradually pulled from the server. As illustrated in Figure 12.2, you can set the number of scans the progressive JPEG will display. Five scans will result in faster display of the first image but will take longer to display the final image because of the five incremental passes of the scans. Some say four is a good number but only because it's in between three and five. Thank goodness, Adobe didn't allow for more options.

File **Formats**   275

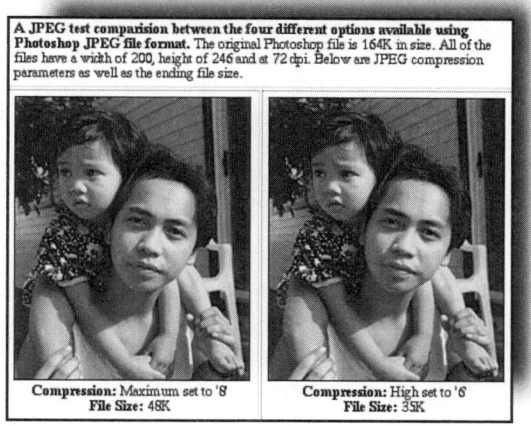

Figure 12.2

Setting the number of scans in the JPEG Options dialog box.

Now, let's take a look at the four JPEG images with different compression settings. For consistency sake, let's clarify that this test was done using Photoshop 4.0 and on an original 164K file. All of the images have a width of 200 points, height of 246 points, and a resolution of 72 dpi.

Figure 12.3

The image on the left has a maximum compression at 8 for a file size of 48K. The image on the right has a maximum compression at 6 for 35K.

Figure 12.4

The image on the left has a maximum compression at 3 for 8K; the one on the right has a maximum compression at 1 for 25K.

After a closer look at the image above, the left-hand image in Figure 12.4 is a good compromise of retaining quality while compressing to an acceptable rate. Some may argue, however, that 35K may still be pretty high, but at the same instance, Image 4 just doesn't produce the same quality of continuous colors that you would want in any publication.

I would optimally target JPEG image sizes to 30–35K. Displaying an image at more than 40K is hitting the limit for your user's patience.

Progressive JPEG

Everything that we have mentioned so far is considered to be "baseline" JPEG. "Baseline" JPEG is basically encoded and then decoded and displayed from top-to-bottom. You can usually notice if a photograph is saved as a "baseline" JPEG as opposed to a "progressive" JPEG according to how it displays itself onscreen. If it displays straight top-to-bottom, it's baseline. If it displays slightly blurred at first and then increases in quality over time, then the file is progressive. (GIF formats may also be displayed in a similar fashion, although instead of progressive, they are called interlaced). File size is not compromised when using progressive JPEG. It should be noted, however, that versions of Netscape Navigator earlier than 2.0 could not read progressive JPEGs, but in these ever-changing browser war days, this really doesn't matter.

Why use progressive JPEG? Basically, it gives your user a preview of what the image will become. Though it may be a very low resolution image at first, the user will have an idea what she is waiting on. It's worth noting that the time it takes a browser to compute the full resolution image is basically the same time it takes a "baseline" JPEG to fully load an image from top to bottom. Also, for faster connection such as a T1 or ISDN, these progressive JPEG displays will hardly be noticeable. On the other hand, on dial-up modems such as 14.4 or 28.8, downloading these progressive images can gradually give the user a glimpse of what's to come. And in my opinion, giving your user that power is what the Web is all about. One key to remember about trying to control display on the Web is that we really don't have any. The user can turn off images if they want to, change the color of hyperlinks, or change HTML typefaces. So when it comes to progressive displays, let's think about our user.

Equilibrium's DeBabelizer

Although Photoshop has been an image processing standard for the Internet, another powerful conversion/batch-processing utility out in the market is DeBabelizer from Equilibrium. I've found through large usage and testing that DeBabelizer has greater success in compression than any other product available, including Photoshop JPEG file format. The true beauty of DeBabelizer has always been its efficient compression as well as its ability to batch multiple files, although Photoshop 4.0's new Action palette is very powerful. These two techniques, DeBabelizer's batching and Photoshop's Action palette, give you the ability to basically record a macro once and apply it to many files automatically.

DeBabelizer's compression compabilities for JPEGs works the same as Photoshop in that it can compress images in percentages, as shown in Figure 12.5.

Now let's take a look at some image comparisons between Photoshop and DeBabelizer (see Figure 12.6).

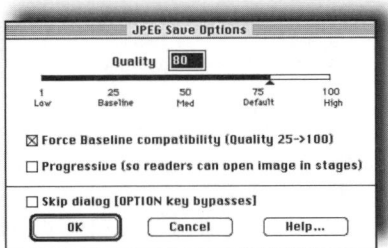

Figure 12.5

DeBabelizer's JPEG Save Options box.

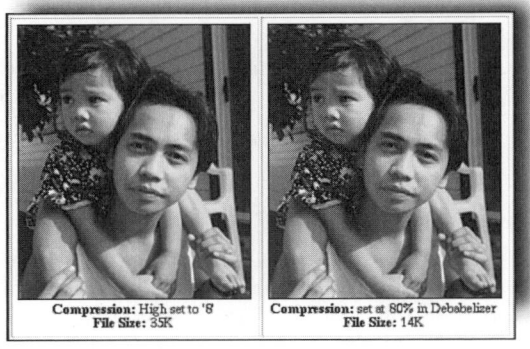

Figure 12.6

Photoshop JPEG (left) and DeBabelizer JPEG compared.

The file size difference between the two images is 21K. That's a major page load difference. Both images have the same dimension, resolution, and color depth parameters. To compare the two while retaining the same image quality, I've actually compressed the JPEG in DeBabelizer at 80% while keeping with the High—set at 6—in the Photoshop file. As you can see, DeBabelizer beats Photoshop JPEG in downsizing the file.

Graphics Interchange Format

GIF, or Graphics Interchange Format, is probably the most popular format for graphic transfers across the Web. By definition, GIF defines a protocol intended for the exchange of raster graphic data regardless of which platform the image will be used in or created on. Most, if not all, icons and navigational buttons on the Web are GIFs. Backgrounds of Web pages are GIFs. To set HTML imagemap codes, the ability to allocate different areas of the image to separate hyper-links, the image has to be a GIF. And you know those animated ads or animated informational graphics you might see here and there? Those are done using the GIF format.

GIF, simply, is the format to use when you have type present in your image. Type is probably the most recurring reason why there are hard edges in your graphic. And because most navigational icons also re-quire some combination of letters or numbers to describe the func-tion of the button, the best solution for file formats, for now, is GIF.

The technology behind GIF is defined in terms of blocks and sub-blocks. In simple terms, computer information or data are stored in blocks. Again, the details of how GIFs actually work is beyond the scope of this type of book. However, knowing that GIFs make up a GIF Data Stream, a sequence of these protocol blocks, might be critical. Because of this fundamental relationship with each other, GIFs work faster and better when this relationship is recognized. For example, this understanding can be useful in color tables.

GIF uses color tables to render graphics. This color table acts like a small chart in the system to record which color is being used in the image. Although color tables are broken down to both local and global areas of control, it is important to understand that discrete bits of GIF Data Stream information that proceed or follow one another can affect one another (and download time) in their use of palettes, again stored in the color table. More precisely, as a GIF passes through an encoder, and this encoder reads a particular color table, it is not re-quired to encode the color table again if the proceeding GIF in the data stream has the same color table. Hence, consistent color palettes in the design of a Web page offer not only good clean design, but also streamline downloading, resulting in faster page loads for the user.

GIF Quality

One of the most frustrating functions of GIF is its inability to reduce file size without reducing the color-depth. As is, compressing an image into a GIF requires you to reduce to a maximum of 8-bit color or 256 colors. The minimum you should reduce to range from 4-bit color (16 colors) or 5-bit color (32 colors). In Photoshop, the only way to save an image as a GIF is to reduce it to index color first. To get to the indexed color dialog box as shown in Figure 12.7, choose Image➡Mode➡Indexed Color... in Photoshop.

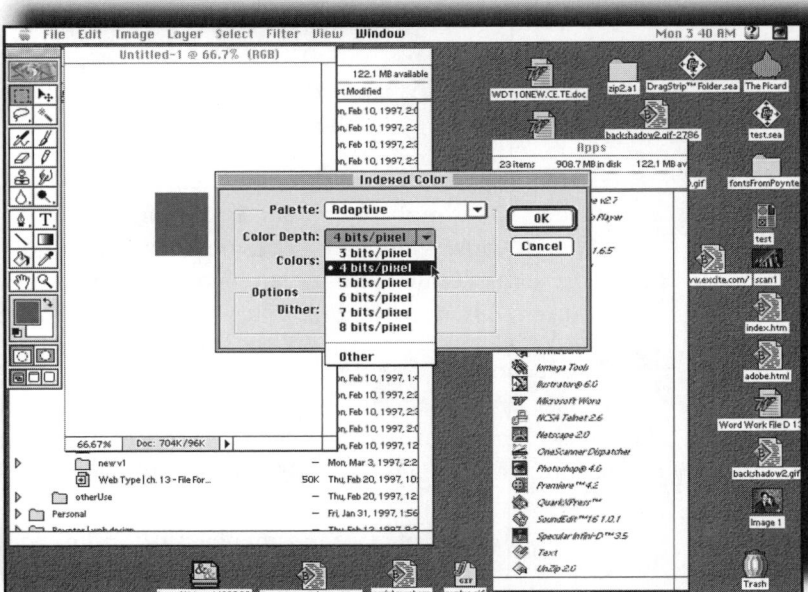

Figure 12.7

The Indexed Color dialog box.

Although this format is limiting to color quality, it unfortunately also serves as a reminder that most people do not surf the Internet with nice monitors.

Interlaced GIFs

Just as with progressive JPEGs, interlaced GIFs enable the browser to display a rather low resolution version of the image that is followed by gradual improvements to the final image.

In most cases, I set larger GIF images to interlace. Large being anything bigger to 25×25 pixels in dimension. I wouldn't, however, bother interlacing background GIFs or place holder GIFs. The whole process of everything on the screen interlacing would appear to be longer. Interlacing small graphics is basically unnecessary.

Transparent GIFs

Transparent GIFs enable an image or parts of the image to appear invisible. Why do this? This will enable the image to become part of the background rather than be surrounded by a box on a background as shown in Figure 12.8.

Figure 12.8

Comparing transparent GIFs to GIFs that aren't.

Most GIF generating applications, such as Photoshop and DeBabel-izer, enable you to set one color or several colors of an image as transparent. Keep in mind, however, that each pixel is either transparent or not. So the level of opacity is only at two levels. Achieving translucency is not possible. In creating a transparent GIF from an image with a drop shadow on a white background, white pixels become transparent whereas the grays in the shadows become opaque.

Note

After taking a closer look at Figure 12.8, you might notice a small white glow around the transparent GIF. This file format's inability to create translucent images results in these nasty white glows (or whatever color the original document had). Because each pixel is either transparent or not, there's a certain visual limit of grays that question whether you should set it as transparent or not. There's a small way around that.

Let's take a look at Figure 12.9, the GIF 89a Export dialog box in Photoshop, for clarification. Notice that as I drag the Eyedropper tool over the once white area around the type and click, it will turn to that browser gray to indicate that that color in the image (white in this instance) will now be transparent. The set of boxes at the bottom of the dialog box also display which color(s) is transparent. Also notice, however, that there ghosted areas of white around the type.

That's because those pixels actually have a small tint of black. It is not pure white.

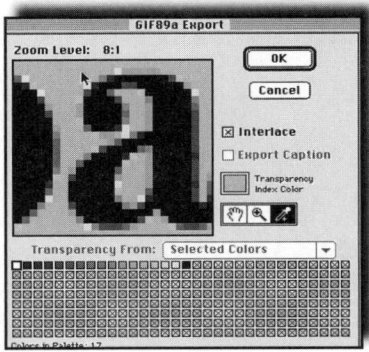

Figure 12.9

Photoshop's GIF89a Export dialog box.

To capture these additional colors simply hold the Shift key and click the desired color for transparency again as shown in Figure 12.10. Notice that the colors that are now transparent are again browser gray and the number of color boxes in the bottom have 4 colors (levels of gray) highlighted.

Warning

Be careful on how much you set for transparency. You might actually hit a pixel carrying a true value of your image resulting in some loss of detail. This multiple color selection for transparency is not a solution for translucent images. PNG, introduced later in this chapter, will be that solution.

Figure 12.10

Multiple colors changed to transparent in the GIF 89a Export dialog box.

JPEG/GIF Usage

When comparing the compression of JPEGs and GIFs, JPEG does a better job of making a file small and retaining better color. JPEG often times can bring down a file at a 20:1 ratio, whereas GIF can compress at a 4:1 ratio. Also, JPEG format stores 24 bits/pixels (16 million colors), whereas GIF can only store 8 bits/pixels or 256 (or fewer) colors.

Note

Decoding and viewing a JPEG file takes longer than viewing a GIF. Ultimately, the time saved by moving a smaller file can actually be greater than the time needed to encode and display a file.

As mentioned earlier, deciding on whether to use JPEG as your file format depends on the type of image. Photographic or reality-based images are compressed better using JPEG, the format that has a difficult time with very sharp edges. Vector-based graphics or icons that use little color are better compressed and continue to maintain good quality in GIF format. Halftones or simple black-and-white images such as a cartoon should always be saved as a GIF. An image needs at least 16 levels of gray for JPEG to be useful in the compression.

Let's compare two images, a photograph and a type image, and run both of them through the JPEG and GIF process as shown in Figures 12.11 and 12.12.

Figure 12.11

Comparing JPEG and GIF compression of a photograph.

Figure 12.12

Comparing JPEG and GIF compression of a graphic.

The rule of thumb here is if it's a photograph use JPEG; if it's graphic type use GIF. As you can see in the comparison of the photograph, the JPEG retains the quality of the image, whereas the GIF created pixelation around the faces and the girl's right arm (see Figure 12.13). The GIF is smaller by 8K, but I don't think the compromise of reduced image quality to file size difference is worth it.

Figure 12.13

Pixelation in GIFs.

Similarly with the graphic, the loss in image quality when it goes through the JPEG process creates a distorted pattern around solid colors as well as blurs the edges of the words "making type in style." Although I compressed the image to its lowest possible setting in Photoshop, the file size at 27K is much higher than the GIF size of 7K.

Figure 12.14

Distortion patterns on solid colors in JPEGs.

However, there are times when you want both, either as type over an image or type masked out by a type. In each instance, I would experiment with both and decide which serves best in quality and file size. Ultimately, it depends on the image and which area of the image overpowers which.

PNG

PNG (Portable Network Graphics, pronounced "Ping") was designed to outperform and replace the aging GIF format. Hence, its unofficial abbreviation for "PNG, Not GIF."

The story behind the rush of a new format was started from Unisys and CompuServe's 1995 announcement that any program implementing GIF would require royalties because of Unisys' patent on the LZW compression method used in the GIF format. Regardless, however, the need to replace or upgrade from GIF's image compression was duly required. PNG, because of its better as well as patent-free technology, will probably be the standard in the future.

The future will be up to the community, of course. At the time of this writing, the two major browsers, Netscape Navigator and Microsoft IE, only offer limited support to this new format. Navigator 3 requires a plug-in to be able to read PNG. Future versions of both browsers promise greater PNG support. Photoshop 4.0, however, does offer PNG format saving compability.

PNG specifications

Some of the GIF features retained in PNG include:

➡ Indexed color up to 256 colors

➡ Interlaced display (the capability to view a low-resolution image immediately followed by gradual improvements to the final image)

➡ Transparency

➡ Effective 100% lossless compression

The new features offered in PNG and not found in GIF include:

➡ True color images of up to 48 bits per pixel

➡ Gray scale images of up to 16 bits per pixel

➡ Transparency masks (alpha channel support, which ultimately could give a translucent image, a definite plus for designers. Imagine Photoshop layers and creating translucency between each layer and you'll get what PNG can do)

Transparency masks are a true life saver for designers. They will eliminate those irritating white glows around transparent GIF images.

➡ Image gamma information

➡ More dependable file corruption detection

➡ Faster progressive display

PNG is a single-image format which basically does not support multiple images in a single file. In English, no more gif Animation type of images.

PNG Quality

As it is touted, PNG will support much more colors than GIF. Because it does not use JPEG's loss compression, however, this will mean somewhat larger file sizes than GIF with the exception of gray scale images. PNG's specifications sound very promising...once it's used in the general public.

Conclusion

In this chapter, we derived the basic understanding of file formats, and that displaying type on the Web requires interlaced, transparent GIFs at 4-bit color (16 colors) or 5-bit color (32 colors). And eventually, PNG will offer an excellent alternative.

CHAPTER 13

Animated Typographic Images

Animations are becoming a vital part of Web page design. The movement across your Web page catches the reader's eye. To view a static page and then see it come to life with moving images is very exciting. Such dynamic images provide a much more interesting Web presence, enhancing the content. This is true of type as well. Animated type is dynamic. It performs for its audience. Whether it is a news flash whose text fades in and out or letters that tumble across the page spelling out a company's name, the animation of text has a dramatic effect on the Web page and its audience.

Companies' Web pages as well as personal Web documents are more frequently introducing animation as a visual lure, attempting to hold the reader's attention that much longer.

Animated images can be both simple and basic in design or complex in nature. Some of the most engaging animations on the Web consist of small icons that load quickly. With animated text, you must be aware of the composition of your Web document. Do not use so much animation that it becomes a distraction.

Unfortunately, there were not many choices when it came to building animation into Web documents in the past. Animation tools and utilities that were available tended to be complex and difficult for the beginner.

Many products now exist—both commercially and as shareware. These tools enable the designer to develop animated typographic images from simple icons and logos to intricate images. Now that these tools are available, the question becomes, which ones should I use? And which file format and technology should I work with?

The animation technology you decide to develop with will determine what set of tools you will use. The complexity (or lack thereof) of the typographic images factors into this decision.

Probably the most important factor to consider when building animated typographic images is whether they suit the needs of your audience. Always remember, it is your audience who you are creating for. They need to view these images as informative as well as entertaining. In this chapter, we will cover the tools and technology available for Web animations, the animating of typographic images, and how file size and compression play a part in choosing to use an animated image.

Animation Formats

Some of the formats you can embed into your Web documents include .AVI, .MOV, .QT, .MPEG, and .GIF files as well as Java applets and other objects that combine audio and video effects.

The .AVI format is Microsoft's digital video standard. Microsoft has since developed ActiveMovie, a cross–platform digital video technology that will be included with Internet Explorer. Both .MOV and .QT are QuickTime movie formats. MPEG, short for Motion Pictures Expert Group, had until recently required additional hardware to be viewed. There are now plug-ins available for browsers to display .MPEG files.

Animated GIFs

The GIF format is a graphical format that also allows for animation. GIFs are easy to develop and are also quite simple to add to your HTML. GIF technology has been around for some time and it is probably the most basic way to develop an animated typographic image. Developing a typographic image is similar to developing a regular graphic image. If there is an area where the GIF format falls short, it may be that it does not provide for sound. However, if you are looking to animate something as basic as an icon, button, or border, an animated GIF is definitely the way to go.

The animated GIF format (which is technically called GIF89A) is now supported by all of the major Web browsers (Netscape

Navigator, Microsoft's Internet Explorer, as well as browsers from Mosaic, AOL, and Prodigy). It is the most widely used format. The extensive support of this format's specification ensures the designer that most Web page readers will be able to view the animation of this dynamic image. For those browsers that do not support the GIF technical specification, the animated image will present itself as a static image (the MacWeb browser does not support GIF).

There is another version of the GIF format, known mainly as GIF, but also known as GIF87a. It does not support animation. But like the animated GIF, it contains 256 colors or less and offers lossless compression, a compression method of reducing the size of the original image without losing too much quality. However, since GIF images are at best 8-bit (256 colors) images, the quality may not be as high as that of another image format that uses lossy compression (greater compression but greater loss of quality) but can be up to 24-bit in color (16 million+ colors).

Tools for Creating Animated GIFs

Not only can a GIF89a image be animated, but this format provides for transparency. One color within the image can be chosen for transparency. When the image is used within a browser, that color drops out, allowing the background to show through.

Depending on the application you use, it can be quite simple to create GIF images. Again, keep an eye on the size of your animated files. Although you may have designed a great looking image, if it is too large and downloads slowly, the viewer may lose interest. An animated image over 100K in size will take a while to run through its sequence. Consider your audience and the quality of the image. Working with fewer frames in an animation will keep the file size smaller. The following tools can be used to create animated typographic images. Some are freeware/shareware and some are available at a software retailer.

GIFBuilder

GIFBuilder is an easy-to-use freeware utility that makes animated GIFs. Both beginners and experienced Web designers will find it to be a resourceful tool. What is really nice about GIFBuilder is that it enables you to import different formats of artwork, including

Photoshop files, QuickTime movie files, PICTs, and sequential GIF files. To save these formats into the animated GIF format, you need only use the tool's Save command. It's that simple.

One of GIFBuilder's features is to turn on or off a background transparency. You can also import your own custom color palettes. One of GIFBuilder's compression features lets you store a static background and then develop transparency whenever an overlying frame does not alter that background. This reduces the size of the file significantly. Figure 13.1 shows an animated GIF file created by using GIFBuilder.

Figure 13.1

An animated GIF file made in GIFBuilder.

Note

For more information on obtaining and learning about GifBuilder, go to this URL:

```
http://iawww.epfl.ch:80/Staff/Yves.Piguet/clip2gif-home/
GifBuilder.html
```

GIFMation

This utility (from Box Top Software, for about $49) requires a bit more skill than using GIFBuilder. GIFMation provides some high-level color control and cropping techniques. GIFMation accepts many different graphic file formats as well as animated formats. Photoshop, GIF, and JPEG formats can be imported.

To provide for smaller file sizes, GIFMation has a robust color reduction mechanism. If you have an image with transparent edges, GIFMation has a utility that assists in removing fringe pixels. Transparency can be set on each frame separately. Although more complex than GIFBuilder, GIFMation is fairly easy to use.

> **Note**
>
> For more information on obtaining and learning about GIFMation, go to this URL:
>
> `http://www.boxtopsoft.com:80/GIFmation/welcome.html`

Adobe Photoshop

Adobe Photoshop enables a designer to develop a series of images as individual frames of a sequence. Each frame/image can be rotated so that the total of all the images provides a series of an image going around and around. You can also fade each sequential image so that, in total, the image will look like it is fading out. Using the layers and actions palettes as well as the GIF89a format within Photoshop, the designer can take the exported frames into a tool such as GIFBuilder for the animating of these frames.

One of the newest features of Photoshop 4.0 is the Actions feature. Actions allows the designer to record a sequence of actions or steps that can then be applied to other tasks. If a designer is performing the same process when animating his images, the Actions features acts like a shortcut to help the designer streamline his development process. Photoshop 4.0 also supports transparent and interlaced GIFs as well as other image file formats like PNG (Portable Network Graphics) and Progressive JPEG.

> **Note**
>
> For more information on obtaining and learning about Photoshop, go to this URL:
>
> `http://www.adobe.com/prodindex/photoshop/`

QuickTime Movie Format

The QuickTime movie format is more complex to develop than animated GIFs. This movie format provides both dynamic images as well as sound. There are two different ways to provide QuickTime movies within your Web documents. The first way does not require the reader to have a QuickTime plug-in for viewing the file. Unfortunately, the reader will have to wait for the movie file to be downloaded. When it is downloaded, the file will not play within the Web browser. Rather, it will play in a separate application. If this type of

QuickTime movie file method is going to be supported, the designer should provide the reader with a warning that reports the size of the file and the length of time it may take to download the animated image.

The newer method allows for QuickTime files to be viewed within the Web browser. The reader must initially download the QuickTime plug-in (which is available free) to view these inline images. This newer option is supported by all Web browsers that have plug-in capabilities. Using a plug-in allows for the QuickTime movie to be viewed immediately. There is no downloading required.

Note

> To make a QuickTime movie, you need to obtain QuickTime software (which is available at `http://www.quicktime.apple.com:80`).

You can create a QuickTime movie using the movie software. For a QuickTime movie to be viewed on more than one platform (it is native to the Mac) the movie needs to be flattened (a process that takes out data resident in the file that tags it as just a Macintosh file).

Note

> Flattening can be done in Adobe Premiere's software (available at `http://www.adobe.com/prodindex/premiere`).

Web Painter

Totally Hip Software's Web Painter provides the designer with an easy to use tool that makes basic cel-style animations. Cel-style animation is when each separate image changes, frame to frame. This is how cartooning is done. In Web Painter, the designer finds it easy to paint the animations as well as export them in a number of formats. These include QuickTime, animated GIFs, and PICs (which are sequences of PICT files).

One of Web Painters features includes a process called "onion-skinning." Onion-skinning is similar to using tracing paper to redraw. You can also take multiple frames and edit them simultaneously.

Web Painter provides an extensive tutorial that explains how to use the product. This makes the job of making cel-style animation both understandable and easy to develop.

> **Note**
>
> For more information on obtaining and learning about Web Painter, go to this URL:
>
> `http://www.totallyhip.com:80/`

Specular's 3D Web Workshop

Wow! Specular's entry into the Web design field is quite a set of tools. 3D Web Workshop's specialty, as the name suggests, is developing three-dimensional images (including typographic images) and animation. The two integral products that are bundled within 3D Web Workshop are LogoMotion and TextureScape. LogoMotion is the animation arm of 3D Web Workshop. TextureScape is a design tool for creating textures for backgrounds as well as placing texture upon images.

There is also a clip art collection within 3D Web Workshop WebHands, a pre-existing set of editable clip art and animation. These images have already been optimized for Web use. 3D Web Workshop also lets designers create their own 3D animated typographic images within LogoMotion. These images are then saved as either animated GIFs or QuickTime movies.

> **Note**
>
> For more information on obtaining and learning about 3D Web Workshop, go to this URL:
>
> `http://www.specular.com/products/3dww`

Plug-Ins

For readers to play any animation that needs a browser plug-in, they must first download the plug-in, install it into their respective browser's plug-in folder, and then restart that browser. Plug-in technology is only a year or so old. Browsers are still in their infancy in their support of plug-ins. Because of this, the implementation of the plug-ins is not always adequate. Readers who have older browsers will probably not be able to view animations that require plug-ins. They will not be a part of your audience if your animated typographic images require them.

Shockwave/Afterburner Plug-ins

Macromedia, whose products include a suite of design, illustration, and presentation applications, makes a product called Director. Director is a high-end movie and animation application.

Director provides two sets of its own plug-ins, namely Shockwave and Afterburner. If you have experience with Director and decide to use it as the basis for you Web animation projects, you will need to use Shockwave.

Shockwave plug-ins are multimedia players. Shockwave can present and playback multimedia such as live audio and interactive games. All of the content presented by Shockwave has to be created within Macromedia authoring tools, such as Director. The family of Shockwave plug-ins is known as Essentials.

Afterburner is a post-process utility that has to be run on Shockwave files before using them in the Web environment.

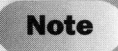

For more information on obtaining and learning about Shockwave, go to this URL:

`http://www.macromedia.com/shockwave/download`

Sizzler

Sizzler is both an animation editor and a plug-in. Using the Sizzler editor is an easy way to convert QuickTime movies or PICs into streamable animations that include sound. The animation files must first be converted into Sizzler's own proprietary file format. Sizzler provides interlacing, which enables the images to slowly come into focus, instead of having to wait until the image is ready to present itself on screen. This gives the reader something to view, instead of waiting. And you never want your reader to wait, if possible.

After readers download the Sizzler plug-in, they can view the animations as they materialize on the screen.

The other feature of Sizzler is that you can export animation files not only to the Sizzler file format, but as Java applets or ActiveX applets (which is Microsoft's version of the Java applet).

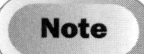

> For more information on obtaining and learning about Sizzler, go to this URL:
>
> `http://www.totallyhip.com:80/Products/Products.html`

Java—Powerful Programming

The latest and greatest choice in creating interactive Web animation is to use Java, a revolutionary programming language. Java outputs mini programs that are called "applets." These "applets" are platform-independent and are small enough in size to travel freely over the phone lines. Microsoft's Internet Explorer and Netscape's Navigator, the two browsers used by most readers, support Java applets.

For anyone interested in learning Java, they should recognize that the technology is in its infancy and there are still some problems with the programming language. However, there are a few tools that have been created to assist the Java designer to make applets, without having to learn the entire programming language.

WebBurst

WebBurst (which lists for about $299) enables the designer to import PICT or GIF formats and export to the Java applet, without Java programming experience. The tool does have a graphical user interface (GUI), but it is not easy to use. One of the features of Web-Burst is that it makes its Java applets perform with shorter download times than most other Web animators. WebBurst includes a selection of its own clip art. Although WebBurst provides an environment to make Java applets without programming experience, there still is a steep learning curve.

 **Note** For more information on obtaining and learning about WebBurst, go to this URL:

`http://www.powerproduction.com/tech/wbnew.html`

Conclusion

Though it may seem we have journeyed quite a distance from the primary focus of the book, typography for the Web, it is very important to understand what tools are available to the Web designer so she or he can add them to her or his arsenal. The tools we have mentioned in this chapter can take typographic images and bring them to life. GIF animations can be small in size, yet can provide just the right amount of animation to an otherwise static page.

Tools such as GIFBuilder and GIFMation make it easy to create animated images. Tools such as QuickTime and WebPainter can export other formats than GIFs, giving the designer some choice over which tools he decides to use. Plug-ins such as Shockwave and Sizzler and Java applets open the door to true multimedia viewing, with animation as well as live audio and interactive media.

These tools provide the Web designer with an opportunity to orchestrate his static typographic image through movement.

PART 4

Building a Bridge

CHAPTER 14

OpenType: A New Font Format

L ong ago there was one font outline format that most applications
and systems software supported—Adobe Systems' Type 1 (Post-
Script). PostScript printers and software made it easy for fonts to be
downloaded to printers for high-quality printed output. PostScript
has always been known for providing great looking results on the
printed page, which requires much higher resolutions (300–1200
dpi) than the computer screen.

Then along came TrueType. The TrueType font format, originally
developed by Apple and fully supported by Microsoft and its Windows software, hit the computer world with a bang. TrueType is
much more than a font. It is its own font program, enabling the font
developer to incorporate additional data to the font. TrueType fonts
can contain hinting information that enable them to look better
onscreen at low resolutions. They also can contain data tables that
speed up the rasterizing process and unicode encoding that enables
the developer to make a very large character set available.

Unicode encoding is a mapping system in which the computer system's software can understand where a character is mapped or positioned within a font.

Type 1 and TrueType were, at their own respective times, the superi-
or font format in the market. Both formats are still quite successful.
Because the Type 1 font format came out first, it has a very large
following. With the largest portion of the computer market being
Windows 3.1, Windows 95, or Windows NT users, however,

TrueType has eclipsed PostScript as the market leader. TrueType has also been known to provide better screen quality output, when compared to PostScript.

Both Adobe and Microsoft seem happy developing and marketing their own formats. The question the Web designer has, however, is "What format is best suited for onscreen use and delivers the quality needed for Web documents?"

The feeling among designers and other professional users has been that PostScript fonts render better than TrueType when output to a printer. TrueType has a much better reputation for superior screen quality or use on the computer. The question of better quality and concerns by users as to the future of their own font libraries is a valid one. And would a designer who had purchased a large PostScript library continue to be able to purchase PostScript fonts in the future? OpenType provides a solution as to which of these two formats to use.

As the computer screen and the Web become the tools and environment more and more people communicate with (while continuing to print hard copy), there seems to be a need for a more global solution, one that would solve the issues of high screen quality (such as legibility at small sizes, colored type), as well as provide superior printed output. OpenType is the proposed answer to that concern.

The OpenType font format has been developed to provide support for high-quality typographic output in print and on the computer screen. It will improve the legibility and readability of documents published on the Web, as well as provide other benefits:

➡ Broader multi-platform support

➡ Better support for international character sets

➡ An enhanced capability to subset characters

➡ Robust font compression technology, which is vital for keeping the size of the fonts down so that they render faster to the screen and on the Web

➡ Support for multiple master PostScript fonts

➡ Font security signature (better protection of font data)

➡ Greater capability for glyph substitution

➡ Much more streamlined font solution for the customer

OpenType builds on the existing TrueType architecture. It maintains all of its fonts in a unified registry, thereby ridding it of any compatibility issues that might arise between TrueType and PostScript.

Joint Venture—Adobe and Microsoft

OpenType is being developed jointly by Adobe and Microsoft. It is due to be released early summer 1997. Before you begin to worry about the probability that this may yet be a third major font format, relax. OpenType is an extension of Microsoft's TrueType Open format. It also enables for the introduction of Type 1 data within the font file. Think of OpenType as a wrapper that cloaks an existing TrueType or Type 1 font. Don't be mistaken, OpenType can do more than either of the other formats as a stand-alone font technology. OpenType is a container within which you can have just Type 1 data, just TrueType data, or both at the same time. The OpenType format is a superset of both existing formats.

Both Adobe and Microsoft decided that the proper solution was not to compete with their different font formats. By merging the two font technologies, both are supported by Macintosh and Windows platforms.

Adobe and Microsoft have an agreement to share their respective font technologies. All existing PostScript fonts and TrueType fonts will be supported by OpenType. Within this agreement, Adobe agreed to convert their popular Type 1 fonts to OpenType. Both Microsoft and Adobe are to co-promote the further development of OpenType fonts. The OpenType specification will be made available to other font developers (type designers and font foundries making OpenType fonts) as well so that they may develop and support OpenType as Adobe and Microsoft does.

OpenType will initially be supported by a suite of core fonts designed with the intention of using them in Web documents.

Support for OpenType

Though the OpenType font will be available during the second half of 1997, you may need to make font format decisions before then. For the Web designer whose main concern is their environment, the screen, TrueType is the best choice.

Font developers will continue to be able to develop for Type 1 and TrueType if they so desire. They will, however, be able (as well as software) to convert their existing and new font libraries to OpenType. This also gives the smaller font foundries a way to get their fonts into the hands of the public.

With the possibility for such dramatic growth of OpenType compatible libraries, it should only be a matter of time until the onscreen developing world supports it. The World Wide Web Consortium will be compelled to further their support for more font tags within the Web document. This will make for better Web pages and a greater availability of fonts that look great onscreen.

Rasterization

Rasterization is when the scalable outline font is going to be sent to the printer with instructions to render (draw) it at a specific point size. The scalable outline is first converted to a bitmap image (black pixellated image) and that bitmap is transferred to the printer and printed on the page.

The PostScript data held in an OpenType font can be rasterized by a Type 1 rasterizer such as Adobe's Type Manager (ATM), as long as ATM is installed on your computer system. If a Type 1 rasterizer such as ATM is not present on your computer, the Type 1 data can be converted to TrueType data (through OpenType conversion utilities) and rasterized by the TrueType rasterizer.

System Compatibility

Because OpenType supports both TrueType and PostScript fonts, customers need not change anything about their computer systems. OpenType fonts will act the same whether they are being used on a Mac, Windows 95, or Windows NT. Any upgrade of system software will not affect the fonts. As in the past, the font is separate from the system software, although many fonts ship with the system software. The application and system utilities will change around the Open-Type font format, not the other way around. The user will not have to do anything but load the fonts onto his system as he normally would.

How OpenType Affects the Web

As Web designers continue to create online documents, they will be able to include high-quality fonts with them, providing an opportunity for great, eye-catching documents. OpenType fonts will take less time to render and display within the documents. An agreement is in the works between Adobe and Microsoft that would allow standardization of OpenType font embedding. OpenType enables fonts to be embedded and made inseparable from the Web document. This calms some concerns over the stealing of fonts and font licensing. A license is given when a font is purchased by a user. That user has an agreement with the developer of that font to use the font but not to copy, manipulate, or resell it. Nor can the user give it to another user. Under normal circumstances, a font is purchased from the foundry that made it or one of its resellers.

The printed page contains a printed representation of the font the page designer has used. There is no way for the reader to gain access to the fonts used within that printed document. It is different on the Web. When a font is downloaded to the screen for use on the Web, part or all of the font file is available to the audience, which brings about security concerns. Are fonts used on the Web secure from those who want to steal the data? We will speak further to this issue when we describe the "digital signature" table later on.

OpenType Tables

What makes the OpenType format so functional is the addition of more data tables, which enable the increased functionality. This section looks at those tables specific to the OpenType spec. This new font format contains most of the existing TrueType tables that make such fonts work as well as they do. We will concentrate on the OpenType tables, as well as a few tables that provide an environment for the PostScript format to exist.

OpenType tables are invisible to the font user. They are hidden within the header of the font file. It is important, however, to understand how the OpenType format provides its many new font capabilities. The figures within this chapter, which illustrate some of the capabilities of the OpenType format, were culled from Microsoft's Web site at `www.microsoft.com/truetype`.

Character Alignment

Different languages have different baselines upon which their characters align. If you are using glyphs from differing scripts and/or languages (such as Latin and Arabic fonts) and different point sizes as well, an adjustment must be made to fix any internal line spacing problems or alignment issues. If you use a character from a Latin font followed by a Kanji character (a Japanese font), normally the Kanji character is going to base align on the alignment of the Latin. This is incorrect alignment. Figure 14.1 shows how this can be a problem.

Figure 14.1

Alignment of varying languages can be tricky.

The BASE table, or Baseline table, is new to the OpenType font format. It provides information needed to align characters of differing scripts (and sizes) when they are both included on a line of text. This table provides a minimum and a maximum glyph extent for each of the scripts or language systems.

OpenType works to provide the font with baseline positions and minimum and maximum extents for each of the differing languages. If needed, these extent values are available for modification. Figure 14.2 shows the results of using the BASE table in the OpenType font.

Figure 14.2

Correct alignment of varying languages.

The BASE table makes a number of assumptions. It assumes that one of the scripts or languages is the dominant of the two or more that exist. Then all of the other baselines are positioned with regard to that initial baseline.

Character Positions

OpenType gives a lot of control when placing glyphs as well as when rendering each language that the typeface supports.

When dealing with foreign writing systems, the position of glyphs can become a nightmare. Positioning is critical, however, especially when it comes to languages whose diacritical marks and their proper placement provides both readability and legibility. There is also the issue of accuracy in placement; the incorrect placement of a diacritic mark can lead to a different meaning for a word.

Below you will see how several foreign glyphs are positioned incorrectly (Figure 14.3) and correctly (Figure 14.4).

Figure 14.3

Incorrect alignment of foreign glyphs.

Figure 14.4

Correct alignment of the same glyphs.

The developer can create an entire set of position adjustments that are assembled by script systems and languages.

Substitution of Characters

OpenType contains data for making glyph substitution in an effort to render any scripts or languages supported within the font. Some languages have glyphs that, based on their position within a word or phrase, will change shapes. Figure 14.5 shows how the combination of characters provide for glyph substitution.

f + i = fi

Figure 14.5

The glyph substitution of an "f" and an "i."

Justification of Text

OpenType carries information that provides font designers with even more control over how their glyphs should be either substituted or positioned.

When you are working with justified text, the application places the characters in a line so that a specific length of line is filled. The justification of words in the line can make for spotty text and uneven line breaks.

To correct this problem, the user can make changes within an application to shrink or grow the white space between words. Words can also be hyphenated to better adjust for the spacing.

Another way to help alleviate the justification problem is to use an OpenType font that enables or disables individual character substitution and positioning.

An example of enabling glyph substitution would be to use a ligature glyph (such as an "ffi" ligature) instead of multiple glyphs. Figure 14.6 illustrates this.

the same difficulties as before

the same difficulties as before

Figure 14.6

The top line uses a ligature glyph. The bottom line uses multiple glyphs.

Font Security

OpenType carries a Digital Signature that contains information protecting the font from being changed or manipulated after the font's designer has developed it. This will become an effective way to inhibit any font thief from stealing a font and/or keep unauthorized people from accessing a font they do not own. All OpenType fonts will contain the Digital Signature. Digital Signatures will contain the following information:

➡ Content information

➡ A graphical certificate that will come to the screen and display the designer/publisher, expiration dates, and serial numbers

➡ Attributes that aren't authentic or are authentic to the font

This Digital Signature is based upon Microsoft's Authenticode technology. It protects a font from typographic alteration. Within the Digital Signature, the font designer can provide custom licensing information.

PostScript (Type 1) OpenType Information

The following information deals with the PostScript font data that can be contained within the OpenType font format. The PostScript font data can access all of the previously mentioned tables.

Compact Postscript Data

OpenType can contain a compact representation of a Type 1, Multiple Master, or CID font. The Compact Font Format (or CFF)

information enables more than one Type 1 font to be kept together within the overall font. A compact version of the Type font enables for great space saving. Font data can be shared between Type 1 font data.

Multiple Master Support

OpenType provides additional information for the support of Multiple Master fonts.

Application Use

Any time there is new technology or a new font format, there are issues concerning the seamlessness with which we view a font's capability to work. Extended testing will have to be done in many applications to work the bugs out of a new font format. Because OpenType is based on two existing font formats and with Microsoft's and Adobe's support of its development, there is reason to believe that the ramp up time for OpenType, as opposed to a brand new technology, will be shortened. Both of these companies have a great stake in the development and use of quality type onscreen.

OpenType is an outgrowth of the need for a format that provides great looking screen and printed type. It also incorporates the two most widely used font formats. OpenType has much greater flexibility with regard to character positioning, substitution, and alignment. Its support for foreign languages and their use in conjunction with other languages makes it a font format for worldwide use.

Character Sets

TrueType character set at 24 point

32-47:	!"#$%&'()*+,-./
48-63:	0123456789:;<=>?
64-79:	@ABCDEFGHIJKLMNO
80-95:	PQRSTUVWXYZ[\]^_
96-111:	`abcdefghijklmno
112-126:	pqrstuvwxyz{|}~
128-143:	ÄÅÇÉÑÖÜáàâäãåçéè
144-159:	êëíìîïñóòôöõúùûü
160-175:	†°¢£§•¶ß®©™´¨≠ÆØ
176-191:	∞±≤≥¥µ∂∑∏π∫ªºΩæø
192-207:	¿¡√ƒ≈∆«»… ÀÃÕŒœ
208-223:	—―""''÷◊ÿŸ⁄¤‹›ﬁﬂ
224-239:	‡·‚„‰ÂÊÁËÈÍÎÏÌÓÔ
240-255:	□ÒÚÛÙı ˆ˜¯˘˙˚¸˝˛ˇ

PostScript Template - Standard Mac Type 1 Character Set

Apple character set at 24 point

32-47:	!"#$%&'()*+,-./
48-63:	0123456789:;<=>?
64-79:	@ABCDEFGHIJKLMNO
80-95:	PQRSTUVWXYZ[\]^_
96-111:	`abcdefghijklmno
112-126:	pqrstuvwxyz{|}~
128-143:	ÄÅÇÉÑÖÜáàâäãåçéè
144-159:	êëíìîïñóòôöõúùûü
160-175:	†°¢£§•¶ß®©™´¨≠ÆØ
176-191:	∞±≤≥¥µ∂∑∏∫ªºΩæø
192-207:	¿¡¬√ƒ≈∆«»… ÀÃÕŒœ
208-223:	——""''÷◊ÿŸ⁄¤‹›ﬁﬂ
224-239:	‡·‚„‰ÂÊÁËÈÍÎÏÌÓÒ
240-255:	◆ÔÚÛÙı˜¯˘˙°¸˝˛ˇ

Mac Characters absent from the PostScript Set:

≠	∞	≤	≥	∂	∑	∏	π	∫	Ω	√	≈	∆	◊	◆
173	176	178	179	182	183	184	185	186	189	195	197	198	215	240

NOTE:
- Positions 0-31 are not accessible.
- Positions 127-160 are unencoded and not recommended for substitution.
  - For some standard applications, these positions may not be accessed and/or may have characters of their own substituted.
  - If characters are substituted in these positions, the PostScript names will be that of the accented character shown above.
  - Positions are usable if Customer's proprietary application is designed to access.
- MAC Type 1: 223 accessible characters on the screen.

This table contains character sets of WGL4 (Windows Glyph character) list as decribed for Windows 95), UGL, Windows 3.1x (for U.S. use), and the Macintosh (also for U.S.).

Key

•—Glyph in character set

★—Glyph not accessible from keyboard, only by PostScript name

Special Characters

Min	Unicode	PostScript Name	Descriptive Name	WGL4	UGL	Win31	MacChar	MacIndex
•		notdef		•				0
•		null		•			0×0	1
•		CR		•			0×d	2
•	U+0020	space	space	•	•	•	0×20	3
•	U+0021	exclam	exclamation mark	•	•	•	0×21	4
•	U+0022	quotedbl	quotation mark	•	•	•	0×22	5
•	U+0023	numbersign	number sign	•	•	•	0×23	6
•	U+0024	dollar	dollar sign	•	•	•	0×24	7
•	U+0025	percent	percent sign	•	•	•	0×25	8
•	U+0026	ampersand	ampersand	•	•	•	0×26	9
•	U+0027	quotesingle	apostrophe	•	•	•	0×27	10
•	U+0028	parenleft	left parenthesis	•	•	•	0×28	11
•	U+0029	parenright	right parenthesis	•	•	•	0×29	12
•	U+002a	asterisk	asterisk	•	•	•	0×2a	13
•	U+002b	plus	plus sign	•	•	•	0×2b	14
•	U+002c	comma	comma	•	•	•	0×2c	15
•	U+002d	hyphen	hyphen-minus	•	•	•	0×2d	16
•	U+002e	period	period	•	•	•	0×2e	17
•	U+002f	slash	slash	•	•	•	0×2f	18
•	U+0030	zero	digit zero	•	•	•	0×30	19
•	U+0031	one	digit one	•	•	•	0×31	20
•	U+0032	two	digit two	•	•	•	0×32	21
•	U+0033	three	digit three	•	•	•	0×33	22
•	U+0034	four	digit four	•	•	•	0×34	23

continues

Special Characters, continued

Min	Unicode	PostScript Name	Descriptive Name	WGL4	UGL	Win31	MacChar	MacIndex
•	U+0035	five	digit five	•	•	•	0×35	24
•	U+0036	six	digit six	•	•	•	0×36	25
•	U+0037	seven	digit seven	•	•	•	0×37	26
•	U+0038	eight	digit eight	•	•	•	0×38	27
•	U+0039	nine	digit nine	•	•	•	0×39	28
•	U+003a	colon	colon	•	•	•	0×3a	29
•	U+003b	semicolon	semicolon	•	•	•	0×3b	30
•	U+003c	less	less–than sign	•	•	•	0×3c	31
•	U+003d	equal	equals sign	•	•	•	0×3d	32
•	U+003e	greater	greater–than sign	•	•	•	0×3e	33
•	U+003f	question	question mark	•	•	•	0×3f	34
•	U+0040	at	commercial at	•	•	•	0×40	35
•	U+0041	A	latin capital letter a	•	•	•	0×41	36
•	U+0042	B	latin capital letter b	•	•	•	0×42	37
•	U+0043	C	latin capital letter c	•	•	•	0×43	38
•	U+0044	D	latin capital letter d	•	•	•	0×44	39
•	U+0045	E	latin capital letter e	•	•	•	0×45	40
•	U+0046	F	latin capital letter f	•	•	•	0×46	41
•	U+0047	G	latin capital letter g	•	•	•	0×47	42
•	U+0048	H	latin capital letter h	•	•	•	0×48	43
•	U+0049	I	latin capital letter i	•	•	•	0×49	44
•	U+004a	J	latin capital letter j	•	•	•	0×4a	45
•	U+004b	K	latin capital letter k	•	•	•	0×4b	46

Min	Unicode	PostScript Name	Descriptive Name	WGL4	UGL	Win31	MacChar	MacIndex
•	U+004c	L	latin capital letter l	•	•	•	0×4c	47
•	U+004d	M	latin capital letter m	•	•	•	0×4d	48
•	U+004e	N	latin capital letter n	•	•	•	0×4e	49
•	U+004f	O	latin capital letter o	•	•	•	0×4f	50
•	U+0050	P	latin capital letter p	•	•	•	0×50	51
•	U+0051	Q	latin capital letter q	•	•	•	0×51	52
•	U+0052	R	latin capital letter r	•	•	•	0×52	53
•	U+0053	S	latin capital letter s	•	•	•	0×53	54
•	U+0054	T	latin capital letter t	•	•	•	0×54	55
•	U+0055	U	latin capital letter u	•	•	•	0×55	56
•	U+0056	V	latin capital letter v	•	•	•	0×56	57
•	U+0057	W	latin capital letter w	•	•	•	0×57	58
•	U+0058	X	latin capital letter x	•	•	•	0×58	59
•	U+0059	Y	latin capital letter y	•	•	•	0×59	60
•	U+005a	Z	latin capital letter z	•	•	•	0×5a	61
•	U+005b	bracketleft	left square bracket	•	•	•	0×5b	62
•	U+005c	backslash	backslash	•	•	•	0×5c	63
•	U+005d	bracketright	right square bracket	•	•	•	0×5d	64
•	U+005e	asciicircum	circumflex accent	•	•	•	0×5e	65

continues

Special Characters, continued

Min	Unicode	PostScript Name	Descriptive Name	WGL4	UGL	Win31	MacChar	MacIndex
•	U+005f	underscore	underline	•	•	•	0×5f	66
•	U+0060	grave	grave accent	•	•	•	0×60	67
•	U+0061	a	latin small letter a	•	•	•	0×61	68
•	U+0062	b	latin small letter b	•	•	•	0×62	69
•	U+0063	c	latin small letter c	•	•	•	0×63	70
•	U+0064	d	latin small letter d	•	•	•	0×64	71
•	U+0065	e	latin small letter e	•	•	•	0×65	72
•	U+0066	f	latin small letter f	•	•	•	0×66	73
•	U+0067	g	latin small letter g	•	•	•	0×67	74
•	U+0068	h	latin small letter h	•	•	•	0×68	75
•	U+0069	i	latin small letter i	•	•	•	0×69	76
•	U+006a	j	latin small letter j	•	•	•	0×6a	77
•	U+006b	k	latin small letter k	•	•	•	0×6b	78
•	U+006c	l	latin small letter l	•	•	•	0×6c	79
•	U+006d	m	latin small letter m	•	•	•	0×6d	80
•	U+006e	n	latin small letter n	•	•	•	0×6e	81
•	U+006f	o	latin small letter o	•	•	•	0×6f	82
•	U+0070	p	latin small letter p	•	•	•	0×70	83
•	U+0071	q	latin small letter q	•	•	•	0×71	84
•	U+0072	r	latin small letter r	•	•	•	0×72	85
•	U+0073	s	latin small letter s	•	•	•	0×73	86
•	U+0074	t	latin small letter t	•	•	•	0×74	87
•	U+0075	u	latin small letter u	•	•	•	0×75	88
•	U+0076	v	latin small letter v	•	•	•	0×76	89
•	U+0077	w	latin small letter w	•	•	•	0×77	90
•	U+0078	x	latin small letter x	•	•	•	0×78	91
•	U+0079	y	latin small letter y	•	•	•	0×79	92
•	U+007a	z	latin small letter z	•	•	•	0×7a	93
•	U+007b	braceleft	left curly bracket	•	•	•	0×7b	94
•	U+007c	bar	vertical line	•	•	•	0×7c	95
•	U+007d	braceright	right curly bracket	•	•	•	0×7d	96
•	U+007e	asciitilde	tilde	•	•	•	0×7e	97

Min	Unicode	PostScript Name	Descriptive Name	WGL4	UGL	Win31	MacChar	MacIndex
•	U+00a0	nbspace	no-break space		•	•	0×ca	172
•	U+00a1	exclamdown	inverted exclamation mark	•	•	•	0×c1	163
•	U+00a2	cent	cent sign	•	•	•	0×a2	132
•	U+00a3	sterling	pound sign	•	•	•	0×a3	133
•	U+00a4	currency	currency sign	•	•	•	0×db	189
•	U+00a5	yen	yen sign	•	•	•	0×b4	150
•	U+00a6	brokenbar	broken bar	•	•	•	★	232
•	U+00a7	section	section sign	•	•	•	0×a4	134
•	U+00a8	dieresis	diaeresis	•	•	•	0×ac	142
•	U+00a9	copyright	copyright sign	•	•	•	0×a9	139
•	U+00aa	ordfeminine	feminine ordinal indicator	•	•	•	0×bb	157
•	U+00ab	guillemotleft	left guillemet	•	•	•	0×c7	169
•	U+00ac	logicalnot	not sign	•	•	•	0×c2	164
•	U+00ad	sfthyphen	soft hyphen	•	•			
•	U+00ae	registered	registered trademark sign	•	•	•	0×a8	138
•	U+00af	overscore	macron, overline	•	•	•	0×f8	218
•	U+00b0	degree	degree sign	•	•	•	0×a1	131
•	U+00b1	plusminus	plus–minus sign	•	•	•	0×b1	147
•	U+00b2	twosuperior	superscript two	•	•	•	★	242
•	U+00b3	threesuperior	superscript three	•	•	•	★	243
•	U+00b4	acute	acute accent	•	•	•	0×ab	141
•	U+00b5	mu1	micro sign	•	•	•	0×b5	151
•	U+00b6	paragraph	paragraph sign	•	•	•	0×a6	136
•	U+00b7	middot	middle dot, kana conjoctive	•	•	•		
•	U+00b8	cedilla	cedilla	•	•	•	0×fc	222
•	U+00b9	onesuperior	superscript one	•	•	•	★	241
•	U+00ba	ordmasculine	masculine ordinal indicator	•	•	•	0×bc	158

continues

Special Characters, continued

Min	Unicode	PostScript Name	Descriptive Name	WGL4	UGL	Win31	MacChar	MacIndex
•	U+00bb	guillemotright	right guillemet	•	•	•	0×c8	170
•	U+00bc	onequarter	vulgar fraction one quarter	•	•	•	★	245
•	U+00bd	onehalf	vulgar fraction one half	•	•	•	★	244
•	U+00be	threequarters	vulgar fraction three quarters	•	•	•	★	246
•	U+00bf	questiondown	inverted question mark	•	•	•	0×c0	162
•	U+00c0	Agrave	latin capital letter a with grave accent	•	•	•	0×cb	173
•	U+00c1	Aacute	latin capital letter a with acute accent	•	•	•	0×e7	201
•	U+00c2	Acircumflex	latin capital letter a with circumflex accent	•	•	•	0×e5	199
•	U+00c3	Atilde	latin capital letter a with tilde	•	•	•	0×cc	174
•	U+00c4	Adieresis	latin capital letter a with diaeresis	•	•	•	0×80	98
•	U+00c5	Aring	latin capital letter a with ring above	•	•	•	0×81	99
•	U+00c6	AE	latin capital letter a with e	•	•	•	0×ae	144
•	U+00c7	Ccedilla	latin capital letter c with cedilla	•	•	•	0×82	100
•	U+00c8	Egrave	latin capital letter e with grave accent	•	•	•	0×e9	203
•	U+00c9	Eacute	latin capital letter e with acute accent	•	•	•	0×83	101
•	U+00ca	Ecircumflex	latin capital letter e with circumflex accent	•	•	•	0×e6	200
•	U+00cb	Edieresis	latin capital letter e with diaeresis	•	•	•	0×e8	202
•	U+00cc	Igrave	latin capital letter i with grave accent	•	•	•	0×ed	207
•	U+00cd	Iacute	latin capital letter i with acute accent	•	•	•	0×ea	204

Min	Unicode	PostScript Name	Descriptive Name	WGL4	UGL	Win31	MacChar	MacIndex
•	U+00ce	Icircumflex	latin capital letter i with circumflex accent	•	•	•	0×eb	205
•	U+00cf	Idieresis	latin capital letter i with diaeresis	•	•	•	0×ec	206
•	U+00d0	Eth	latin capital letter eth	•	•	•	★	233
•	U+00d1	Ntilde	latin capital letter n with tilde	•	•	•	0×84	102
•	U+00d2	Ograve	latin capital letter o with grave accent	•	•	•	0×f1	211
•	U+00d3	Oacute	latin capital letter o with acute accent	•	•	•	0×ee	208
•	U+00d4	Ocircumflex	latin capital letter o with circumflex accent	•	•	•	0×ef	209
•	U+00d5	Otilde	latin capital letter o with tilde	•	•	•	0×cd	175
•	U+00d6	Odieresis	latin capital letter o with diaeresis	•	•	•	0×85	103
•	U+00d7	multiply	multiplication sign	•	•	•	★	240
•	U+00d8	Oslash	latin capital letter o with oblique stroke	•	•	•	0×af	145
•	U+00d9	Ugrave	latin capital letter u with grave accent	•	•	•	0×f4	214
•	U+00da	Uacute	latin capital letter u with acute accent	•	•	•	0×f2	212
•	U+00db	Ucircumflex	latin capital letter u with circumflex accent	•	•	•	0×f3	213
•	U+00dc	Udieresis	latin capital letter u with diaeresis	•	•	•	0×86	104
•	U+00dd	Yacute	latin capital letter y with acute accent	•	•	•	★	235
•	U+00de	Thorn	latin capital letter thorn	•	•	•	★	237
•	U+00df	germandbls	latin small letter sharp s	•	•	•	0×a7	137
•	U+00e0	agrave	latin small letter a with grave accent	•	•	•	0×88	106

continues

Special Characters, continued

Min	Unicode	PostScript Name	Descriptive Name	WGL4	UGL	Win31	MacChar	MacIndex
•	U+00e1	aacute	latin small letter a with acute accent	•	•	•	0×87	105
•	U+00e2	acircumflex	latin small letter a with circumflex accent	•	•	•	0×89	107
•	U+00e3	atilde	latin small letter a with tilde	•	•	•	0×8b	109
•	U+00e4	adieresis	latin small letter a with diaeresis	•	•	•	0×8a	108
•	U+00e5	aring	latin small letter a with ring above	•	•	•	0×8c	110
•	U+00e6	ae	latin small letter a with e	•	•	•	0×be	160
•	U+00e7	ccedilla	latin small letter c with cedilla	•	•	•	0×8d	111
•	U+00e8	egrave	latin small letter e with grave accent	•	•	•	0×8f	113
•	U+00e9	eacute	latin small letter e with acute accent	•	•	•	0×8e	112
•	U+00ea	ecircumflex	latin small letter e with circumflex accent	•	•	•	0×90	114
•	U+00eb	edieresis	latin small letter e with diaeresis	•	•	•	0×91	115
•	U+00ec	igrave	latin small letter i with grave accent	•	•	•	0×93	117
•	U+00ed	iacute	latin small letter i with acute accent	•	•	•	0×92	116
•	U+00ee	icircumflex	latin small letter i with circumflex accent	•	•	•	0×94	118
•	U+00ef	idieresis	latin small letter i with diaeresis	•	•	•	0×95	119
•	U+00f0	eth	latin small letter eth	•	•	•	★	234
•	U+00f1	ntilde	latin small letter n with tilde	•	•	•	0×96	120
•	U+00f2	ograve	latin small letter o with grave accent	•	•	•	0×98	122
•	U+00f3	oacute	latin small letter o with acute accent	•	•	•	0×97	121

Min	Unicode	PostScript Name	Descriptive Name	WGL4	UGL	Win31	MacChar	MacIndex
•	U+00f4	ocircumflex	latin small letter o with circumflex accent	•	•	•	0×99	123
•	U+00f5	otilde	latin small letter o with tilde	•	•	•	0×9b	125
•	U+00f6	odieresis	latin small letter o with diaeresis	•	•	•	0×9a	124
•	U+00f7	divide	division sign	•	•	•	0×d6	184
•	U+00f8	oslash	latin small letter o with oblique stroke	•	•	•	0×bf	161
•	U+00f9	ugrave	latin small letter u with grave accent	•	•	•	0×9d	127
•	U+00fa	uacute	latin small letter u with acute accent	•	•	•	0×9c	126
•	U+00fb	ucircumflex	latin small letter u with circumflex accent	•	•	•	0×9e	128
•	U+00fc	udieresis	latin small letter u with diaeresis	•	•	•	0×9f	129
•	U+00fd	yacute	latin small letter y with acute accent	•	•	•	★	236
•	U+00fe	thorn	latin small letter thorn	•	•	•	★	238
•	U+00ff	ydieresis	latin small letter y with diaeresis	•	•	•	0×d8	186
	U+0100	Amacron	latin capital letter a with macron	•				
	U+0101	amacron	latin small letter a with macron	•				
	U+0102	Abreve	latin capital letter a with breve	•	•			
	U+0103	abreve	latin small letter a with breve	•	•			
	U+0104	Aogonek	latin capital letter a with ogonek	•	•			
	U+0105	aogonek	latin small letter a with ogonek	•	•			

continues

Special Characters, continued

Min	Unicode	PostScript Name	Descriptive Name	WGL4	UGL	Win31	MacChar	MacIndex
•	U+0106	Cacute	latin capital letter c with acute accent	•	•		★	253
•	U+0107	cacute	latin small letter c with acute accent	•	•		★	254
	U+0108	Ccircumflex	latin capital letter c with hacek	•				
	U+0109	ccircumflex	latin small letter c with hacek	•				
	U+010a	Cdot	latin capital letter c with dot above	•				
	U+010b	cdot	latin small letter c with dot above	•				
•	U+010c	Ccaron	latin capital letter c with caron	•	•		★	255
•	U+010d	ccaron	latin small letter c with caron	•	•		★	256
	U+010e	Dcaron	latin capital letter d with hacek	•	•			
	U+010f	dcaron	latin small letter d with hacek	•	•			
	U+0110	Dslash	latin capital letter d with stroke	•	•			
•	U+0111	dmacron	latin small letter d with stroke	•	•		★	257
	U+0112	Emacron	latin capital letter e with macron	•				
	U+0113	emacron	latin small letter e with macron	•				
	U+0114	Ebreve	latin capital letter e with breve	•				
	U+0115	ebreve	latin small letter e with breve	•				
	U+0116	Edot	latin capital letter e with dot above	•				
	U+0117	edot	latin small letter e with dot above	•				
	U+0118	Eogonek	latin capital letter e with ogenek	•	•			

Min	Unicode	PostScript Name	Descriptive Name	WGL4	UGL	Win31	MacChar	MacIndex
	U+0119	eogonek	latin small letter e with ogenek	•	•			
	U+011a	Ecaron	latin capital letter e with hacek	•	•			
	U+011b	ecaron	latin small letter e with hacek	•	•			
	U+011c	Gcircumflex	latin capital letter g with circumflex	•				
	U+011d	gcircumflex	latin small letter g with circumflex	•				
•	U+011e	Gbreve	latin capital letter g with breve	•	•		★	248
•	U+011f	gbreve	latin small letter g with breve	•	•		★	249
	U+0120	Gdot	latin capital letter g with dot above	•				
	U+0121	gdot	latin small letter g with dot above	•				
	U+0122	Gcedilla	latin capital letter g with cedilla	•				
	U+0123	gcedilla	latin small letter g with cedilla	•				
	U+0124	Hcircumflex	latin capital letter h with circumflex	•				
	U+0125	hcircumflex	latin small letter h with circumflex	•				
	U+0126	Hbar	latin capital letter h with stroke	•				
	U+0127	hbar	latin small letter h with stroke	•				
	U+0128	Itilde	latin capital letter i with tilde	•				
	U+0129	itilde	latin small letter i with tilde	•				
	U+012a	Imacron	latin capital letter i with macron	•				
	U+012b	imacron	latin small letter i with macron	•				

continues

Special Characters, continued

Min	Unicode	PostScript Name	Descriptive Name	WGL4	UGL	Win31	MacChar	MacIndex
	U+012c	Ibreve	latin capital letter i with breve	•				
	U+012d	ibreve	latin small letter i with breve	•				
	U+012e	Iogonek	latin capital letter i with ogonek	•				
	U+012f	iogonek	latin small letter i with ogonek	•				
•	U+0130	Idot	latin capital letter i with dot above	•	•		★	250
•	U+0131	dotlessi	latin small letter i without dot above	•	•		0×f5	215
	U+0132	IJ	latin capital ligature ij	•				
	U+0133	ij	latin small ligature ij	•				
	U+0134	Jcircumflex	latin capital letter j with circumflex	•				
	U+0135	jcircumflex	latin small letter j with circumflex	•				
	U+0136	Kcedilla	latin capital letter k with cedilla	•				
	U+0137	kcedilla	latin small letter k with cedilla	•				
	U+0138	kgreenlandic	latin small letter kra	•				
	U+0139	Lacute	latin capital letter l with acute accent	•	•			
	U+013a	lacute	latin small letter l with acute accent	•	•			
	U+013b	Lcedilla	latin capital letter l with cedilla	•				
	U+013c	lcedilla	latin small letter l with cedilla	•				
	U+013d	Lcaron	latin capital letter l with hacek	•	•			
	U+013e	lcaron	latin small letter l with hacek	•	•			

Min	Unicode	PostScript Name	Descriptive Name	WGL4	UGL	Win31	MacChar	MacIndex
	U+013f	Ldot	latin capital letter l with middle dot	•	•			
	U+0140	ldot	latin small letter l with middle dot	•	•			
•	U+0141	Lslash	latin capital letter l with stroke	•	•		★	226
•	U+0142	lslash	latin small letter l with stroke	•	•		★	227
	U+0143	Nacute	latin capital letter n with acute accent	•	•			
	U+0144	nacute	latin small letter n with acute accent	•	•			
	U+0145	Ncedilla	latin capital letter n with cedilla	•				
	U+0146	ncedilla	latin small letter n with cedilla	•				
	U+0147	Ncaron	latin capital letter n with hacek	•	•			
	U+0148	ncaron	latin small letter n with hacek	•	•			
	U+0149	napostrophe	latin small letter n preceded by apostrophe	•				
	U+014a	Eng	latin capital letter eng	•				
	U+014b	eng	latin small letter eng	•				
	U+014c	Omacron	latin capital letter o with macron	•				
	U+014d	omacron	latin small letter o with macron	•				
	U+014e	Obreve	latin capital letter o with breve	•				
	U+014f	obreve	latin small letter o with breve	•				
	U+0150	Odblacute	latin capital letter o with double acute accent	•	•			
	U+0151	odblacute	latin small letter o with double acute accent	•	•			

continues

Special Characters, continued

Min	Unicode	PostScript Name	Descriptive Name	WGL4	UGL	Win31	MacChar	MacIndex
•	U+0152	OE	latin capital ligature o with e	•	•	•	0×ce	176
•	U+0153	oe	latin small ligature o with e	•	•	•	0×cf	177
	U+0154	Racute	latin capital letter r with acute accent	•	•			
	U+0155	racute	latin small letter r with acute accent	•	•			
	U+0156	Rcedilla	latin capital letter r with cedilla	•				
	U+0157	rcedilla	latin small letter r with cedilla	•				
	U+0158	Rcaron	latin capital letter r with hacek	•	•			
	U+0159	rcaron	latin small letter r with hacek	•	•			
	U+015a	Sacute	latin capital letter s with acute accent	•	•			
	U+015b	sacute	latin small letter s with acute accent	•	•			
	U+015c	Scircumflex	latin capital letter s with circumflex	•				
	U+015d	scircumflex	latin small letter s with circumflex	•				
•	U+015e	Scedilla	latin capital letter s with cedilla	•	•		★	251
•	U+015f	scedilla	latin small letter s with cedilla	•	•		★	252
•	U+0160	Scaron	latin capital letter s with hacek	•	•	•	★	228
•	U+0161	scaron	latin small letter s with hacek	•	•	•	★	229
	U+0162	Tcedilla	latin capital letter t with cedilla	•	•			
	U+0163	tcedilla	latin small letter t with cedilla	•	•			
	U+0164	Tcaron	latin capital letter t with hacek	•	•			

Min	Unicode	PostScript Name	Descriptive Name	WGL4	UGL	Win31	MacChar	MacIndex
	U+0165	tcaron	latin small letter t with hacek	•	•			
	U+0166	Tbar	latin capital letter t with stroke	•				
	U+0167	tbar	latin small letter t with stroke	•				
	U+0168	Utilde	latin capital letter u with tilde	•				
	U+0169	utilde	latin small letter u with tilde	•				
	U+016a	Umacron	latin capital letter u with macron	•				
	U+016b	umacron	latin small letter u with macron	•				
	U+016c	Ubreve	latin capital letter u with breve	•				
	U+016d	ubreve	latin small letter u with breve	•				
	U+016e	Uring	latin capital letter u with ring above	•	•			
	U+016f	uring	latin small letter u with ring above	•	•			
	U+0170	Udblacute	latin capital letter u with double acute accent	•	•			
	U+0171	udblacute	latin small letter u with double acute accent	•	•			
	U+0172	Uogonek	latin capital letter u with ogonek	•				
	U+0173	uogonek	latin small letter u with ogonek	•				
	U+0174	Wcircumflex	latin capital letter w with circumflex	•				
	U+0175	wcircumflex	latin cmall letter w with circumflex	•				
	U+0176	Ycircumflex	latin capital letter y with circumflex	•				

continues

Special Characters, continued

Min	Unicode	PostScript Name	Descriptive Name	WGL4	UGL	Win31	MacChar	MacIndex
	U+0177	ycircumflex	latin small letter y with circumflex	•				
•	U+0178	Ydieresis	latin capital letter y	•	•	•	0×d9	187
	U+0179	Zacute	latin capital letter z with acute accent	•	•			
	U+017a	zacute	latin small letter z with acute accent	•	•			
	U+017b	Zdot	latin capital letter z with dot above	•	•			
	U+017c	zdot	latin small letter z with dot above	•	•			
•	U+017d	Zcaron	latin capital letter z with hacek	•	•		★	230
•	U+017e	zcaron	latin small letter z with hacek	•	•		★	231
	U+017f	longs	latin small letter long s	•				
•	U+0192	florin	latin small letter script f, florin sign	•	•		0×c4	166
	U+01fa	Aringacute	latin capital letter a with ring above and acute	•				
	U+01fb	aringacute	latin small letter a with ring above and acute	•				
	U+01fc	AEacute	latin capital ligature ae with acute	•				
	U+01fd	aeacute	latin small ligature ae with acute	•				
	U+01fe	Oslashacute	latin capital letter o with stroke and acute	•				
	U+01ff	oslashacute	latin small letter o with stroke and acute	•				
•	U+02c6	circumflex	nonspacing circumflex accent	•		•	0×f6	216
•	U+02c7	caron	modifier letter hacek	•	•		0×ff	225
	U+02c9	macron	modifier letter macron	•	•			

Min	Unicode	PostScript Name	Descriptive Name	WGL4	UGL	Win31	MacChar	MacIndex
	U+02d6	tilde	nonspacing tilde				0xf7	217
•	U+02d8	breve	breve	•	•		0xf9	219
•	U+02d9	dotaccent	dot above	•	•		0xfa	220
•	U+02da	ring	ring above	•	•		0xfb	221
•	U+02db	ogonek	ogonek	•	•		0xfe	224
•	U+02dc	tilde	nonspacing tilde	•	•	•		
•	U+02dd	hung-arumlaut	modifier letter double prime	•	•		0xfd	223
	U+0384	tonos	greek tonos	•				
	U+0385	dieresistonos	greek dialytika tonos	•				
	U+0386	Alphatonos	greek capital letter alpha with tonos	•				
	U+0387	anoteleia	greek ano teleia	•				
	U+0388	Epsilontonos	greek capital letter epsilon with tonos	•				
	U+0389	Etatonos	greek capital letter eta with tonos	•				
	U+038a	Iotatonos	greek capital letter iota with tonos	•				
	U+038c	Omicrontonos	greek capital letter omicron with tonos	•				
	U+038e	Upsilontonos	greek capital letter upsilon with tonos	•				
	U+038f	Omegatonos	greek capital letter omega with tonos	•				
	U+0390	iotadieresistonos	greek small letter iota with dialytika and tonos	•				
	U+0391	Alpha	greek capital letter alpha	•				
	U+0392	Beta	greek capital letter beta	•				
	U+0393	Gamma	greek capital letter gamma	•	•			

continues

Special Characters, continued

Min	Unicode	PostScript Name	Descriptive Name	WGL4	UGL	Win31	MacChar	MacIndex
	U+0394	Delta	greek capital letter delta	•				
	U+0395	Epsilon	greek capital letter epsilon	•				
	U+0396	Zeta	greek capital letter zeta	•				
	U+0397	Eta	greek capital letter eta	•				
	U+0398	Theta	greek capital letter theta	•	•			
	U+0399	Iota	greek capital letter iota	•				
	U+039a	Kappa	greek capital letter kappa	•				
	U+039b	Lambda	greek capital letter lambda	•				
	U+039c	Mu	greek capital letter mu	•				
	U+039d	Nu	greek capital letter nu	•				
	U+039e	Xi	greek capital letter xi	•				
	U+039f	Omicron	greek capital letter omicron	•				
	U+03a0	Pi	greek capital letter pi	•				
	U+03a1	Rho	greek capital letter rho	•				
	U+03a3	Sigma	greek capital letter sigma	•				
	U+03a4	Tau	greek capital letter tau	•				
	U+03a5	Upsilon	greek capital letter upsilon	•				
	U+03a6	Phi	greek capital letter phi	•	•			
	U+03a7	Chi	greek capital letter chi	•				

Min	Unicode	PostScript Name	Descriptive Name	WGL4	UGL	Win31	MacChar	MacIndex
	U+03a8	Psi	greek capital letter psi	•				
	U+03a9	Omega	greek capital letter omega	•				
	U+03aa	Iotadieresis	greek capital letter iota with dialytika	•				
	U+03ab	Upsilond-ieresis	greek capital letter upsilon with dialytika	•				
	U+03ac	alphatonos	greek small letter alpha with tonos	•				
	U+03ad	epsilontonos	greek small letter epsilon with tonos	•				
	U+03ae	etatonos	greek small letter eta with tonos	•				
	U+03af	iotatonos	greek small letter iota with tonos	•				
	U+03b0	upsilon-dieresistonos	greek small letter upsilon with dialytika and tonos	•				
	U+03b1	alpha	greek small letter alpha	•	•			
	U+03b2	beta	greek small letter beta	•				
	U+03b3	gamma	greek small letter gamma	•				
	U+03b4	delta	greek small letter delta	•	•			
	U+03b5	epsilon	greek small letter epsilon	•	•			
	U+03b6	zeta	greek small letter zeta	•				
	U+03b7	eta	greek small letter eta	•				
	U+03b8	theta	greek small letter theta	•				

continues

Special Characters, continued

Min	Unicode	PostScript Name	Descriptive Name	WGL4	UGL	Win31	MacChar	MacIndex
	U+03b9	iota	greek small letter iota	•				
	U+03ba	kappa	greek small letter kappa	•				
	U+03bb	lambda	greek small letter lamda	•				
	U+03bc	mu	greek small letter mu	•				
	U+03bd	nu	greek small letter nu	•				
	U+03be	xi	greek small letter xi	•				
	U+03bf	omicron	greek small letter omicron	•				
•	U+03c0	pi	greek small letter pi	•	•		0xb9	155
	U+03c1	rho	greek small letter rho	•				
	U+03c2	sigma1	greek small letter final sigma	•				
	U+03c3	sigma	greek small letter sigma	•	•			
	U+03c4	tau	greek small letter tau	•	•			
	U+03c5	upsilon	greek small letter upsilon	•				
	U+03c6	phi	greek small letter phi	•	•			
	U+03c7	chi	greek small letter chi	•				
	U+03c8	psi	greek small letter psi	•				
	U+03c9	omega	greek small letter omega	•				
	U+03ca	iotadieresis	greek small letter iota with dialytika	•				
	U+03cb	upsilondieresis	greek small letter upsilon with dialytika	•				

Min	Unicode	PostScript Name	Descriptive Name	WGL4	UGL	Win31	MacChar	MacIndex
	U+03cc	omicron-tonos	greek small letter omicron with tonos	•				
	U+03cd	upsilontonos	greek small letter upsilon with tonos	•				
	U+03ce	omegatonos	greek small letter omega with tonos	•				
	U+0401	afii10023	cyrillic capital letter io	•				
	U+0402	afii10051	cyrillic capital letter dje	•				
	U+0403	afii10052	cyrillic capital letter gje	•				
	U+0404	afii10053	cyrillic capital letter ukrainian ie	•				
	U+0405	afii10054	cyrillic capital letter dze	•				
	U+0406	afii10055	cyrillic capital letter byelorussian-ukrainian i	•				
	U+0407	afii10056	cyrillic capital letter yi	•				
	U+0408	afii10057	cyrillic capital letter je	•				
	U+0409	afii10058	cyrillic capital letter lje	•				
	U+040a	afii10059	cyrillic capital letter nje	•				
	U+040b	afii10060	cyrillic capital letter tshe	•				
	U+040c	afii10061	cyrillic capital letter kje	•				
	U+040e	afii10062	cyrillic capital letter short u	•				
	U+040f	afii10145	cyrillic capital letter dzhe	•				
	U+0410	afii10017	cyrillic capital letter a	•				

continues

Special Characters, continued

Min	Unicode	PostScript Name	Descriptive Name	WGL4	UGL	Win31	MacChar	MacIndex
	U+0411	afii10018	cyrillic capital letter be	•				
	U+0412	afii10019	cyrillic capital letter ve	•				
	U+0413	afii10020	cyrillic capital letter ghe	•				
	U+0414	afii10021	cyrillic capital letter de	•				
	U+0415	afii10022	cyrillic capital letter ie	•				
	U+0416	afii10024	cyrillic capital letter zhe	•				
	U+0417	afii10025	cyrillic capital letter ze	•				
	U+0418	afii10026	cyrillic capital letter i	•				
	U+0419	afii10027	cyrillic capital letter short i	•				
	U+041a	afii10028	cyrillic capital letter ka	•				
	U+041b	afii10029	cyrillic capital letter el	•				
	U+041c	afii10030	cyrillic capital letter em	•				
	U+041d	afii10031	cyrillic capital letter en	•				
	U+041e	afii10032	cyrillic capital letter o	•				
	U+041f	afii10033	cyrillic capital letter pe	•				
	U+0420	afii10034	cyrillic capital letter er	•				
	U+0421	afii10035	cyrillic capital letter es	•				
	U+0422	afii10036	cyrillic capital letter te	•				
	U+0423	afii10037	cyrillic capital letter u	•				

Min	Unicode	PostScript Name	Descriptive Name	WGL4	UGL	Win31	MacChar	MacIndex
	U+0424	afii10038	cyrillic capital letter ef	•				
	U+0425	afii10039	cyrillic capital letter ha	•				
	U+0426	afii10040	cyrillic capital letter tse	•				
	U+0427	afii10041	cyrillic capital letter che	•				
	U+0428	afii10042	cyrillic capital letter sha	•				
	U+0429	afii10043	cyrillic capital letter shcha	•				
	U+042a	afii10044	cyrillic capital letter hard sign	•				
	U+042b	afii10045	cyrillic capital letter yeru	•				
	U+042c	afii10046	cyrillic capital letter soft sign	•				
	U+042d	afii10047	cyrillic capital letter e	•				
	U+042e	afii10048	cyrillic capital letter yu	•				
	U+042f	afii10049	cyrillic capital letter ya	•				
	U+0430	afii10065	cyrillic small letter a	•				
	U+0431	afii10066	cyrillic small letter be	•				
	U+0432	afii10067	cyrillic small letter ve	•				
	U+0433	afii10068	cyrillic small letter ghe	•				
	U+0434	afii10069	cyrillic small letter de	•				
	U+0435	afii10070	cyrillic small letter ie	•				

continues

Special Characters, continued

Min	Unicode	PostScript Name	Descriptive Name	WGL4	UGL	Win31	MacChar	MacIndex
	U+0436	afii10072	cyrillic small letter zhe	•				
	U+0437	afii10073	cyrillic small • letter ze					
	U+0438	afii10074	cyrillic small letter i •					
	U+0439	afii10075	cyrillic small letter short i	•				
	U+043a	afii10076	cyrillic small letter ka	•				
	U+043b	afii10077	cyrillic small letter el	•				
	U+043c	afii10078	cyrillic small letter em	•				
	U+043d	afii10079	cyrillic small letter en	•				
	U+043e	afii10080	cyrillic small letter o	•				
	U+043f	afii10081	cyrillic small letter pe	•				
	U+0440	afii10082	cyrillic small • letter er					
	U+0441	afii10083	cyrillic small letter es	•				
	U+0442	afii10084	cyrillic small letter te	•				
	U+0443	afii10085	cyrillic small letter u	•				
	U+0444	afii10086	cyrillic small letter ef	•				
	U+0445	afii10087	cyrillic small letter ha	•				
	U+0446	afii10088	cyrillic small letter tse	•				
	U+0447	afii10089	cyrillic small letter che	•				
	U+0448	afii10090	cyrillic small letter sha	•				

Min	Unicode	PostScript Name	Descriptive Name	WGL4	UGL	Win31	MacChar	MacIndex
	U+0449	afii10091	cyrillic small letter shcha	•				
	U+044a	afii10092	cyrillic small letter hard sign	•				
	U+044b	afii10093	cyrillic small letter yeru	•				
	U+044c	afii10094	cyrillic small letter soft sign	•				
	U+044d	afii10095	cyrillic small letter e	•				
	U+044e	afii10096	cyrillic small letter yu	•				
	U+044f	afii10097	cyrillic small letter ya	•				
	U+0451	afii10071	cyrillic small letter io	•				
	U+0452	afii10099	cyrillic small letter dje	•				
	U+0453	afii10100	cyrillic small letter gje	•				
	U+0454	afii10101	cyrillic small letter ukrainian ie	•				
	U+0455	afii10102	cyrillic small letter dze	•				
	U+0456	afii10103	cyrillic small letter byelorussian-ukrainian i	•				
	U+0457	afii10104	cyrillic small letter yi	•				
	U+0458	afii10105	cyrillic small letter je	•				
	U+0459	afii10106	cyrillic small letter lje	•				
	U+045a	afii10107	cyrillic small letter nje	•				
	U+045b	afii10108	cyrillic small letter tshe	•				

continues

Special Characters, continued

Min	Unicode	PostScript Name	Descriptive Name	WGL4	UGL	Win31	MacChar	MacIndex
	U+045c	afii10109	cyrillic small letter kje	•				
	U+045e	afii10110	cyrillic small letter short u	•				
	U+045f	afii10193	cyrillic small letter dzhe	•				
	U+0490	afii10050	cyrillic capital letter ghe with upturn	•				
	U+0491	afii10098	cyrillic small letter ghe with upturn	•				
	U+1e80	Wgrave	latin capital letter w with grave	•				
	U+1e81	wgrave	latin small letter w with grave	•				
	U+1e82	Wacute	latin capital letter w with acute	•				
	U+1e83	wacute	latin small letter w with acute	•				
	U+1e84	Wdieresis	latin capital letter w with diaeresis	•				
	U+1e85	wdieresis	latin small letter w with diaeresis	•				
	U+1ef2	Ygrave	latin capital letter y with grave	•				
	U+1ef3	ygrave	latin small letter y with grave	•				
•	U+2013	endash	en dash	•	•	•	0xd0	178
•	U+2014	emdash	em dash	•	•	•	0xd1	179
	U+2015	afii00208	horizontal bar	•				
	U+2017	underscoredbl	double low line	•	•			
•	U+2018	quoteleft	left single quotation mark	•	•	•	0xd4	182
•	U+2019	quoteright	right single quotation mark	•	•	•	0xd5	183
•	U+201a	quotesinglbase	single low-9 quotation mark	•	•	•	0xe2	196

Min	Unicode	PostScript Name	Descriptive Name	WGL4	UGL	Win31	MacChar	MacIndex
	U+201b	quote-reversed	single high-reversed-9 quotation mark	•				
•	U+201c	quotedblleft	left double quotation mark	•	•	•	0xd2	180
•	U+201d	quoted-blright	right double quotation mark	•	•	•	0xd3	181
•	U+201e	quote-dblbase	double low-9 quotation mark	•	•	•	0xe3	197
•	U+2020	dagger	dagger	•	•	•	0xa0	130
•	U+2021	daggerdbl	double dagger	•	•	•	0xe0	194
•	U+2022	bullet	bullet	•	•	•	0xa5	135
•	U+2026	ellipsis	horizontal ellipsis	•	•	•	0xc9	171
•	U+2030	perthousand	per mille sign	•	•	•	0xe4	198
	U+2032	minute	prime	•				
	U+2033	second	double prime	•				
•	U+2039	guilsinglleft	single left-pointing angle quotation mark	•	•	•	0xdc	190
•	U+203a	guilsingl rightsingle	right-pointing angle quotation mark	•	•	•	0xdd	191
	U+203c	exclamdbl	double exclamation mark	•	•			
	U+203e	radicalex	overline	•				
	U+2044	fraction	fraction slash	•				
	U+207f	nsuperior	superscript latin small letter n	•	•			
•	U+20a3	franc	french franc sign	•	•		★	247
	U+20a4	afii08941	lira sign	•				
	U+20a7	peseta	peseta sign	•	•			
	U+2105	afii61248	care of	•				
	U+2113	afii61289	script small l	•				
	U+2116	afii61352	numero sign	•				

continues

Special Characters, continued

Min	Unicode	PostScript Name	Descriptive Name	WGL4	UGL	Win31	MacChar	MacIndex
•	U+2122	trademark	trademark sign	•	•	•	0×aa	140
•	U+2126	Ohm	ohm sign	•	•		0×bd	159
	U+212e	estimated	estimated symbol	•				
	U+215b	oneeighth	vulgar fraction one eighth	•				
	U+215c	threeeighths	vulgar fraction three eighths	•				
	U+215d	fiveeighths	vulgar fraction five eighths	•				
	U+215e	seveneighths	vulgar fraction seven eighths	•				
	U+2190	arrowleft	leftwards arrow	•	•			
	U+2191	arrowup	upwards arrow	•	•			
	U+2192	arrowright	rightwards arrow	•	•			
	U+2193	arrowdown	downwards arrow	•	•			
	U+2194	arrowboth	left right arrow	•	•			
	U+2195	arrowupdn	up down arrow	•	•			
	U+21a8	arrow-updnbse	up down arrow with base	•	•			
•	U+2202	partialdiff	partial differential	•	•		0×b6	152
•	U+2206	increment	increment	•	•		0×c6	168
•	U+220f	product	n-ary product	•	•		0×b8	154
•	U+2211	summation	n-ary summation	•	•		0×b7	153
•	U+2212	minus	minus sign	•	•		★	239
•	U+2215	fraction	division slash		•		0×da	188
•	U+2219	period-centered	bullet operator	•	•		0×e1	195
•	U+221a	radical	square root	•	•		0×c3	165
•	U+221e	infinity	infinity	•	•		0×b0	146
	U+221f	orthogonal	right angle	•	•			
	U+2229	intersection	intersection	•	•			
•	U+222b	integral	integral	•	•		0×ba	156
•	U+2248	approxequal	almost equal to	•	•		0×c5	167
•	U+2260	notequal	not equal to	•	•		0×ad	143

Min	Unicode	PostScript Name	Descriptive Name	WGL4	UGL	Win31	MacChar	MacIndex
	U+2261	equivalence	identical to	•	•			
•	U+2264	lessequal	less-than or equal to	•	•		0×b2	148
•	U+2265	greaterequal	greater-than or equal to	•	•		0×b3	149
	U+2302	house	house	•	•			
	U+2310	revlogicalnot	reversed not sign	•	•			
	U+2320	integraltp	top half integral	•	•			
	U+2321	integralbt	bottom half integral	•	•			
	U+2500	SF100000	box drawings light horizontal	•	•			
	U+2502	SF110000	box drawings light vertical	•	•			
	U+250c	SF010000	box drawings light down and right	•	•			
	U+2510	SF030000	box drawings light down and left	•	•			
	U+2514	SF020000	box drawings light up and right	•	•			
	U+2518	SF040000	box drawings light up and left	•	•			
	U+251c	SF080000	box drawings light vertical and right	•	•			
	U+2524	SF090000	box drawings light vertical and left	•	•			
	U+252c	SF060000	box drawings light down and horizontal	•	•			
	U+2534	SF070000	box drawings light up and horizontal	•	•			
	U+253c	SF050000	box drawings light vertical and horizontal	•	•			
	U+2550	SF430000	box drawings double horizontal	•	•			
	U+2551	SF240000	box drawings double vertical	•	•			

continues

Special Characters, continued

Min	Unicode	PostScript Name	Descriptive Name	WGL4	UGL	Win31	MacChar	MacIndex
	U+2552	SF510000	box drawings down single and right double	•	•			
	U+2553	SF520000	box drawings down double and right single	•	•			
	U+2554	SF390000	box drawings double down and right	•	•			
	U+2555	SF220000	box drawings down single and left double	•	•			
	U+2556	SF210000	box drawings down double and left single	•	•			
	U+2557	SF250000	box drawings double down and left	•	•			
	U+2558	SF500000	box drawings up single and right double	•	•			
	U+2559	SF490000	box drawings up double and right single	•	•			
	U+255a	SF380000	box drawings double up and right	•	•			
	U+255b	SF280000	box drawings up single and left double	•	•			
	U+255c	SF270000	box drawings up double and left single	•	•			
	U+255d	SF260000	box drawings double up and left	•	•			
	U+255e	SF360000	box drawings vertical single and right double	•	•			

Min	Unicode	PostScript Name	Descriptive Name	WGL4	UGL	Win31	MacChar	MacIndex
	U+255f	SF370000	box drawings vertical double and right single	•	•			
	U+2560	SF420000	box drawings double vertical and right	•	•			
	U+2561	SF190000	box drawings vertical single and left double	•	•			
	U+2562	SF200000	box drawings vertical double and left single	•	•			
	U+2563	SF230000	box drawings double vertical and left	•	•			
	U+2564	SF470000	box drawings down single and horizontal double	•	•			
	U+2565	SF480000	box drawings down double and horizontal single	•	•			
	U+2566	SF410000	box drawings double down and horizontal	•	•			
	U+2567	SF450000	box drawings up single and horizontal double	•	•			
	U+2568	SF460000	box drawings up double and horizontal single	•	•			
	U+2569	SF400000	box drawings double up and horizontal	•	•			
	U+256a	SF540000	box drawings vertical single and horizontal double	•	•			
	U+256b	SF530000	box drawings vertical double and horizontal single	•	•			

continues

Special Characters, continued

Min	Unicode	PostScript Name	Descriptive Name	WGL4	UGL	Win31	MacChar	MacIndex
	U+256c	SF440000	box drawings double vertical and horizontal	•	•			
	U+2580	upblock	upper half block	•				
	U+2584	dnblock	lower half block	•				
	U+2588	block	full block	•				
	U+258c	lfblock	left half block	•				
	U+2590	rtblock	right half block	•				
	U+2591	ltshade	light shade	•				
	U+2592	shade	medium shade	•				
	U+2593	dkshade	dark shade	•				
	U+25a0	filledbox	black square	•				
	U+25a1	H22073	white square	•				
	U+25aa	H18543	black small square	•				
	U+25ab	H18551	white small square	•				
	U+25ac	filledrect	black rectangle	•				
	U+25b2	triagup	black up-pointing triangle	•				
	U+25ba	triagrt	black right-pointing pointer	•				
	U+25bc	triagdn	black down-pointing triangle	•				
	U+25c4	triaglf	black left-pointing pointer	•				
•	U+25ca	lozenge	lozenge	•			0xd7	185
	U+25cb	circle	white circle	•				
	U+25cf	H18533	black circle	•				
	U+25d8	invbullet	inverse bullet	•				
	U+25d9	invcircle	inverse white circle	•				
	U+25e6	openbullet	white bullet	•				
	U+263a	smileface	white smiling face	•				
	U+263b	invsmileface	black smiling face	•				

Min	Unicode	PostScript Name	Descriptive Name	WGL4	UGL	Win31	MacChar	MacIndex
	U+263c	sun	white sun with rays	•				
	U+2640	female	female sign	•				
	U+2642	male	male sign	•				
	U+2660	spade	black spade suit	•				
	U+2663	club	black club suit	•				
	U+2665	heart	black heart suit	•				
	U+2666	diamond	black diamond suit	•				
	U+266a	musicalnote	eighth note	•				
	U+266b	musical-notedbl	beamed eighth notes	•				
•	U+f000	applelogo	apple logo				0×f0	210
•	U+f001	fi	fi ligature[1]	•			0×de	192
•	U+f002	fl	fl ligature[2]	•			0×df	193
•	U+fb01\ure			•		0×df	193	

[1] In order to preserve compatibility with HP printers, the fi ligature has two different unicode values associated with it, yet references a single glyph.

[2] In order to preserve compatibility with HP printers, the fl ligature has two different unicode values associated with it, yet references a single glyph.

APPENDIX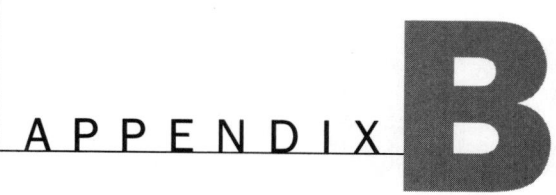

Browser Capabilities and Comparison Chart

Windows

Browsers	Supporting Elements
Netscape Navigator 3.0	Java, frames, tables, plug-ins, font size, font color, font face, colored table data cells, columns, compacted lists, JavaScript, animated GIFs
Netscape Navigator 2.0	Java, frames, tables, plug-ins, font size, font color, compacted lists, JavaScript, animated GIFs
Netscape Navigator 1.1	Tables, font size
Microsoft Internet Explorer 3.0	Java, frames, tables, plug-ins, font size, font color, font face, colored table data cells, compacted lists, JavaScript, animated GIFs, style sheets
Microsoft Internet Explorer 2.0	Tables, font size, font color
Microsoft Internet Explorer 1.0	Tables, font size, font color
Mosaic 2.1.1	Tables
Mosaic 1.0	None
AOL Browser 3.0	Frames, tables, font size, font color
AOL Browser 1.0	None

Macintosh

Browsers	Supporting Elements
Netscape Navigator 3.0	Java, frames, tables, plug-ins, font size, font color, JavaScript, animated GIFs
Netscape Navigator 2.0	Frames, tables, plug-ins, font size, font color, JavaScript, animated GIFs
Netscape Navigator 1.1	Tables, font size
Microsoft Internet Explorer 2.1b1	Tables, plug-ins, font size, font color
Mosaic 3.0b4	Frames, tables, font size, font color
Mosaic 2.0	Tables
Mosaic 1.0	None
AOL Browser 2.7	None
AOL Browser 1.0	None

Note

Data obtained from *Webmonkey Browser Kit*, October, 1996. For more up-to-date browser capabilities see `http://www.webmonkey.com/browserkit/`.

HTML Reference Chart

Table C.1

Main Tags

Element	Description
<HTML></HTML>	Start/End tags of the HTML document
<HEAD></HEAD>	Identifies the document head
<META>	Meta-info about document (must be in head)
<META HTTP=EQUIV="name">	Binds element to HTTP response header
<META HTTP=EQUIV="Refresh" _CONTENT=n>	Refresh page every n seconds
<META HTTP=EQUIV="Refresh" _CONTENT=n; URL>	Refesh page in n seconds by jumping to URL
<TITLE></TITLE>	Denotes title of HTML page (must be in head)
<BODY></BODY>	Specifies body of document
<BODY BACKGROUND="URL">	Background texture
<BODY BGCOLOR=="#RRGGBB" _or "colorname" ></BODY>	Background color
<BODY TEXT="#RRGGBB" _or "colorname"> </BODY>	Text Color
<BODY LINK="#RRGGBB" _or "colorname" ></BODY>.	Link Color

continues

Table C.1   **continued**

Main Tags

Element	Description
<BODY VLINK="#RRGGBB" _or "colorname" ></BODY>	Visited Link Color
<BODY ALINK="#RRGGBB" _or "colorname" ></BODY>	Active Link Color

Type Related	Description
<Hn></Hn>	Heading (n=1–6 with 1 as the largest heading)
<Hn ALIGN=LEFT|CENTER| _RIGHT|NOWRAP|CLEAR></Hn>	Align heading 3.0
<CODE></CODE>	Text in monospace computer code
<TT></TT>	Teletype font
<FONT SIZE=n></FONT>	Font Size (n ranges from 1–7; default is 3)
<FONT COLOR=="#RRGGBB" _or "colorname"></FONT>	Font Color
<FONT FACE="fontname"> _</FONT>	Specify Font (ususally common system fonts)
<BASEFONT SIZE="n">	Changes the base font value (where default basefont is 3) n=1–7
<B></B>	Bold
<I></I>	Italic
<U></U>	Underline text
<S></S>	Strikeout text
	Subscript text
	Superscript text

Layout	Description
<BLOCKQUOTE></BLOCKQUOTE>	Block indent
 	Line break
<BR CLEAR=LEFT|RIGHT|ALL>	Clearing line break
<CENTER></CENTER>	Center
<DIV>	Division of a document

Layout	Description
<HR>	Horizontal rule
<HR ALIGN=LEFT|RIGHT| _CENTER>	Aligns horizontal rule
<HR SIZE=n>	Thickness of horizontal rule (n=number in pixels)
<HR WIDTH=n>	Width of horizontal rule (n=number in pixels)
<HR WIDTH=n%>	Width of horizontal rule defined by percentage of page
<HR NOSHADE>	Solid black horizontal rule
<NOBR>	Prevents line break
<P>	Paragraph return
<P ALIGN=LEFT|CENTER|RIGHT>	Align paragraph
<PRE></PRE>	Preformatted (displayed with browser default font, usually Courier)

Links	Description
<A HREF="url"></a>	Hypertext link
<A HREF="url" TARGET= _"window">	Link opens a new browser window
<A HREF="url" TARGET= _"framename">	Link loads in a frame specified by frame name
<A HREF="url" TARGET= _"_self">	For Frames: link loads in frame where the link was clicked
<A HREF="url" TARGET=_"_parent">	For Frames: link loads in the immediate FRAMESET parent of document
<A HREF="url" TARGET=_"_top">	For Frames: link loads in the full body of the window

Images	Description
<IMG SRC="URL">	Display image
<IMG SRC="URL" ALIGN=TOP| _BOTTOM|MIDDLE>	Align image relative to text baseline
<IMG SRC="URL" ALIGN= _LEFT|RIGHT>	Align image relative to page

continues

Table C.1	continued

Main Tags

Images	Description
<IMG SRC="URL" ALT=_"alttext">	Alternative/Descriptive Text displayed when images are turned off
<IMG SRC="URL" ISMAP>	Image is an image map
<IMG SRC="URL" USEMAP>	Image is a client-side image map
<IMG SRC="URL" WIDTH="n" _HEIGHT="n">	Image dimensions (in pixels)
<IMG SRC="URL" BORDER=n>	Image border (in pixels)
<IMG SRC="URL" HSPACE=n _VSPACE=n>	Specifies horizontal or vertical spacing (in pixels)
<IMG LOWSRC="URL" SRC=_"URL">	Specifies low-resolution load of image

Lists	Description
<DL></DL>	Definition title
<DD>	Definition
<DT>	Definition term
<LI>	List item (bullet when used with <UL>, numbered list with <OL>
<OL></OL>	Ordered list
<OL COMPACT></OL>	Compact ordered list
<OL TYPE=A|a|I|i|1>	Format of list items (caps, small, numerical, roman, or default)
<LI TYPE=A|a|I|i|1>	Controls format of list item
<UL></UL>	Unordered list
<UL COMPACT></UL>	Compact version of unordered list
<UL TYPE=DISC|CIRCLE|_SQUARE>	Specifies bullet style

Forms	Description
<FORM ACTION="URL" _METHOD=GET|POST></FORM>	Define form
<INPUT TYPE="TEXT|_PASSWORD|CHECKBOX|RADIO|_SUBMIT|RESET">	Input field for HTML form

Forms	Description
<INPUT NAME="fieldname">	Field name forms
<INPUT CHECKED>	Checked checkboxes or radio boxes forms
<INPUT SIZE=n>	Field size (in characters)
<INPUT MAXLENGTH=n>	Maximum length (in characters)
<OPTION>	Option (items that can be selected forms)
<SELECT></SELECT>	Selection list forms
<SELECT NAME="listname">_</SELECT>	Name of list forms
<SELECT SIZE=n></SELECT>	n=number of options
<TEXTAREA ROWS=n COLS=n>_</TEXTAREA>	Input box size
<TEXTAREA NAME="boxname">_</TEXTAREA>	Name of box forms

Tables	Description
<TABLE></TABLE>	Defines table
<TABLE BORDER></TABLE>	Table border (on or off)
<TABLE BORDER=n></TABLE>	Table border (width of table border)
<TABLE CELLSPACING=n>	Spacing between cells
<TABLE CELLPADDING=n>	Thickness of cell borders
<TABLE WIDTH=n>	Desired width (in pixels)
<TABLE WIDTH=%>	Width percent (percentage of page)
<TD></TD>	Table cell (must appear within table rows)
<TD ALIGN=LEFT|RIGHT|CENTER _VALIGN=TOP|MIDDLE|BOTTOM>	Alignment
<TD NOWRAP>	No linebreaks
<TD COLSPAN=n>	Columns to span
<TD ROWSPAN=n>	Rows to span
<TD WIDTH=n>	Desired width (in pixels)

continues

Table C.1	continued

Main Tags

Tables	Description
<TD WIDTH=n%>	Width percent (percentage of table)
<TH></TH>	Table header
<TH ALIGN=LEFT|RIGHT|CENTER _VALIGN=TOP|MIDDLE|BOTTOM>	Alignment
<TH NOWRAP>	No linebreaks
<TH COLSPAN=n>	Columns to span
<TH ROWSPAN=n>	Rows to span
<TH WIDTH=n>	Desired width (in pixels)
<TH WIDTH=n%>	Width percent (percentage of table)
<TR></TR>	Table row
<TR ALIGN=LEFT|RIGHT|CENTER _VALIGN=TOP|MIDDLE|BOTTOM>	Alignment
<CAPTION ALIGN=TOP|BOTTOM> _</CAPTION>	Specifies table caption

Frames	Description
<FRAMESET></FRAMESET>	Hosts the frame elements (must be placed in the header)
<FRAMESET COLS=n>	Column Widths
<FRAMESET ROWS=n>	Row height
<FRAMESET SPACING=1|0>	Frame Spacing adds additional space between frames
<FRAME SRC="URL">	Single frame
<IFRAME SRC="URL">	Floating frame
<FRAME ALIGN=left|center| _right>	Frame alignment
<FRAME FRAMEBORDER=1|0>	Frame border (1 is default, 0 is no border)
<FRAME NAME="name">	Frame name
<FRAME NORESIZE>	Prevents resizing of frame
<FRAME SCROLLING=yes|no>	Scrolling frame
<FRAME MARGINHEIGHT="n">	Frame height (in pixels)
<FRAME MARGINWIDTH="n">	Frame width (in pixels)

Multimedia	Description
<EMBED SRC="url" WIDTH=	Indicates an embedded object (used for n _HEIGHT=n> Shockwave)

Style Sheets	Description
<STYLE TYPE="text/css">	Start and closing tags for the style element _</STYLE> (must live in the head of the document)

Paragraph Style Properties	Description
P{ color: color name }	Text color of paragraph
P{ background: color }	Background color of paragraph
P{ padding: length, %, _auto }	Controls spacing between text and border of paragraph; can specify up to four values in order of padding for top, right, bottom, left
P{ font-size: size in }	Font size of text in paragraph (must have pt or _points or pixels px suffix)

Style Properties	Description
P{ font-family: font name }	Specifies font
P{ letter-spacing: }	Controls spacing of letters
P{ text-align: left| _right|center|justify }	Alignment of paragraph
P{ text-indent:length _or % }	Controls indent of first line of paragraph
P{ border-color: color }	Specifies color of border
P{ border-width: thin| _medium|thick }	Specifies width of paragraph border

Link Style Properties	Description
A:link {color: color name}	Link color
A:link {font-size: size in _points or pixels}	Size of font (must have pt or px suffix)
A: link {font-family: _font name}	Specifies font

INDEX

C